CRAFTY MAMA

CRAFTY MAMA

Makes

49 FAST, FABULOUS, FOOLPROOF (BABY & TODDLER) PROJECTS

by Abby Pecoriello

Lily and Sasha's Crafty Mama

WORKMAN PUBLISHING ♥ NEW YORK

FOR LILY AND SASHA

This book references websites and retail locations that may be of interest to the reader. Every effort has been made to ensure that the information about these resources is correct and up-to-date as of press time.

Library of Congress Cataloging-in-Publication Data is available.

ISBN-13: 978-0-7611-4022-1

Workman books are available at special discounts when purchased in bulk for premiums and sales promotions as well as for fund-raising or educational use. Special editions or book excerpts can also be created to specification. For details, contact the Special Sales Director at the address below.

Cover design: Janet Vicario
Book design: Janet Parker

Workman Publishing Company, Inc.
225 Varick Street
New York, NY 10014-4381
www.workman.com

A NOTE ABOUT SAFETY: The safety of items made for infants and toddlers should always be kept very much in mind and common sense should prevail. Be sure that all materials you obtain to make these items are lead-free. Be extra careful when sewing on buttons, gluing ornamentation, or using other objects that may be small enough to be swallowed; make sure they won't come off with all the chewing and pulling you can expect from your child. And, of course, you alone can decide which of the items suggested in this book are appropriate for your child's use.

Printed in the United States of America

First printing April 2008

10 9 8 7 6 5 4 3 2 1

ACKNOWLEDGMENTS

I'm starting to really empathize with all those people who win an Oscar because it's *impossible* to thank everyone who had a hand in helping you create something special. That said, I'll give it a try! First and foremost, I must thank my daughter, Lily Skye Pecoriello, for being the utter genesis of this book. If you weren't born . . . and didn't have such dynamic energy and spirit (even at 2 days old), I'd never have turned to crafts! I love every single speck of your exuberant, dramatic, intense little being!

Thanks to my husband, Mike, for schlepping to pretty much every craft store in the entire tri-state area, for trying his hardest to help me decide which rhinestones look best in what places, for dealing with hot glue blobs and tons of other crafty remnants around the apartment, and for supporting me, believing in me, and loving me more than anyone else on the planet.

Thanks to Hindi and baby Natan, my first mommy/baby craft partners. I never would have thought our early morning breastfeeding/tie-dye sessions would have morphed into this. Thank you Ange and baby Cayla, Renee and baby Stephanie, and Amy and babies Max 'n' Hannah for showing up at every CM event and constantly reminding me that I might actually have a good idea (especially when my mommy hormones made me forget!). Thanks to everyone who attended my classes and workshops, Jocelyn and Stacey for helping me teach, and Dana and Elana at the JCC for taking a chance on my idea.

Thanks to my little chub-a-lub Sasha, who was in my belly, pushing on my bladder every 15 minutes as I wrote this book. And thanks to Grandma Susan, Papa D, Grandma Iris, and Oompa for babysitting so I could teach, craft, and write to my heart's content.

Thanks to my not-so-crafty, but oh-so-supportive friends Ciulla, Mander, and Jeweley-Jewels. You guys are awesome. Thanks to my sister-in-law, Sherri, for being such a fan and always offering to help me out.

Stay with me . . .

Thanks to Becky for introducing me to my wonderful agent, Katherine Fausset. And super mondo thanks to Katherine for helping me, selling me, and smiling at me.

Thanks to Raphael and Sylvie Buchler, and Deborah Ory and their respective crews for styling and taking such gorgeous photographs . . . and thanks to all the moms and babies in the photographs for your positivity and gorgeousness! A special thanks to Haley Pelton for being the best and most dedicated editorial intern on the planet. And thanks to Alicia Matusheski, Elaine Pumarejo, and José Vegas for helping out with too many things to mention. Thanks to my brilliant and patient production editor, Carol White; the artistically gifted Janet Parker, John Gilman, and Janet Vicario; the photography goddesses, Leora Kahn and Anne Kerman; typesetting and production gurus, Barbara Peragine, Jarrod Dyer, and Doug Wolff; my amazing publicist, Kim Small; Jennifer Griffin, my first friend at Workman; ALL of the folks in sales and marketing, and the big daddy of Workman, Peter Workman—if you didn't start such an amazing company, I wouldn't have a book!

And a big, juicy thanks to my fabulous editor, Megan Nicolay. Without her constant support, patience, words, attitude, and big cookies, this book would be a big messy jumble of hot glue and rhinestones.

Oh no, the music is starting to play and I need to get off the stage! Thanks to everyone I know, ever knew, and will know one day! You all rock!

TABLE OF CONTENTS

WHEN THE GOING GETS TOUGH,
THE TOUGH GET
CRAFTING

Every time I've been incredibly overwhelmed in life, I've turned to crafts. When all of my friends in seventh grade hated me, I made tons of ribbon barrettes. When I couldn't deal with the stress of the SATs or the college essay, I made beaded rings. And when I worked on the very first season of *The Ricki Lake Show* and had to find spandex-clad "hoochie moms" willing to fight with their disapproving kids on national TV, I made charm necklaces and eyeglass chains. My craft binges lasted anywhere from a week to six months—enough time for me to escape my reality and engage in a simple, pressure-free project that I could admire. After finishing, I'd look at my creation, touch it, look in the mirror, try it on again and again, and think, "Everything's going to be okay." My stress miraculously faded into the background. I was no longer a seventh-grade loser, a stressed-out senior, or a struggling associate producer; I was a productive, creative, and viable human being. I like to call this phenomenon—the Power of Crafts.

The Power has to do with crafting being incredibly forgiving, uncompetitive, very accessible, and easy. You don't need to be fantastically artistic (I'm not!), or exceptionally innovative (I'm not!), or even overly patient (I'm *really* not!). It's something you can pick up whenever you have a spare moment, or put down (without feeling guilty about not finishing it) when you're not in the mood. To sum it up: Crafting rocks! And it's helped me get through some of the hardest and most stressful periods of my life. So you can imagine how incredibly crafty I became on July 6, 2003, when my first daughter, Lily Skye, was born.

Talk about overwhelming! There you are, big and pregnant one day, and a week later, you're sitting in your house—uterus still swollen—with this very real, very helpless little baby sucking on pretty much everything in sight. What's more, you're responsible for making it thrive. (The SATs never looked so good!) I couldn't stop Lily from crying; I couldn't get her to wake up during the day and sleep during the night; and I couldn't (quickly) figure out how to fix her like I'd fixed every other situation in my life thus far. (Note: Everyone started liking me again in seventh grade, I got into a good college, and, as it turned out, plenty of hoochie moms jumped at the chance to have it out on national TV!)

My work as a freelance producer didn't exactly offer "maternity leave" or a place to go back to. So, if I wanted to work, I had to find a freelance gig. But was I ready? If so, who would watch Lily? Could I leave her with a nanny? Would she be mad at me? Would I be mad at me? Unfortunately, no answers immediately came. (And my thought process wasn't helped by my lack of downtime— for the first eight months of her life, Lily napped *only* in a moving stroller.) So I took on the role of "stay-at-home mom." I was excited to be with Lily, but I wasn't convinced I was going to be very good at it.

In all of my postpartum confusion, I dug out my hot-glue gun from the bottom of the diaper-crammed linen closet and started to create. I knew my first project had to be something simple and quick, but attractive enough to warrant the "oh-my-goodness-I-can't-believe-you-made-that" response. The Photo Bragnets (page 197) were my solution. I made fifty-six (enough for all of Lily's grandparents, great-grandparents, aunts, and uncles). People couldn't believe that I was awake, let alone crafting. But the fact that I could make cute projects starring Lily made me feel good, even when I was feeling so uncertain about, well, everything else.

Still trying to figure out my new role as "Mom," I moved on to iron-ons (pages 28–30). I downloaded free fonts and photos from assorted sites on the web to decorate every blank onesie, burp cloth, T-shirt, sweatshirt, and blanket Lily had. Everyone on the Upper West Side of Manhattan knew her name and that she liked (okay, *I* liked) *The Facts of Life*, the Fonz, and Tootsie Pops. I got compliments galore, and it made me feel like I was really getting somewhere. What can I say? I'm a validation junkie! For more than ten years, I had bosses who told me they were proud of me and that I was doing a great job. But with Lily as the boss now, advanced as she was, she didn't say anything of the sort. (Unless, of course, that's what "WAAAAH!" really means?) I know, I know: She was healthy and happy, and indeed I felt blessed and grateful (almost) every second of the day, but I missed the validation. People would say things like, "Oh, she's got such great neck control," and that was a testament to Lily, not me. How could I possibly take credit for the strength of her neck? That said, I was more than happy to take credit for her mama-made onesies, barrettes, and burp cloths. Each creation made me feel productive, positive, and, most importantly, successful as a mom. This Crafty Mama was here to stay. And now I wanted to spread the love.

It was time to find a playgroup. I peered into strollers on the street and picked up moms who had babies around the same age as mine. I went to a few "mommy lunches," and I signed up for a baby massage class. Many of the moms I met were refreshingly honest about their new reality. Each of us was navigating her way through new motherhood, and there was just so much to talk about and figure out. Thankfully, I connected with a great bunch of women who were interested in trying to figure it out together.

We met every Thursday and, in between talking about sleep, our in-laws, "the Donald," and how addictive apple cinnamon soy chips are, they remarked how much they liked Lily's embellished goodies. (By this time I'd added personalized diaper wipe boxes, brag books, and fleece hats to my repertoire.) They all wanted to buy my snazzy creations for their little nuggets! But when it occurred to me that I didn't want to become a one-woman craft factory, I thought it'd be great if other moms could experience the Power of Crafts for themselves. So one Thursday, we all got crafty together.

As I gave my mommy friends the Photo Bragnet "how-to" (page 197), baby Noah slept in the swing, Lily and Stephanie lay under the Gymini, Jaden and Aidan snoozed in their strollers, Elizabeth gurgled from her bouncy seat, and Cayla hung out in the Bjorn. They all cried and pooped, and needed to be fed and loved—as babies do—so

Abby and Lily in NYC.

we paused from time to time, and then started crafting again. Two hours later, everyone had a fabulous set of Bragnets to display proudly on the fridge! The fact that we were actually making something while bonding and commiserating made motherhood seem lighter and easier to deal with. Everyone was amazed at how satisfied they felt post-crafting, and they couldn't wait to show off their Crafty Mama creations to their family and friends. As more and more moms joined our weekly craft fests, my apartment got smaller and smaller. So I pitched the idea of a "Bond-with-New-Moms-as-You-Make-Cute-Stuff-for-Your-Baby" class to a community center nearby. Three weeks later, I started teaching Crafty Mama classes every Monday afternoon to eleven new moms at the JCC Manhattan.

Mind you, these moms are not artists. Most of them hadn't done anything crafty since fifth grade and had never even used a glue gun! But it didn't matter. Crafty Mama gatherings aren't about making the perfect project. They're about connecting with people who are going through the same thing as you and using your hands for something other than changing a diaper. Besides, I hate the word "perfect" these days.

Lily is now four and has a little sister, Sasha. Over the last three years, I've been freelance producing, teaching crafty mamas, having a baby, and . . . writing this book so all of you elated, frustrated, overjoyed, overwhelmed, sleep-deprived, busy moms can experience the Power of Crafts for yourselves! Just when I think I've figured my kids out, they hit a new stage, and I have to start all over again. But rather than let it get me down, I get crafty. ♥

THOSE WHO COO TOGETHER, GLUE TOGETHER

Connect with other creative moms, preggy pals, and PNMFs (Potential New Mommy Friends)— and start your own Crafty Mamas group.

Crafting is good. But crafting with other sleep-deprived, overwhelmed yet overjoyed moms is even better. There are many ways to go about starting your own Crafty Mamas playgroup. If you already get together with a bunch of moms, see if they're interested in adding some hot glue and fleece to your weekly rendezvous. That's how mine started. For the first few weeks, we hung out, ate Jelly Bellys, and talked about *Oprah,* our couch stains, and the defective wheels on our strollers. None of the women considered themselves particularly crafty, but since they loved the idea of making stuff for their little ones, I planned an easy (but boutique-worthy) craft for each week's meeting. We found that crafting while bonding made us feel great. Not only did we get stuff off our engorged chests, but we also had a fabulous keepsake to show for ourselves at the end of the Momfest.

the dating game

Making new mommy friends after you have a baby is just like dating. If you want to succeed, you need to make the approach, get a number, and then go through that awkward "getting to know you" stage. Personally, I was always a lousy dater. I never made the first move, plus I'm emotional and needy, which is a bad combination when you're twenty-four and going after a hottie in a bar. But the good thing about "dating" other moms is that this time around, *everyone* is emotional and needy. For me, the need to discuss sore nipples, lack of sleep, and the latest guest on *Ellen* was greater than all my former dating fears, so I aggressively sought out a playgroup!

Now, I'm no parenting expert. (Please—I didn't even know that there was more than one size bottle nipple, so when Lily was eight months old, she was still slurping from a size one!) But I do feel comfortable giving this piece of advice to new moms: Hang out with other new moms. Even if every one of your old friends already has kids, talking to someone who's going through the same things as you, *at the same time as you,* is healthy. Yes, the dating part of putting yourself out there at one of the most vulnerable times in your life is less than desirable, but meeting new mamas and realizing that (almost) everyone is just as overwhelmed and amazed as you are—well, it's a tremendously empowering feeling. And when you find the right people, the bad parts of dating disappear, and you find yourself surrounded by some really wonderful, interesting, supportive new mommy friends.

So get ready to face the world with your new, adorable baby and "in-between" jeans. Get ready, get set, get out there, and be social. You da mom!

PREGGY PALS!

If you're still "with child," sign up for a prenatal yoga or birthing class. Not only will you stretch your already stretching body and learn about newborn umbilical care (fun!), but you'll also get to bond with other women who have tiny elbows jabbing them in the stomach! Stay in touch with your preggy pals and once your babies are born, you'll instantly have new moms to hang out with when you're trying to figure out how to unfold your stroller with one hand.

TAKE A WALK

Whether you live in the city or the 'burbs, take a walk on the streets, in the mall, or at the park, and you're sure to see dozens of moms doing the same. Target a Potential New Mommy Friend (PNMF) and think of a good conversation starter. I once made a friend on the street by commenting on how well she had tied the sunshade onto her stroller. (It really was impressive!) If your convo goes well, get her number and put it someplace safe (and that doesn't include scribbling it on a wipe or gum wrapper at the bottom of your diaper bag). If you're feeling super-ambitious, make up some "mommy calling cards" with your name, your baby's name, your e-mail address, and your cell number on them. I received a few of them from some über-organized moms, and I really appreciated them.

TAKE A NEW BABY CLASS

I took a baby massage class when Lily was about three months old. Although I can't say that I'm now an ace at soothing my baby through gentle touch, I did meet most of my playgroup there! Music classes, postnatal yoga, mommy-and-me exercise, and baby sign language classes are great places to pick up new moms. Check out your local community center, pediatrician's office, place of worship, or mall to find classes near you.

GO TO THE MOVIES

Several cinema chains have added special daytime screenings for moms with their babies. The lights are brighter, the movie isn't as loud, and screaming and pooping are more than welcome. Look into: Lowe's "Reel Moms," Cineplex Odeon's "Stars and Strollers," Clearview Cinema's "Mommie Matinees," National Amusements' "Baby Pictures," or Consolidated Theatres' "Movie Mom's Club." There are often activities before or after the movie so you can socialize with the other new (and sleepy) moms.

STOP AND READ THE FLIERS!

And while you're at it, smell the flowers, too. There are pamphlets and fliers displayed all over your pediatrician's office that advertise groups and activities for new moms. Since you're going to have plenty of spare time in the waiting room, pick one up and see if it's advertising a group or activity that's right for you. If you want to get in on the action *before* you have a baby, check your OB's office for literature about prenatal or postnatal groups.

GO "MOMLINE"

If you're dying to connect with other moms, but the thought of getting out of your stretchy PJs makes you want to cry, don't you worry. First, it's normal. Second, just pull your glider up to the computer and log on to a website to chat with other new moms and check out the local playgroups and moms' groups. There's no pressure to join anything or get out of the house just yet, but it's

great to know that there are people out there just waiting to meet you and your precious little bambino!

babyzone.com This site connects you to kid-friendly *events* in your area, which will connect you to *people* in your area who are great candidates for a *playgroup* in your area!

cafemom.com Journals, photos, and groups . . . This site is wall-to-wall moms—talking, sharing, emoting, and connecting—from the same people who started clubmom .com. At cafemom.com, you can find local groups or virtual groups with the same interests as you.

childavenue.com Log on, click on "playgroups," choose a state, and—voilà!—playgroups at your fingertips. Even though your baby's only, say, three months old, you can also check out their cute ideas for birthday themes while you're there. It's never too early to start planning her first!

matchingmoms.org Just type in your ZIP code and find mama members near you. They also have message boards and practical information about playgroup etiquette.

meetup.com Do you want to hang out with other Veggie Moms, Political Moms, or Punky Moms? Then join one of the already existing mom "meet-ups" or start your own. (Crafty Mamas group anyone?)

mommyandme.com After you join (no worries, it's free), you can search the National Playgroup Directory to locate a playgroup in your 'hood. How's that for convenience?

mothersclick.com This forum allows moms to mingle in cyberspace, ask questions, and share stories and experiences with other moms all over. Sign up and read or post group activities, recipes, toy and product reviews, and other resources!

myplaydate.com Did you meet your significant other online? Then try this on for size: Fill out a profile for your baby (photo optional), browse other babes' stats, and then make a connection.

nomotc.org If you have twins, triplets, quads, quints, or more, then the National Organization of Mothers of Twins Club is the group for you! Find local support, playgroups, and tons of resources for parents of multiples.

parentsconnect.com This is a great site from the fine folks at Nickelodeon for parents to . . . connect. But you probably figured that out already. Hook up with like-minded mamas by entering your ZIP, your kid's age, and a few things you like. You'll be connected to members who live near you and groups with the same interests as you. A bonus: Tons of recipes, tips, and crafts to do with your kids!

"I often leave my Crafty Mama posse with paint under my fingernails, but a huge grin on my face." —CRAFTY MAMA JEN

playgrouptoday.com Log on, log in, and search for one of many playgroups near you. If you don't find one that speaks to you and your lifestyle, start one. There's also a chat forum so you can bond with moms all over the U.S.

thenestbaby.com Chat with other hopeful parents, parents-to-be, and parents of kids of all ages and get tips from experts on every stage from preconception to six-plus months. Find or post about recommended baby-related services in your area—including the ever-challenging search for kid-friendly eateries.

yahoo.com/group While you're at Yahoo searching for a Squirrel Nut Zippers image to iron on to your baby's onesie, join the site for free and check out the groups. No matter where you are, you can probably hook up with a group of mamas that dig the Zippers too! (Then kick off your new playgroup with a Squirrel Nut Zippers onesie craft party!)

great expectations

Playgroups are a great forum for sharing your honest feelings about being a mom, but expect some differences of opinion. By the time Lily was about five months old, I was so totally stressed out. Whenever I expressed my frustration to my husband, he'd say, "Oh

say what?

Whether you're going "momline" to find a playgroup or just want to find out if anyone ever really put cabbage leaves on their boobs, you might be a little confused by what you read on the message boards. For instance, one poster writes, "Three weeks AB and my DH (who's a WAHD) is already begging for LO, but GMAB—all he's getting is a GBH&K." What does it all mean? Here's a guide to some commonly used momcronyms!

AB = After Baby

AF = Aunt Flo (menstruation)

BB = Before Baby or Bulletin Board

BCP = Birth Control Pills

BD/BMS = Baby Dance/ Baby-Making Sex

BF = Breastfeeding

BFN/BFP = Big Fat Negative/ Positive (pregnancy test)

BM = Breast Milk or Bowel Movement

BTDT = Been There, Done That

CIO = Cry It Out

DD/DS/DC = Dear or Darling Daughter/Son/Child or Day Care

DH/DP/DW = Dear or Darling or Damn Husband/Partner/Wife

EBF = Exclusively Breastfeeding

EDD = Estimated Due Date

FF = Formula Feeding

FV = Fertile Vibes

GBH&K = Great Big Hug & Kiss

GD = Gestational Diabetes

GMAB = Give Me a Break

HMP = Help Me Please

HS = Homeschool

HTH = Hope This/That Helps

IF = Infertility

IME = In My Experience

KF = Kid-less Friends

LO = Love Olympics (sex)

MC, m/c, misc. = Miscarriage

MG = Mother's Group

MIL/FIL = Mother-/Father-in-Law

ML = Maternity Leave

MNO = Mom's Night Out

MS = Morning Sickness

MW = Midwife

NH/NP/OP = New Here/ New Poster/Original Poster

OMG = Oh My Gosh, or God

OT = Off Topic

PG = Pregnant or Playgroup

PPD = Postpartum Depression

ROTFLMAO = Rolling On The Floor Laughing My Ass Off

SAHD/SAHM = Stay-At-Home Dad/Mom

TFTT = Thanks for the Tip

TMI = Too Much Information

TTC = Trying to Conceive

US, u/s = Ultrasound

VR = Vasectomy Reversal

WAHD/WOHM = Work At/Outside Home Dad/Mom

Abby, all moms feel the same way." Well, they don't. Some *do*, and they'll say so. Some *do*, but they'll keep it to themselves. And some honestly aren't stressed out at all. We're all different, from the type of pasta we prefer (I'm a ziti gal) to the movies we watch (I still love the teen flicks). We all married different types of people, dress our kids in different outfits, and feel differently about the president of the United States. And that's part of the fun. While it's incredibly comforting to know that many of the moms are having the same doubts and fears as you are, it can be refreshing (and inspiring) to hear other people's points of view.

"It's one thing to drop $25 on a kid's T-shirt at a store; it's a whole different sensation to tie-dye it yourself. There's a great sense of pride that goes along with creating like this." —CRAFTY MAMA AMY

crafty mamas playgroup policy

Before you start crafting, there are a few things to think about and decide upon. Nothing major— just a few details that will make your playgroup easier in the long run—and they shouldn't take more than two hours to figure out. But keep in mind, those two hours do include diaper changes, feedings, and discussions about your husband (who, as wonderful as he is, often "just doesn't get it"), so you're making good time.

TAKE ME TO YOUR LEADER

Many new moms are super-happy to leave the corporate world, but they often miss that fancy title at work. See if one of those high-powered women wants to be the CEO (Crafty Executive Officer) of your Crafty Mamas group. The CEO organizes the finances, buys materials, and sends out weekly e-mail craft briefs about what you're making and what you need to bring. It does take up some time, but it's not too much responsibility. Plus, if you happen to visit your old office and a former coworker asks, "So, what are you doing these days?" you can proudly say, "I'm at home raising my darling daughter, but I also just took this great job as the CEO of a small arts organization for women!" Impressive, no? Having one super-organized person in charge of everything will save you tons of time, headache, and cash. Make sure you frequently tell the CEO how helpful, wonderful, and beautiful she is! (Oh, and if you do elect a CEO, don't be surprised if every once in a while she wears a classy suit to your playgroup and whips out her laptop for a quick PowerPoint presentation. Old habits die hard.)

An alternative to a CEO is the rotating position of the "weekly leader." A different mama (perhaps the host) is responsible for sending out the e-mails, shopping for the materials, and getting everything prepared for the project each week. We tried this in my group, and it was a disaster: Some projects cost more than others so the Crafty Mama who had to schlep to the 'burbs and spend $94 on twenty-four yards of Swanky Blanky fleece (page 41) harbored some resentment for the mama who took the subway to 34th

Street and spent $37 on twelve packs of mitten clips and three spools of ribbon for the Insta-Bibs (page 107). And then there were the wonderful moms in the group who, while very excited to craft 'n' bond, found that getting all the stuff and preparing it was just not among their strengths.

So, talk to your group. If this way works best for you guys, please send an e-mail (via craftymamas.com) and tell me how you did it so I can post it on my website for others to see!

TO CRAFT WITH OR WITHOUT BABY? *THAT* IS THE QUESTION!

Most Crafty Mamas *playgroups* (the ones *with* the babies) take place during the day. You get out of the house and make something fabulous while you gripe about your lack of sleep, and Junior bonds with other drooling cuties. Most Crafty Mamas *mom's groups* (the ones *without* the bambinos) take place at night. Dads, partners, or grandparents do the sitting while Mom has both hands free to craft (or craft with one hand and sip red wine with the other)—while griping about your lack of sleep, of course.

If you decide to do a daytime playgroup, there are benefits to hiring a sitter or mother's helper to assist with the babies. Or, invite a Crafty Nana to come along to look after the tykes and offer pearls of wisdom on crafting (and everything else). Most of the projects take approximately two hours to make in a Crafty Mamas playgroup, and about one-and-a-half hours in a mom's group. That said, feel free to make your sessions last as long as you want. *Note:* Crafting with baby means you have to be extra

diligent about your materials. Make sure you keep them on the table and away from little hands and mouths, since some embellishments do present a choking hazard.

WHEN AND WHERE (WE KNOW WHY!)

Pick a place. You can rotate houses or apartments, or you can do it at the same joint every week. If you're dying to get out of the house, see if your local community center or place of worship has a room for you. Just remember that you need an outlet and a sink for 99 percent of the projects. (Unfortunately, that rules out a trip to the park, unless you bring along a generator.) Holding your Crafty Mamas group at the same place each week will be easier because you won't have to schlep your supplies around. Just be considerate and make sure that that same host doesn't get stuck setting up and cleaning up after each meeting.

Once you're all in agreement about location, figure out a regular day and time. Avoid flip-flopping the days around because it always ends up a mess and someone gets left out.

THE DETAILS

Will you have snacks, lunch, or martinis at your weekly meeting? What are the rules about sick babies or sick mommies? (In my Crafty Mamas group, runny noses are okay; fever and vomit, no way.) How does everyone feel about pets? Bringing an older sibling along in case of an emergency? Popping in a video? (The babies in my Crafty Mamas group were mesmerized each week by *Baby Bach*.) Who is going to step up if the CEO is sick or out of town?

Perhaps you want to elect a CFO (Crafty Fill-in Officer). Figuring out all of these details beforehand will limit any potential frustration and not-so-friendly gossip later on. **Baby Steps** During one of your weekly meetings, have everyone consult this book to figure out what three things you want to make over the next three weeks. (One project a week!) You'll learn a lot in your first few sessions about time, supplies, organization, and crafting with a bottle in one hand. If you need to make adjustments to the time or location or logistics—do it. If your three-week trial period goes great, keep on crafting. **Moolah!** First, let's *save* some. Once you're all settled on what you're going to make for the next three weeks, the CEO should e-mail your group a list of all the supplies you'll need to make the three projects. Many of the mamas may already have some of the materials and hardware in their personal craft stashes, and not having to buy fabric scissors or a glue gun will save you cash in the long run! Another way to save money is to pick projects that use similar materials so you don't have to go shopping as frequently. The My Bragamuffin Brag Book (page 209), Lite the Nite (page 81), Wipey Clutch (page 115), and Foxy Boxes (page 73), for instance, all use the home decorator's fabric, ribbons, and hot glue. Make sure the CEO checks your craft inventory before shopping so you don't buy something you already have. And always check out your local craft stores for specials. Sign up for a weekly sales flier (it's free!) online or in stores, and get coupons galore!

Now, let's *spend* some. Figure out approximately how much each member wants to spend on all three projects combined. It's realistic for each person to contribute $10 to $20, but it really depends on the crafts you choose. The Photo Bragnets (page 197), My Bragamuffin Brag Book (page 209), and I Dream of Jeany Bib (page 99) are all less than $5 each, while the No-Sew Swanky Blanky (page 41), Photo a-Go-Go (page 217), and Hasta la Poncho (page 177) projects can run up to $15 each. You can always scale down or jack up a project's cost according to the quality of the materials, the amount of available embellishments, and your ability to bargain hunt. Once you decide on a price, the CEO collects the cash from everyone. If you have some money left over after the shopping's done, you can decide whether you want to divide it up and redistribute it, put it toward another project, or use it for snacks during your playgroup or a wild mom's night out!

Shopping Therapy! It's the next best thing to crafting therapy. Since the CEO holds the cash, she makes the shopping plan. She can go shopping alone, go with everyone, or designate another Crafty Mama to get the materials for the week. If you're the super-shopper elected, look at the supply list first to see if there is one store or website that has everything you need. Dashing from Michaels to Jo-Ann to the Dollar Store to A. C. Moore to Pearl Paint to Ikea in one afternoon is not everyone's idea of fun! Also, make sure there's an approximate budget for each project, so the group doesn't overspend on one and then have to skimp on another. If people are available and into it, I like to make shopping a group activity; everyone goes to the craft store(s) and decides on fabrics, gems, and beads, and then it's chow time at the local pizza joint.

"P" IS FOR PREPARATION

Do your homework: You've got to be ready for anything! If a Crafty Mama arrives at your house with a soundly sleeping baby, chances are she's going to want to dive right into the week's project. Be prepared by appointing at least one person (maybe the host, the CEO, or an appointed Craftista) to check out the project's instructions the night before so she can guide the eager mama.

Find the Cybermama When it's time to prepare personalized craft ingredients like iron-ons and decoupage images, see how your group wants to handle this. Most likely, there'll be a cybermama who is a whiz at finding, fixing, sizing, and printing pics who will emerge naturally as your go-to gal. Otherwise, see if you can find someone in your group who is a quick study. (It's not hard, I promise.) Just make sure you set aside some money for her computer ink and paper—that stuff's expensive!

Details, Details I do all of the prep and setup for my group because I find cutting rectangles out of home décor fabric and alphabetically separating letter beads therapeutic. You may have a freak or two like me in your playgroup, or you may have to assign someone to step up and prepare the supplies. Talk amongst yourselves.

reality check

Once you decide upon the day, time, and place, buy all of the supplies, and assign roles (for now), release your inner crafty mama and make stuff! Oh dear, is that *your* baby getting unpacifiably hysterical just as you're ready to create an amazing decoupage masterpiece? Don't be alarmed. Babies are just like us; they have their good days and their bad. Actually, forget days—they're on a minute-to-minute basis. If your little one has a meltdown, ask a friend with a sleeping beauty to get your project

"Crafting makes me feel like a kid again— something I need now that I'm a real grown-up with all of these new grown-up responsibilities."

—CRAFTY MAMA SARAH

started (and possibly even finished) for you. Never feel bad that your kid is the one crying. Chances are someone else's munchkin will have a meltdown next week.

IF IT'S BROKE, FIX IT!

Again, it's like dating: You go out with a guy and think things are great because you're all caught up in having a boyfriend, only to realize one day that he's all wrong for you. The same goes for a playgroup. Some groupmates, whom you met at a time when you were desperate for human interaction, may not make you feel good about yourself now. Remember, if you don't click, you can always end the relationship. There are a lot of great moms out there looking to connect. You wouldn't settle on a mate who makes you unhappy, so why settle for friends who do?

have it your way

Now that you've read all of this, I want you to know that there's no "right way" to have a Crafty Mamas playgroup. Craft at every playgroup or craft just once a month. Have two women there or sixteen. As with everything in motherhood, you gotta do what feels right for you!

CRAFTY MAMA 101

**A crash course on all the tools, techniques,
and tips for getting crafty, mama-style.**

Not only have you gotten out of your pajamas, but you've
gone out of your house, met some really great friends,
organized a Crafty Mamas playgroup, and even put on a little
lipstick to boot (yes, Chapstick counts!). Let me just say, I am very
impressed. Now all you have to do is craft. But before you plug in
your hot-glue gun and get out your rickrack and rhinestones, read
this chapter. Crafty Mama 101 is a crash course on the basic tools
and techniques you'll need to know to make all the projects in the
book. Refer back to it whenever your "mommy brain" kicks in and
you can't remember if you packed a bottle, let alone how to make a
cow hitch on your mama-made fleece hat.

Speaking of know-how, worry not: You don't need to know how to knit, draw, or even cut in a straight line to make cute stuff! Many of the projects in this book are about jazzing up or personalizing an existing item, rather than starting completely from scratch. The real key to making fabulous Crafty Mama creations is finding great fabric, ribbon, trim, and embellishments. With the right materials, even the sleepiest, uncraftiest mama can make a wipe box go from plastic to fantastic.

Although I give fairly explicit instructions for the base of each project, I intentionally leave the embellishment steps less specific. I've provided examples of how I chose to make each project, but I want you to make what *you* like. After all, just as there's no one way to be a parent, there's also no one way to decorate a jean bib. By choosing your own fabrics and embellishments, your creation is going to reflect awesome you!

That said, some days "awesome you" is awesomely tired, and the thought of deciding what to put on your baby's booties is awesomely overwhelming. In this case, check out the archives of some trendy baby sites to get style, color, pattern, and decoration ideas (try www .urbanbaby.com, www.coolmompicks.com, www.daily candykids.com, and www.thedailystroll.com), or make exactly what your friend is making! Imitation *is* the sincerest form of flattery, and with a different set of hands (yours) working on the project, it will still be unique.

If at the end of the day you hate the way your project came out, let it go. Sometimes your craft is going to rock, and sometimes it's gonna look like one. If you can talk yourself out of tossing it, you might want to keep it to share with your child when he's older and feeling imperfect. Or donate it, as chances are there's a Madison somewhere who needs a picture frame!

using this book

I know, I know, you just want to get to the crafting, but before you take off, hot-glue guns ablaze, there are just a few things more that I promise will make everything easier as you go. You'll learn the staple ingredients every Crafty Mama should keep stocked in her craft pantry (so she can serve up a project at a moment's notice) as well as several crafting techniques that can be applied to many projects throughout this book. Rather than explaining them in great detail every single time they're used, I'm going to lay them all out for you up front. So when you see the word *decoupage* in the instructions, instead of responding with a "What

the . . . ?," you'll be all, "Decoupage? Bring it on. My middle name is Decoupage!"

RATED C FOR CRAFT

Cost: .... $

Time: .... ⏱ ⏱

Skill: .... ✂ ✂ ✂

How ga-ga they'll go: ... ♥ ♥ ♥ ♥ ♥

Before each project, you'll notice this lovely little rating chart. Each "cost" unit represents $5. Each "time" unit represents approximately half an hour. Each "skill" unit represents level of difficulty (one unit is easy, five units is more challenging), and each "ga-ga" unit represents how impressed everyone's going to be when they find out what an incredible Crafty Mama you are! *Note:* "Time" and "Skill" ratings do account for diaper changes and minor tantrums, but if your baby happens to be crankier than usual, or you've had fewer than five hours of sleep, time and level of difficulty *are* subject to change.

CRAFTYPEDIA

If there's ever a time when you're looking at the list of supplies for a project and find yourself saying, "What on earth is that?," simply dance your itsy bitsy spiders to the back of the book for a look at the Craftypedia. It's an easy-to-use glossary of nearly every material you need to make any project in this book, along with a brief description of each, how to use it, approximate cost, where to buy it, and which projects you need it for. Alternatively, if you find yourself with leftover fabric or ribbon, turn to that entry in the Craftypedia to figure out what else you can make!

SAFETY MAMA

Glue guns, and rhinestones, and scissors—oh my! There are a lot of craft tools and materials that you'll use in this book that aren't exactly child friendly. Please be conscious of all the hot, sharp little things around you at all times. If possible, set up your craft station in the kitchen while the babies play in a craft-free room nearby. Just make sure there's one brave mama always looking after the kids ('cause crafts aren't the only thing in your house that you don't want your kids getting into!). Or, set up shop at a table that your child can't reach. No matter where you set up, always clean up immediately and thoroughly to account for any dropped jewels, ribbons, or beads. There are some projects that, when completed, can fit through a toilet paper roll (the universal indicator for being a choking hazard). Those are the projects that are meant for you or grandma to enjoy (bracelets and necklaces); let your baby enjoy the blankets and bibs (no small parts there!).

"In the first few months of motherhood, where everything is a challenge, being successful at creating something so concrete as an embellished diaper wipe box—well, it just made me happy!"

—CRAFTY MAMA LIZ

the craft pantry

You have all the little jars of pureed carrots, peas, and apples you could ever need in your kitchen pantry, but how's your craft pantry holding up? Like the chefs who recommend that you keep your kitchen well stocked with olive oil and garlic at all times, I'm here to tell you that there are items equally essential to being a Crafty Mama. These are tools or materials that you'll use in virtually every project. They're going to be your best friends, so let's get you introduced.

SCISSORS

You can't use just any pair of "grown-up" scissors to cut fabric. Trust me; I learned the hard way when I tried to trim some quilting cotton with my orange-handled office scissors. In order to easily get a straight, non-frayed cut of fabric or ribbon, a pair of bent-handled, stainless steel 8" shears is the best. (Shears are defined by having two different sized finger holes and an offset blade longer than 6".) Now, I am all about a bargain, but don't buy a pair that costs less than $5 because chances are the blades aren't as sharp, and they won't cut through fabric. (That was the problem with my $2.99 office pair!) A good pair of shears will cut through fabric, ribbon, paper—even craft wire. Many people who work with fabric professionally may pop a button to hear me say this, but for the casual crafter, one pair of sharp shears *can* do the trick. Personally, I love

Fiskars brand shears because they're durable, come in great colors (I have pink and purple pairs), and some even have nonstick blades (so they don't get gummed up when I cut contact paper). Admittedly, I have many pairs of scissors for multiple craft needs (and classes), but I will repeat: One sharp pair is all you need to start off. Eventually, you may decide to invest in specialized scissors for fabric, paper, or multipurpose use (to keep each pair sharp). And there is no shortage of places to find them; they're available at most craft, fabric, and mass merchant stores, as well as online!

FABRIC

If a *Project Runway* episode was the only time you've ever seen the inside of a fabric store, I can see how you might be a little intimidated. But fear not! Your local retail fabric store probably isn't tremendously massive, and they don't make you pick everything out in fifteen minutes (although you might need to 'cause chances are Junior's going to want to eat the second you get there).

Most fabric stores are arranged by fabric type, such as quilting cotton, home décor fabric, fleece, felt, and tulle—which happen to be the ones you need to gravitate toward for the projects in this book. The first are quilting cottons, which are cute, printed, thin cotton fabrics.

Home décor fabric is bold, graphic, and a thicker, more durable, canvaslike fabric. Fleece is a warm, fuzzy, slightly stretchy, no-fray fabric that's easy to maneuver. You'll probably recognize felt as the same no-fray, easy-to-cut stuff you used in first grade. And tulle is that pretty netted tutu fabric. Fabric generally comes on a "bolt"—the fancy name for "wrapped around a piece of cardboard"—and is sold by the yard.

And even though most parenting experts shun the words *right* and *wrong*, they admit that it is okay to use them when referring to fabric! The "right" side of the fabric is the one where the print is clearest; the "wrong" side is the one where there is no print or where the print is fuzzier or blurrier.

And now let's talk about stretching—something you might not do, but something your fabric does, especially fleece. If you pull your fleece vertically and horizontally, you'll see that it is much more stretchy in one direction. (I'm telling you this now so you don't think you're going crazy the next time you're doing a fleece project and one side is way easier to manipulate than the other.) Quilting cotton, home décor fabric, tulle, and felt all stretch on the "bias," a fancy word for "diagonal."

Now that you know all this, you'll be a pro at making everything . . . and you'll be able to watch *Project Runway* in a whole new light!

RIBBON

I've had a love affair with ribbon ever since I first learned to tie a yarn bow in my hair in the second grade. But since

dollars and sense!

If there's one thing I hate, it's paying too much for craft supplies. Luckily, there are a bunch of places to find fantastic sales and bargains on great craft stuff. To cut costs, sign up for sales fliers and web coupons, look in sale bins, and scour the aisles for deals. Here are a few stores that I love:

• Jo-Ann
• Michaels Arts and Crafts
• A. C. Moore
• Ikea
• Pearl Paint
• Wal-Mart (It has a great craft section!)
• Any 99 cent or dollar store
• Staples

Here are sites that I love:
• www.createforless.com
• www.dickblick.com
• www.orientaltrading.com
• www.save-on-crafts.com
• www.ssww.com
• www.discountschoolsupplies.com

(Just make sure not to pay more for shipping than the cost of your item!)

then, I've come to understand that ribbon is more than a hair tie. So, so much more.

Like fabric, there are all different kinds of ribbon—thick or thin, textured or smooth, embroidered or printed—which means your embellishment options are endless. There's grosgrain ribbon, with a matte finish and a crisp, ribbed weave. Satin ribbon is smooth, shiny, and lightweight. Jacquard is a thick, woven ribbon that is distinguished by its two visibly different "sides"; the "right" side has an intricate design resembling embroidery, while the "wrong" side reveals all the chunky, funky strings of the underbelly. Organza and nylon ribbon are sheer, thin, and shimmery, and velvet ribbon has (surprise!) a soft, velvet finish.

Most ribbons fray when you cut them—it's almost unavoidable. But there are easy fixes. I often stop the fray with a gluey solution like No Fray, Fray Stop, or Fray Check. Alternatively, I'll sometimes squeeze a dab of fabric hot glue at the very end of a ribbon and fold it over. Or, on lighter weight ribbons, I brush clear nail polish on the ends. Each technique comes in handy because I cut ribbon a lot! If you plan on doing several projects (chances are you're going to need some ribbon at a later date for one of those projects, a present, or a hairdo), buy ribbon on spools, rather than by the yard, because it's cheaper. Being the thrifty mama that I am, I can't be a stronger advocate for buying in bulk.

EMBELLISHMENTS

I got an early start at embellishing. From the ages of nine to nineteen, I went to an all-girl, two-month sleep-away camp in Maine that had a uniform. A uniform! So every year, I'd figure out a new way to jazz it up and make it more "me." One year, I puffy-painted over my camp logo to make it 3-D. Another year, I chopped up the uniform to make it look distressed. And then there was my trim phase, my beading phase, and let's not forget the bedazzling-rhinestones-and-studs-on-everything-I-wore phase (that one lasted about three years). Indeed, some things should be kept plain and simple, but others, if you listen closely enough, are just crying out for some pizzazz!

Welcome to the wonderful world of embellishments—little things that transform the most "blah" object into an "a-ha!" masterpiece. An embellishment can be anything—

some ribbon, buttons, a Matchbox car, a pendant, a bottle cap, rhinestones, beads, a Super Ball, a plastic bug, even a broken cufflink—you name it. If you like it and it's the right size to hot glue onto your picture frame, bootie, or wipe box, go for it! You can find embellishments at the dollar store, the toy store, the supermarket, the stationery store, the craft store, mass merchant stores, fabric stores, thrift stores, and even your junk drawer at home. You can embellish modestly with one tiny silver star or a small piece of plain ribbon, or go all out bling-tastic with zillions of rhinestones, polka-dotted bows, and Barbie heads! Whether your style is preppy, jazzy, sporty, simple, punk, retro, or goth, there is an embellishment out there for you that's going to take your project to a whole different level!

Ribbon or rickrack, sequins or silk flowers, plastic buttons or plastic bugs— anything can serve.

et tu, hot glue?

Having kids blew my mind, but to be honest, it was not my first life-altering experience. Another one came about eighteen years earlier when I discovered . . . the hot-glue gun! All of a sudden I was able to do things that I never could do before: I decorated twenty-seven different cheap hats to hide a hideously traumatic haircut, I reupholstered the skanky couch that my roomies and I inherited from a skanky ex, and I was finally able to fix things that had fallen apart over the first seventeen years of my life. I said good-bye to needles, Krazy Glue, and frightening staple guns, and hello to hot glue, the easiest way to fix anything and everything in the world.

HOT AND COLD

First things first: When purchasing your first hot-glue gun (available at most craft, drug, mass merchant, or hardware stores), I recommend buying one that is labeled "hot" and not "low temp." "Low temp" glue guns, as you may have guessed, don't get nearly as hot. So although you have less of a chance of getting burned (a plus), the glue doesn't stick as well, so there's a higher chance of your project falling apart (a minus). Also, the cool-melt sticks sometimes dry a little bit milky, so it's more visible if you overdo it.

SIZE *DOES* MATTER

Large hot-glue guns range anywhere from $8 to $30 at most craft or hardware stores. Usually, the more expensive they are, the hotter they get, which is helpful in making things stick more permanently. Some of the newer and craftier models come with separate nozzles for gluing ribbons and fixing things in hard-to-reach, small places. Some also come cordless, but while they are easier to use, they're also easier to leave lying around, so I don't recommend them if you're crafting with free-roaming babies. I've had several different large hot-glue guns over the years, but I'm a big fan of Aleene's glue guns and Stanley glue guns.

Mini hot-glue guns range in price from $1 to $5, and work well for attaching embellishments and trim. The nozzle is smaller, and the glue flows out slowly, giving you more control and fewer opportunities to burn yourself. I don't recommend any particular brand, but I do suggest getting about five of them so that several people in your Crafty Mamas group can glue at the same time. One time I found them on sale for 99 cents at A. C. Moore, so I bought about forty-seven of them! I continue to use them and give them out to glue-gunless people who visit my home.

keep it clean!

To clean one of your hot-glued creations, gently wipe it down with a wet, soapy cloth. Don't scrub it too vigorously or put it in the (gasp!) dishwasher because something might peel off.

TWO IS BETTER THAN ONE

Asking "Do I really need two glue guns?" is sort of like asking, "Do I really need two pairs of black boots?" Realistically and practically, you don't. That one pair of hot black boots you splurged on this season looks great with pretty much everything. That said, the black suede ones (that are *totally* on sale) look better with a few outfits, and will make you feel good and sexy while putting less stress on that lonely black pair, so they'll last longer. But enough about boots. At publication time, the specialty glue sticks (fabric, glitter-infused, etc.) needed for several projects in this book aren't available in mini glue gun sizes. So if you only want one, buy a large one. I promise you won't regret investing a few more bucks in a mini hot-glue gun, though, because changing from the clear hot melt sticks to the fabric glue sticks can be incredibly messy, sticky, and *hot*! Both glue guns will get plenty of use; there's never a shortage of things that need to be fixed, hemmed, or embellished.

HOW TO USE YOUR GLUE MACHINE

Before you even start gluing, get your workspace ready. If your surface isn't used exclusively for crafting, it's a good idea to protect it. Cut a 5" square from an old cardboard box (a cereal box works great). This square will protect your rug, table, countertop, or floor from getting all gluey. No matter where you decide to glue, make sure your glue gun is completely out of any baby's reach. Now for the gluing:

1 Set the hot-glue gun on its stand on the cardboard square. If there's no stand attached, simply lay it on its side on the cardboard. *Note:* Whenever the glue gun is on, and not in your hand, it should be on the cardboard.

2 Plug in your hot-glue gun and push a glue stick all the way into the hole in the back of it. If needed, push in another right behind it so its end is sticking out.

3 Wait about seven minutes for the glue to warm up. You'll know your glue gun is ready when a little bit of glue

not to nag, but . . .

Hot glue guns are HOT! Please, please, please be super-careful when you're gluing and never have them anywhere within your baby's reach.

leaks out of the nozzle. Whatever you do, don't touch the metal nozzle—it's hot!

4 Before you tackle a big project, practice. Take a spare embellishment, turn it over, and press the gun's trigger to release a small dab of glue. Quickly stick it onto a scrap of fabric or paper.

5 Note the amount of pressure you apply to squeeze the right amount of glue on the object. If you squeeze too hard, you'll end up with too much glue blobbing over the edges, which is painful to your fingers, and aesthetically . . . blobby. If you don't squeeze hard enough, too *little* glue comes out, and it might not stick. Getting the right amount of glue is an acquired skill; keep practicing with scraps to get it right.

6 Practice sticking your glued item to your project quickly. The hotter the glue is, the better it sticks, and the faster it cools. Regular hot-melt glue sticks only have a five-second window to stick. But if you wait too long and it doesn't stick, don't worry. Wait two minutes until the glue dries and then pick it off. Or, carefully place the heated nozzle of the glue gun against the dry glue. As the nozzle melts the dry glue, squeeze a small amount of new glue over the area. Turn the embellishment over *immediately* and stick it on.

crafty computer

Figuring out your computer (much like figuring out your child!) can be frustrating, but once you get the hang of it, it gets easier, better, and far more rewarding. Plus, you get the added benefit of being (briefly) more computer savvy than your two-year-old! (Warning: It won't last long. My sister-in-law constantly bemoans the fact that ever since my nephew turned three, he knows how to use the computer better than she does!)

Some people have their own hyper-organized way of storing things on their computer. But others, like my mom, my friend Bindi, and many, many more, just save everything to their desktop (or wherever else it might randomly end up on their computer) and then get really annoyed when they can't find what they're looking for later! I recommend making a folder for each chapter in this book—that way, you can easily identify and access an image, font, or photo that suits the project you want to make. Within each chapter folder, create three subfolders: "Fonts and Text," "Photos," and "Decoupage." So if you happen upon the perfect picture of John Travolta circa his *Saturday Night Fever* years, you'll be able to find it in a snap next time you get the urge to make an iron-on tee (page 133) for your little dancing queen.

THE LITTLE SEARCH ENGINE THAT COULD

Brainstorm about the images you want to download for placement on a plate, a onesie, a toy bucket, or even a dresser drawer. Your image selection can include anything or anyone, from Duran Duran to Ganesha the Hindu elephant god, from Frida to Elmo—or how about a tractor? Totally up to you. Head to your computer, sit down, and get comfy.

Log on to one of the large search engines, such as Google (www.google.com) or Yahoo (www.yahoo.com), and click on "Images" (right above the little search bar). Type in the name of the person or thing you want (aka "search word"), and hit enter/return. It's doubtful that you'll stump the World Wide Web completely. Tons of images matching your search criteria will pop up. Find one you like, open it, view it as a full-size image, and save it to the appropriate Crafty Mamas chapter folder. Just note that an image that is at least 200 x 200 pixels will work best (as an iron-on or other crafty piece). And even if you're practically positive that you've got it right, print test photos at low resolution on regular paper to check.

RESIZE

Whether you're using your own photo or an image found online, you want the resolution to be as high as possible for it to look its best on your iron-on or decoupage project. That said, the size of the image may need to change. If you're planning to decorate a onesie, your iron-on image should be smaller than, say, a photo you put on a personalized placemat. To resize, "insert" your picture (from one of your Crafty Mama folders) into a Word document (nothing fancy!). Click on a corner (rather than a side) to maintain the image's proportions, and use the arrow to drag until you find the best size for your project. Reduce your margins allowing for just .3 clearance all around to fit the maximum number of images per page. Since iron-on transfer and fancy photo papers don't come cheap, resizing also allows you to fit several images on one page, helping you save the environment and your pennies.

A CLICK IN THE RIGHT DIRECTION

Not everyone's computer (or brain) is set up the same way.

If your machine's got you stumped, don't freak out. You do have options! Call a friend, your hubby, your partner, your mom, your local computer store, your thirteen-year-old computer geek neighbor, or search online for help. There are several sites (such as www.computerhope.com or www .cybertechhelp.com) that can offer you free step-by-step instructions on exactly how to do what you want to do.

FONTASTIC

If you're content to use all of the fonts already on your computer for your iron-on and decoupage projects, fine. If you're looking to upgrade, download from sites like www.1001freefonts.com and www.fontface.com. Feel free to peruse all of the fonts on these sites, or if you want to direct your search within a font site, try my very unscientific "letter theory." Let me explain: If you're thinking, "I really want to write something in the *Star Wars* font. I wonder if they have it," try clicking on "S" (for *Star Wars*) and be pleasantly surprised when you find "Star Jedi," the font that looks like the movie title. Want something with flowers? Try "F." Want something with hearts, hands, or a little Hawaiian punch? Try "H." The technique has a few glitches, and sometimes you need to think a little outside the box. For instance, in order to find a *Flintstones* font, I tried "F," but after finding nada, I tried "prehistoric" before I finally ended up finding the Caveman font under "C."

photo phabulous

You just had a baby and you hardly have the time to shower and brush your teeth, let alone take a photography class to learn how to take great pictures of your gorgeous new addition who, frankly, isn't much into

sitting and posing just yet anyway. Lucky you: There are all sorts of computer programs that can turn those adorable off-center, red-eyed, dull, faraway, and slightly blurry shots of your little one into fantastic photos for your projects.

A good photo editing program allows you to crop your shots (to avoid that big box of diaper wipes in the background), fix the colors and/or contrast (so your baby doesn't look green), make the shot black-and-white, sepia, or tinted, and yes, even fix those devilish red eyes. Best of all, it's low-stress. Most photo editing programs these days are user-friendly, even for the technologically spastic (like me).

DOWNLOAD OR UPLOAD NOW

If you have a digital camera, chances are it came with a photo editing program that can help you do all this. However, if you're looking for more ways to punch up your photos, search online for "photo editing program." I did and downloaded a whole bunch of software to help fix my photos. The one that I found was the best and most user-friendly is Picasa. It's a great (and at this point, free) online service available at www.picasa.com. So, do your photos and your crafts a favor and download a program now!

BASIC FIXES

Here are a few basic solutions to common picture problems that will make your images (whether from your camera or the web) look better instantly! Sit down with your computer and photo editing program and experiment.

Crop Cropping means you're trimming any unnecessary background distractions from the photo's edges. I'm not saying your walls aren't gorgeous, but in these photos, you really want to show off your baby's deliciousness, so zoom in tight! If you're not happy with how you cropped things, press "undo," "redo," or "recrop," and try, try again.

Red-Eye Many programs have a miraculous feature that allows you to get rid of your little angel's devilish red eyes. Use it! It makes a world of difference.

Auto Color and Auto Contrast As a mom, your time is limited, and you need to set priorities. If laundry and dinner are all ahead of "tweaking the color and contrast in my photos," let your computer do it for you. Some photo editing programs have an "auto" function. Click on it and your photo will look at least a little bit better.

TUNING

If you've conquered the basics and you're ready to keep on tweaking, try some of the following functions. Every program is different, however, so your photo editing program might not have all of the options listed here.

Color For super-juicy photos, bring up the color bar a teensy bit at a time. For black-and-white images, bring down the color bar all the way. For the best final result, play with the "brightness" and "contrast" after you adjust the color.

Brightness If your photo is too bright (as if you took it outside on a super-sunny day), bring down the brightness level to fix it. On the other hand, if your picture is a little dark because there wasn't enough light when you took it, increase the brightness to make it look just right. If things still don't look right, play with the contrast button.

Contrast If your picture is too dark or too gray, boost the contrast to make it look brighter, clearer, and more colorful. Actually, even if your photo isn't so dark or gray, crank up the contrast a little bit in all of your photos (except the really bright ones). Contrast makes photos look sharper and clearer, which makes them look better on your projects—and they're more easily spotted from far away! If you already used "Auto Contrast," don't be afraid to push the contrast even more for a dramatic look.

Color Temperature Sometimes your baby can look a little blue or yellow in a photo. Adjusting the color temperature can usually correct that. Add a little more blue to the yellow or more yellow to the blue registers. *Note:* Don't be fooled by the name; this function is totally different from the "Color" function.

Saturation This button, on the other hand, *is* similar to the "Color" function. Bring the saturation all the way up for juiced-up, hyper-vibrant pictures. However, if your babe is a wee bit blotchy, bring the saturation all the way down to make your photo black and white. (And don't forget, any break-out looks better in black and white!)

Shadows/Fill Light/Highlights All three of these buttons work together to create the same results as "Brightness" and "Contrast." "Fill Light" and "Highlights" brighten up your photos. "Shadows" gives your pictures a nice dose of contrast to make the subject of the image more pronounced and clear. Use all three of these buttons together for really great-looking pictures.

EFFECTS

If you've mastered the basics, tuned up your pics, and are still hungry for more, most photo-editing programs have a few buttons that can totally transform your photos from iffy to spiffy—perfect for your next project.

Sepia If you want your baby's baby pictures to look like your grandparents' baby pictures, then make them sepia. "Sepia" is like a black-and-white photo with a yellow tint.

Tint If you want your tyke's baby pictures to look like

alien baby pictures, use the tint button to make your little ET green or blue! "Tint" tints your black-and-white pictures any color of the rainbow.

Sharpen This function makes a slightly out-of-focus picture look remarkably *in focus*! Use "Sharpen" on your fuzzy images, and you'll be amazed at how much clearer everything becomes. It's like LASIK, but for pictures!

The Rest There are a few more minor functions like "Warmify," "Soft Focus," and "Film Grain" that are fairly self-explanatory, but the best way to see if you like the effects is to experiment with all of the different features. Don't be shy! But as you explore, be sure to always save your souped-up images with a new name so you can revert to your originals if you want to!

PHOTO MAKEOVER

More than making your snapshots frame-worthy, the application of these techniques and tips will prime your pics for greatness when they appear on your crafty projects. Whether you're decorating a onesie, a wipe box, a placemat, or brag book, the right cropping, color saturation, and contrast will take your photos to the next level.

Before the Edit Here's a photo from a Crafty Mama whose daughter, Paige, is adorable in her mama-made tie-dye. But you can't really tell *how* adorable she is from this picture until you jazz it up a little.

As it is, there's too much room over her head and at her sides, and her teensy little feet are cut off. The background is dark, and the colors aren't as juicy as they could be. You can't really tell that Paige has gorgeous blue eyes and strawberry blond hair. Plus, she looks a little bit out of focus (or maybe that's just me because I've been staring at my computer all day).

BEFORE

After the Edit Now we're talking. The picture is cropped so Paige is what you see (and not her mom's floor moldings). I saturated the colors of the picture and sharpened the photo as well, so the image is crisper. Unfortunately, the software couldn't bring back her chopped-off feet! It's good, but not *that* good.

AFTER

sweet irony

After you've fixed up your photos or collected images online, it's time to learn how to apply them to your decoupage, jewelry, and . . . iron-ons. In the immortal words of Barbra, "We've only just begun."

When's the last time you saw a baby wearing a plain onesie or tee? For me, I think it was 2002. These days, every store everywhere sells teensy babywear with cheeky sayings like: "Boobman," "Word to Big Bird," "Mullets Rule," or "Listens to Black Sabbath." Or they sport pictures of Dora, Chewbacca, Gary Coleman, or, every baby's favorite revolutionary, Che Guevara. But don't fret, there's no reason to pay $20 or $30 for a teeny T-shirt with a swanky saying or decal that's just going to get stained, when you can *make* one (and so many, many more) with iron-on transfer paper. And the fun doesn't stop there. You can easily whip up an iron-on with your baby's picture or name so you can personalize your fabric-covered diaper wipe box, shoes, pillows, purses, brag books, and more! What are you waiting for?

IRON-ON TRANSFER PAPER

I love the Avery brand ink-jet transfer papers, so if you choose to use them, allow me to share with you some things that I've learned from printing for both light- and dark-colored fabrics.

For Light-Colored Fabrics Ink-jet T-shirt transfer paper for light-colored fabrics works best for text, photos, or designs you plan to use on white or light-colored cotton or cotton/poly fabrics. When ironed on, an image will look more like a silk screen print, rather than a traditional, rubbery iron-on. If there is some ribbing on your garment, the ink won't seep into the little grooves. People like this type of paper because it makes your design look a little distressed, in a stylish, I-paid-good-money-for-a-pair-of-ripped-jeans kind of way. The thing to know about this paper is that you must print your designs *in reverse*! I've messed up many a tee by forgetting this little detail.

Most packaging instructions ask that you wait until the paper completely cools before you peel off the backing paper. In my experience, however, this sometimes makes the iron-on crackle or deteriorate. If you want your iron-

"Even when your brain has turned to mush, you can still use your hands to make something comment-worthy." —CRAFTY MAMA CAROL

ons to look more like silk screens (with just the ink on the shirt), pull the paper off five to ten seconds after you iron. If there's a little bit of ink on the paper backing, it's okay.

For Dark-Colored Fabrics Ink-jet dark T-shirt transfers work well on thin bright or dark-colored fabrics, as well as fabrics that you want to embellish with your baby's picture, like Bootie-licious shoes (page 183), Hip Purse (page 205), and My Bragamuffin Brag Book (page 209). When ironed on, these look like traditional '70s-style iron-ons because the image is printed on top of a white piece of rubbery paper. You don't have to reverse these iron-ons when you print them, and the images are much clearer and more vibrant than the light-colored ones. (That's probably why this paper is also two to three times the price of the paper for light-colored tees!) Oh, and this kind of paper smells funky when you iron it on, so open a window when you're making your stuff!

Even if the colors appear duller than expected on your printout, be patient. They will come to life when you iron them from this type of paper. And when it's time to peel the paper backing from the iron-on, peel slowly and carefully from the sides rather than the corners—it will separate cleanly and easily.

TRICKS OF THE TRADE

Keep the following tips in mind before, during, and after

ironing on with light- or dark-colored fabrics.

Practice Makes Perfect I like to test my technique before I iron on. I print up a few low-res images, and then iron them onto one of my husband's stained undershirts to see what timing, temp, and pull-off time work best.

The Time/Heat Phenomenon The longer you leave the iron on, the hotter it gets, and the less time it takes for iron-ons to transfer to a T-shirt. If you're making a few T-shirts, the third one will take less time to iron on than the first two. Be mindful of this when creating your baby's new wardrobe.

Don't Get Burned! If you hold down the iron too long in one place, you can burn your iron-on and the T-shirt. Move the iron around a lot. Burnt tees look and smell horrible.

For Keeps Sometimes after you wash your T-shirt, the iron-on wrinkles a bit. To restore its fabulousness, save a piece of the parchment that you originally used to iron your images on, place it on top of your design, and iron over it for a few seconds to smooth it out.

The Truth About Crack If you wash your iron-ons too much, they will crack. To ensure a long life, try to make a point of washing them inside-out and always, always adjust your machine settings to "low" when drying them.

HOW TO PRINT ON IRON-ON TRANSFER PAPER

Once your images are uploaded or downloaded and edited to perfection (see pages 24–27), check your paper to make sure you're printing on the correct side. If you're printing onto light-colored fabric, remember that you need to print your image in reverse, and proceed with step 1. If you're printing onto dark-colored fabric, skip to step 2.

1 Click on "Print" in the File menu, then "Properties," and then click on the different tabs to find the option that says "T-shirt transfer paper" or "iron-on paper" or "print in reverse" or "flip horizontal" or "mirror image" or "mirror print." If you don't see one of these tabs, check the manual, or log on to your printer's website to get online help or a toll-free number you can call.

2 Print a test sheet to make sure the image is on the right side of the paper and is sized correctly (and, if destined for light-colored fabric, is in reverse). Regular printer paper is far less expensive than iron-on transfer paper, so it's worth it to take the time. Since this is just a test, click on "Properties" on your print menu to change the quality of the image—choose the lowest quality possible to save ink. Only one side of the sheet will work, so load the paper according to how your test goes.

3 Settle on the desired sizes for all of your images. Change your page margins to .3 on all sides, then rearrange the images to fit the maximum number onto one sheet. Sometimes it helps if you make your paper horizontal. Click "File," click "Page Setup," and then click on "Landscape."

4 Click "Print" when you're ready to print your image (either regular or reversed, depending on your paper). Look in your basic "Print Preferences" to see if you can find "Quality" (or something similar). Locate the highest quality option available or something that says "Photo" and then click "Okay." This will make your iron-ons look all nice and professional!

5 Wait a few minutes for the ink to dry, and then cut out your iron-ons, leaving a ⅛" to ¼" border around all sides. *Note:* Any white that you leave around the edges on the paper for *dark-colored* shirts *will* appear as a white border around your design when you iron it onto your shirt. A little white around the edges of the iron-on paper for *light-colored* fabrics *will not* show.

6 Plug in your iron and read the iron-on instructions in the package to get your designs off the paper and onto something that could actually hold up in a spin cycle!

☞ **READING IS FUNDAMENTAL!** *No matter which type of paper or brand you buy, make sure to read all of the instructions before you iron them on your projects. Different brands have different prepping, ironing, and washing rules.*

voulez-vous decoupage avec moi?

The word *decoupage* sounds far sexier than it really is. Literally, it means "cut out," and that's exactly what you do—cut out stuff and then stick it on things. How's that for sexy? Decoupage will most likely do nothing to spice up your life in the bedroom, but it will spice up a whole lot of boring objects you have lying around your house.

SURFACE SAVVY

You can decoupage almost any surface—wood, metal, glass, or plastic. And while the name sounds all mysterious and complicated, the concept is pretty basic: It's collage with a layer of glue *on top*. So, if you ever made a magazine cutout tribute to Kirk Cameron, New Kids on the Block, or Tom Cruise back in middle school, then you're sure to be a pro!

That said, here are a few things to keep in mind: A decoupage surface should be dry and clean, so once you've picked the item you want to spice up with decoupage, wipe away the dust and polish up the smudges. If it's wooden, and it's rough, sand it a bit. If you want to paint your object first, go for it. Wood, especially, looks great when you put down a coat of color before decoupaging. Aluminum, too!

DECOUPAGE PICTURES

You can buy papers and die-cuts made especially for decoupage at almost any craft store, but if you don't even have the time to tuck your tiny tyke into his stroller for a walk down those aisles, why not browse your own home for some equally great materials? Wondering what to do with that third copy of *Goodnight Moon*? Books are an excellent source for cool, kid-friendly decoupage images. Haven't actually been able to *read* the *New Yorker* since little Suki was born? Cut out those hilarious cartoons and decoupage your changing table. Now you can laugh, instead of cry, when you have to change yet another diaper. Old calendars,

"Whether I'm making something my daughters will wear or something we'll hang on the wall, it's something we can keep forever."

—CRAFTY MAMA MINDY

travel brochures, or catalogs also come in handy when you get a decou-craving. Or try using that gorgeous wrapping paper you saved after your baby shower (you did that, right?), or the extra wallpaper you have left over from redoing your hallway. If your household excavation leaves you wanting more (but with her sleeping on your shoulder, a walk around the house could be risky), check out the Internet. You can find tons of prints, images, and even fabric swatches that can be in your hot little hand with just the push of a button ("Print," that is). So get creative, and get your cut-and-paste on!

copy cat

If you want to decoupage several projects with the same great images, stick or arrange your images onto a few sheets of paper and make color copies (or scan them in and print them with your color ink-jet printer). Now your mirror has the potential to match your garbage can, which can in turn match your nightstand!

glass globs on the job

Ever wondered who buys those flat-on-one-side glass marble thingies that they sell in fish and flower stores? Well, even if you never have, the answer is me—and now you! No, I don't have any amphibians or flowers, but as you might have guessed, I use them in many of my craft projects.

Some people call them accent marbles, some call them glass gems, and some call them glass nuggets, flat glass marbles, glass gem marbles, craft marbles, crystal accent flats, vase gems, or, my personal fave, *glass globs.* If you're looking to buy them, ask a craft store clerk or search online using any or all of the above names before you get discouraged that they don't really exist—they're out there!

But no matter where you buy them or what you call them, *please keep them away from your young kids.* I am the glass glob queen, but I am very careful about where I place the projects I make with them since they're very small and present a major choking hazard. My magnets (Photo Bragnets, page 197) are high on the fridge; Lily's barrette holder is inside her closet; and the bubble letter globs picture frame is sitting safely on my husband's desk at work.

WHAT'S THE DEAL?

Here are a few important facts that every glass glob lover should know:

• They're made in every color imaginable, from ice clear to electric brick swirl. Take your pick!

• They come in a bunch of different sizes from small (½") to medium (¾") to large (1" to 1½") to jumbo (2⅓"). Know what you want to use them for before buying them. For instance, if you're making magnets with photos underneath them, you'll want the large or jumbo clear ones. If you're using them to decorate a frame, try the mediums or smalls in any color.

• You can choose from three different finishes: clear (surprise, it's clear), frosted (matte and frosty on top), and iridescent (shiny with a hint of rainbow). But if you want a picture to show through, you need to use clear without a finish.

• They are available in a whole lot of shapes: squares, hearts, stars, and moons. But if circles are more your speed, you still have options with perfectly molded circles or more free-form, blobbier ovals.

BUBBLE LETTERS

If bubble letters make you think of the ones you used to scrawl over the cover of your notebook in middle school, go with it! Embrace your inner sixth-grader and make a prank phone call, pass a note, and smear on some watermelon-flavored lip gloss. Then, snap out of it and check out *these* bubble letters. Updated and less complicated (you don't have to know how to draw!), this technique is great for making personalized accents for picture frames, shadow boxes, barrette holders, and more. Just some clear hot glue, some alphabet stickers (⅛" to ¼" high), and, yes, some glass globs.

1 Plug in your hot-glue gun and insert one glue stick.

2 Find a piece of paper that you'd like to use as the background—colored or patterned.

3 Press each letter sticker on the paper at least 1½" apart.

4 Place a large dab of hot glue on the flat side of one glass glob. Quickly turn it over and *firmly* press it down on top of one of the letters. (It's okay if some glue blobs over.) Continue to glue glass globs onto each letter. Then wait a minute or two for all of the glued pieces to dry.

5 Use all-purpose scissors to cut around all your glass globs, removing the excess paper. If you experienced any spillover with the glue, cut it off as well.

6 Add your bubble letter accents to, well, just about anything: picture frames, shadow boxes, mirrors, brag books, buckets . . .

BUBBLE PAINTS

As far as I'm concerned, "crafty" and "artistic" are two entirely different things. I consider myself crafty, but totally not artistic. I'm incredibly fearful of painting; I never know what design or picture to make, and I'm always bummed with how it turns out. But many of the mamas in my classes are super-skilled with a paintbrush, so in honor of those ladies, I present this artsy glass glob option to you.

1 Choose a glass glob and paint a design, pattern, or color onto the flat side of the glob. If you prefer a more complicated look, paint in layers. For example, paint your little darling's name in a dark color, wait for it to dry, and then paint over her name with a lighter color as background. Cute!

2 Let it dry and repeat, decorating as many glass globs as you want.

3 Use your artsy globs to accent frames, coasters, mirrors, jewelry, or vases.

STICKY WICKET

Some people just can't get the hot glue to stick to their glass glob. Maybe it's altitude, maybe it's a faulty gun, junky glue, or just plain crappy luck. In any case, if you find yourself in this not-so-sticky situation, tune in to these troubleshooters:

- Double-check that your glue is hot-melt glue and not low-temp glue.

- Try using a different brand of glue stick.

- Try using a large, hotter glue gun.

- Buy a tube of thick Weldbond Glue. It doesn't have the immediate pay-off that hot glue does, but if you're willing to wait for it to dry, it shouldn't give you any grief! You can find it online or at most craft stores.

be jeweled

Even though making jewelry was among my favorite crafting projects in my stressed-out past, it never occurred to me to make mommy jewels until my neighbor got a schmancy $75 bracelet emblazoned with her kid's name for Mother's Day one year. I took one look at it and said, "I could so make that!" Twenty minutes later, my ten-month-old daughter and I were on the subway to the garment district in Manhattan for beads. I bought all of the supplies I needed, and later that night, I made a nearly identical bracelet (the only real difference was that mine had my kid's name on it). It only cost me $11 to make—and that's including my $4 round-trip subway fare!

The next week, I made mommy bracelets in my Crafty Mamas class, and they were a huge hit! Over time, the style evolved and I started adding photo charms into the mix. All of the jewelry projects in this book are very easy to make, but if your last beading project involved stringing painted ziti onto yarn, keep reading! There are a few basic pieces and techniques you should be familiar with.

JUMP RINGS

Jump rings are a staple in all jewelry-making. The little loops come in a variety of diameters and thicknesses in both gold and silver tones. A jump ring has a teensy slit so you can pry it open and use it as a connector to hang a charm on a chain or attach a clasp to a bracelet or necklace. Here's how to use them:

1 Use your round-nose pliers to pry the slit open just a bit.

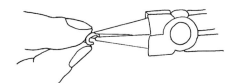

2 Hook one end of the opened ring through the charm loop.

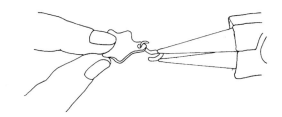

3 Use your pliers to carefully close the jump ring.

4 For a secure close: Use your pliers to "over-close" the ring so the two ends overlap slightly. This will ensure that

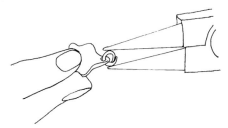

the jump ring won't open up if the little lady tugs on it. (And who are we kidding, she's going to tug on it!)

HEAD PINS

Head pins look almost exactly like straight pins for sewing, but less pointy. They're just the things for turning funky beads into funky charms. They come in a variety of lengths and both gold and silver tones. Here's how to use them to create a charm:

1 Slip a bead (or a few beads, for a longer charm) onto a head pin, eye pin, or decorator head pin (see variations in the Craftypedia, page 227). If the bead slides off the flat end, the bead hole is too big. Try a different bead, or put a smaller bead first (so it rests beneath the larger bead) to keep it from sliding off.

2 Hold the pin straight so the bead is sitting nicely on the flat end of the pin. Using regular scissors, trim the point of the pin so there's about ½" of wire sticking out of the bead. *Note:* Be careful when you cut the pin. The extra wire sometimes goes flying across the room!

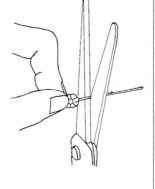

3 Clamp the tips of your round-nose pliers onto the very top of the pin and curl the wire around to create a loop. *Note:* If your loop is tilting to the

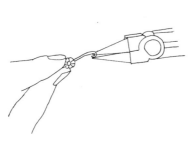

left or the right, use the pliers to gently adjust it.

4 Slip a jump ring through the opening of the loop. Then tighten the loop to finish the charm.

EYE PINS

An eye pin is a fabulous little piece that looks like a sewing needle, but with a loop instead of a hole at one end. Eye pins come in a variety of lengths as well as gold and silver tones. These come in handy when you want to transform a bead (or beads) into a link of a bracelet, earring, or necklace. You can also use them to create a beaded link from which to hang a charm. Here's how:

1 Slip a bead (or a few beads) onto an eye pin.

2 Hold the eye pin straight and make sure the bead is resting nicely against the loop. Using your regular scissors, trim the point of the pin so there's about ½" of wire sticking out above the top bead. *Note:* Be careful when you cut the pin because the extra wire likes to go flying across the room! (And if it does go flying, track down the little piece to dispose of it properly. You don't want your little crawler happening upon your scraps!)

3 Clamp the tips of your round-nose pliers onto the very top of the pin and curl the wire around to create a little loop. *Note:* If your loop is tilting to the left or the right, use the pliers to straighten it out.

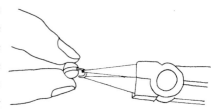

4 Hook the loop onto another link or a charm before tightening it.

knots landing

You're *knot* going to be able to complete all of the fabulous fleece projects or tie off your (gulp!) sewing projects in this book if you don't know how to tie the right knots! There are three in this book that you'll specifically need to know. So read on to learn how, and after you knot your projects together, go ahead and tie one on!

KNOT 1: THE DOUBLE KNOT

This is a your everyday basic knot. You simply take two ends (of fringe, thread, ribbon, or string), wrap them one over the other, as shown, and pull them tight. (This step is commonly known as a "granny knot.") Repeat to complete the double knot. No fancy loops, just a knot. When you're working with fleece fringe, this knot will make for wilder, non-uniform fringe.

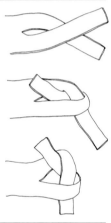

KNOT 2: THE OVERHAND KNOT

A little more time-consuming, and neater, this one's for the type A personalities. You'll use it for tying your sewing thread, ribbon ends, or blanket fringe. Take the two ends, wrap them carefully around your pointer finger, creating a loop, and then carefully stick both ends through the loop. Pull them tight.

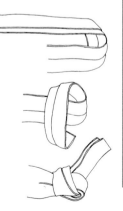

KNOT 3: THE COW HITCH KNOT

This knot is easy, but you have to have a hole to wrap it through or an edge to wrap it around. Take a short 4" to 8" strip, and pinch the two ends of the strip together. Thread both ends through a hole in the side of your blanket (or hat, poncho, etc.) until they're about halfway through (there should be a loop on the other side of your blanket). Stick the two ends through the loop (around the edge) and pull them tight.

sew it up

Now, I know sewing can be intimidating, but I promise you, this won't hurt a bit. In some instances (like the Vinyl Diner Bib, page 95), you won't even recognize that the technique you're using is actually a form of sewing!

RUNNING STITCH

This is the most common, and arguably the easiest stitch—and the only one you really need in this book and for most simple sewing projects.

1 Cut a 24" piece of thread in whatever color matches your project.

2 Thread your needle, pulling the thread all the way through so the two ends meet. Tie the ends with an overhand knot, doubling or tripling it so the knot is big enough that it doesn't slip through your project when you're sewing.

3 Stick the needle up through the two pieces of fabric you're sewing together and pull it until the knot in the bottom of the thread reaches the fabric. Pass the needle down through the fabric about ⅛" from the knot in the direction you're sewing.

4 Draw the needle and thread back up through the fabric ⅛" from the first stitch.

5 Continue threading your needle down and up through the fabric to the end.

OVER-EDGE STITCH (WHIPSTITCH)

I'm going to describe this stitch in sewing terms, but once you get to some of the fleece hat or bib projects, you'll recognize the technique. Instead of using a needle and thread, you'll use a strip of fleece, ribbon, or suede lacing.

1 Thread your needle, following steps 1 and 2 in the running stitch instructions.

2 Stick the needle up through the two pieces of fabric you're binding together, and pull it until the knot in the bottom of the thread reaches the fabric.

3 Draw the needle around the edge of the fabric(s) and stick it up through the bottom again, about ⅛" along the edge in the direction you're sewing.

4 Continue drawing your needle up, around the edge, and through the bottom again to the end. (The needle should only be passing through the fabric from the underside to the top side.)

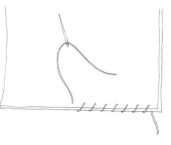

TYING OFF

No matter what stitch you sew, you'll need to finish it when you've reached the end of your stitches, so you can snip your thread and move on to the next project.

1 Make a small loop of a (running) stitch, but don't pull it tight.

2 Draw your needle through the loop, and pull it tight.

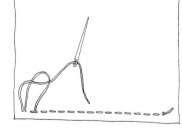

3 Repeat this once or twice over the same knot to reinforce it.

ready to roll!

Are you still with me? Splendid. Now that you know everything, let's get a-crafting!

Oh wait, you have Mommy 'n' Me Yoga right now? And then you need to go to the supermarket? And then she has an appointment at the pediatrician to get her shots? Okay, go. I'll still be here when you get back. Promise!

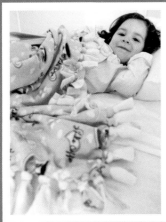

MAKE ROOM FOR BABY

**Blankies and pillows and nightlights, oh my!—
11 fun and funky projects for a one-of-a-kind nursery.**

A bout four or five months into your pregnancy, you finally start to think about sex again (a lot) *and* about cleaning out your office/exercise/guest room to convert it into a nursery. In between bedroom romps, you sell your treadmill on eBay (honestly, when was the last time you used it anyway?). You throw away all the old mags you've been saving for no reason. You move your desk. And you stuff all of your other clutter into random closets and boxes. After it all, you sit back (because your back is killing you) and congratulate yourself. Because, hey, you literally made *room* for your baby! Then you paint the walls, get a crib, a changing table, some cute bedding, and—voilà!—you have a nursery. But still, something's missing. (No, not the baby—something *else*.) It's time to add some mama-made accents to your much-awaited nugget's nesting space.

Tucked into her stroller or tucked into bed, this snuggly blanky will keep her cozy wherever she goes.

NO-SEW SWANKY BLANKY

YOU PROBABLY HAVE ABOUT THIRTEEN (OR MORE) ADORABLE receiving blankets from your registry and random gifts, but there comes a time when the thin cotton cuddlies that once engulfed your little infant barely fit over his five-month-old feet. What's a baby to do for a post-swaddling, pre-comforter blanky? Well, he looks to his mama to make one, of course. Not only are these blankies insanely cuddly, comfy, and cute, but according to the women who invented the Taggie-blankets, pulling and sucking on fringy things helps foster fine motor skill development. So when your little Einstein becomes a famous surgeon, you can attribute her success to the good ol' Swanky Blanky you made her as a baby!

Now, knotting the fringe does take time, but if your baby's in a good mood, put her in the center of your blanket while you make it. If she's in a great mood, try some "tummy time." Just don't be surprised if she spits up on the blanket before you're done.

make it:

PREP

1 Lay the two pieces of fleece on top of each other with the wrong sides facing. (The "wrong side" is the one that looks less finished.) Make sure the "stretch" of both pieces is going in the same direction.

2 Use a ruler, marker, and scissors (or a ruler, rotary cutter, and mat) to trim off the

rate it:

Cost: .... $ $ $
Time: .... 🕐 🕐 🕐
Skill: .... ✂ ✂
How ga-ga they'll go: ... ♥ ♥ ♥ ♥ ♥

To amp up the "aww" factor, get some great fleece. Make a pink striped blanket, and people will think it's cute. Make one with little martinis all over it, and they'll go wild.

need it:

✔ 1⅓ yards patterned fleece*
✔ 1⅓ yards solid fleece*
✔ Fabric scissors
✔ Marker or chalk
✔ Ruler
✔ 5" square scrap cardboard
✔ Rotary cutter (optional)
✔ Cutting mat (optional)

*For a bigger blanky, use more fleece; for a smaller one, use less. You just need equal amounts of patterned and solid fleece.

rolled edges on two sides to create clean, raw edges. Then trim the other two sides of the fabric so both the top and the bottom layers are exactly the same size. Lay the cut-off strips aside to use in step 4. And don't worry if your shape isn't perfect—you'll never be able to tell!

ASSEMBLE

3 Place the 5" cardboard square in one corner of the fabric and hold it down while tracing around it with a marker. Then use scissors to cut out the square through both layers along the marker line. Repeat on the other three corners. (Save the scrap fabric and stuff it in a drawer, so you can use it to make a Pocket Book, page 63.)

4 Take one of the long fleece strips that you trimmed off the edges in step 2 and lay it onto your fabric 5" in from the edge as a guide.

5 Decide how wide you want your fringe. (For chunky fringe, make your cuts 1" to 1½" apart. For linguini-like fringe, make cuts ½" to ¾" apart.) Use a ruler and scissors (or a ruler, rotary cutter, and mat) to mark and begin cutting perpendicularly through both

layers along one edge of the blanket, stopping 5" in at the fleece strip. Continue cutting fringe in this manner around the entire perimeter of the blanket.

6 Tie the top layer of fringe to the bottom layer of fringe all the way around the blanket, using one of the two methods detailed below. *Note:* You're not going crazy—due to the knit of the fleece, two of the sides are significantly more stretchy and easier to tie.

TYING TIP *When tying fringe, you have two options. For a quicker, easier knot, simply take one piece and tie it to the other. Then tie it again to make a double knot.*

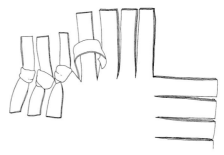

For a neater and more uniform knot, take the two pieces of fringe together, make a loop by wrapping them around your finger, and then pull the ends of both fringes through the loop.

FINISH

7 After you've tied all of the knots, pick up the blanket and hold it up by two corners. (Remove your child from the blanket first, of course!) The knotting sometimes bunches things up, so gently tug on all of the sides and corners to get your blanket into a nice rectangular shape. If you hear teensy ripping noises, no worries—the little tears won't show.

👉 **FRINGE TIP** *If you decided to go with the thick 'n' chunky fringe, but after seeing the results, you are longing for thinner fringe, cut each of your fringe pieces in half (rather than untying, cutting, and then retying them).*

8 Lay your little cutie on top and watch her fine motor skills develop as she plays with your creation!

get fleece!

(But don't *get fleeced*.) The cost of fleece is always variable, depending on when and where you buy it. Most stores sell fleece at full price in July and August when people start prepping for fall and winter, so be ready to stock up on all the cute, discounted ones from November through July.

variation:

Light 'n' Swanky No-Sew Blanky

If you live in a warmer climate and have no need for a double-thick fleece blanky, try a lighter, still fabulously fringy version.

Use one 1⅓-yard sheet of patterned fleece, and then get an additional ½ yard to cut into 1" x 8" fringe pieces. Punch or snip small holes about 1" in from the edge and all around the blanket perimeter. Then loop the cut fringe pieces through the holes using a cow hitch knot, as shown, to create finished fringe.

LITTLE HANG-UPS

DO YOU *NEED* FANCY, MATCHING, ADORABLE HANGERS? NO. Will your mother-in-law be impressed with the stunning set that she finds when she goes snooping around your baby's closet to see if you kept the clothing her friends gave you? Absolutely. So go ahead, get together with friends and make your little fashion plate a designer set!

need it:

✔ Wooden hangers (child size)
✔ Pencil
✔ Scrapbook paper
✔ All-purpose scissors
✔ ¾ cup white glue
✔ Plastic container or paper cup
✔ Stir stick
✔ Wax paper
✔ ¾" to 1" flat paintbrush
✔ Brayer or plastic card
✔ Foam brush
✔ Decoupage medium
✔ Hot-glue gun
✔ Hot-melt glue sticks
✔ Tiny toys or trinkets
✔ Embellishments (optional: ribbon, rhinestones, 3-D letters, bookplates)

make it:

PREP

1 Trace the shape of your hanger carefully onto a piece of scrapbook paper. Position it so you can trace the hanger as many times as possible on one sheet. Keep on tracing until you have as many shapes as you need to cover all of your hangers. (Remember, each hanger needs two hanger-shaped pieces of paper.)

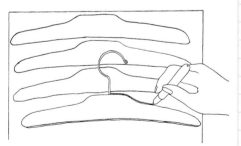

2 Cut out your paper hanger shapes and lay each one, individually, on top of a hanger to see if they need trimming. The paper should not go over the edges of the hanger.

3 In a plastic container or paper cup, mix the white glue with ¼ cup water.

ASSEMBLE

4 Place your hanger on top of a piece of wax paper. Use the paintbrush to brush a thin layer of the white glue solution on one side of the hanger as well as on the back of your paper hanger shape.

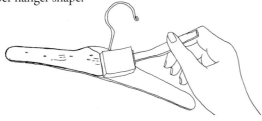

5 Start at one end of the hanger and carefully apply the paper to the hanger, a few inches at a time. Use a brayer or a plastic card to smooth out any bubbles or bumps in the paper.

6 Put the hanger aside to dry for 15 minutes and repeat steps 4 and 5 for all of your hangers.

7 Turn the dried hanger over onto a fresh piece of wax paper and repeat steps 4 and 5 on the opposite side of the hanger. Use the same style paper on both sides, or go for complementary or contrasting ones. Keep gluing until

you've applied paper to both sides of each of your hangers. (Short on time? Just do one side!)

 Wait 10 to 15 minutes for the second side to dry.

9 Use the foam brush and decoupage medium (*not the white glue solution!*) to go over one side of *all* the hangers. Wait 10 to 15 minutes for them to dry, then turn them over, place them on a fresh sheet of wax paper, and apply the decoupage medium to the opposite side of each. Let dry for 10 to 15 minutes.

FINISH

10 Plug in your hot-glue gun while you're waiting for the hangers to dry and insert one glue stick.

11 Squeeze a small dab of hot glue to the underside of a mini car, space shuttle, scorpion, plastic doll, or other tiny toy and attach it to the center of the hanger, below the metal hook. *Optional:* Accent further with rhinestones, googly eyes, 3-D letters, or a metal bookplate, and/or tie a satin ribbon bow around the neck of the hanger.

12 Rummage through your closet, and replace all of the plastic store hangers with the "6–12 mos" tab on them with your gorgeous new hang-ups!

home shopping club!

At the rate your baby is growing, you need to clean out his closet every week. But who has the time? You do! Invite your Crafty Mamas playgroup into your nursery so you can go through his wardrobe as you wait for the glue to dry. Offer the things that don't fit to the moms with tiny tykes or talk about having a clothing swap at your next meeting. Everyone loves to go home from playgroup with a lovely parting gift.

hangin' tough

The possibilities are endless when it comes to enhancing your hangers. Here are just a few ideas to get those creative juices flowing.

A DATE TO PAINT

Paint it instead of decoupaging! Coat a wooden hanger with acrylic paint and then hot glue a trinket at the top  of it. Pick a theme—automobiles, horses, construction, family, candy, princesses, body parts, or whatever your child digs (or maybe whatever *you* dig for your child)—and look for little trinkets that work within your theme. You need one trinket per hanger since you're only placing it on the front of the hanger.

A HANGER'S WORTH A THOUSAND WORDS

Decoupage or paint your hangers and then hot glue a different scrapbook word or phrase embellishment onto each one. The words are generally packaged in sets with words like: "Naughty," "Nice," "Sugar," and "Spice." Punctuate with rhinestones and nothing will say "I'm your hanger for life" quite like these personalized delights.

HIGHWAY TO HANGERS

Decoupage the hanger with road sign or map paper, or paint it black with yellow dotted lines and then glue an inexpensive plastic car (not a heavy metal Matchbox car) from the dollar store to the top/center of the hanger. Vroom-vroom! While you're at

it, try other modes of transport—bicycles, moped, airplane, rocket ship!

ALL DRESSED UP

Decoupage with a pretty argyle, dotted, or paisley paper, or paint each hanger a different color, and then hot glue small doll accessories like hats, shirts, or shoes at the top. (The dollar store has great inexpensive "Barbie-like" outfits and accessories.) Accent with rhinestones. Ooh la la! What a lovely outfit your hanger is wearing!

DINO-MITE

Decoupage your hangers with stone-patterned paper or dino paper, or paint them green, orange, and yellow, and then hot glue a small plastic or rubber dinosaur to the top. It will look out-ROAR-geous. (That actually might be one of my worst jokes ever!)

A-B-C-D-E-F-G . . . H-A-N-G-E-R

Decoupage with baby block paper, or paint any color you like. Hot glue small wooden alphabet block letters or make your own bubble letters to spell out names, words, or just the good ol' ABCs at the top of each hanger.

SCRABBLE BABBLE

Decoupage with Scrabble game board scrapbook paper. (They have it—and Candyland board paper, too!) Then glue on old Scrabble letters to form personalized words—names, nicknames, "son" or "daughter." No need to mess up your own Scrabble set; they make scrapbook embellishments that look just like the game pieces, or you can buy Scrabble letters on eBay for cheap!

HANGIN' OUT IN HOLLYWOOD

Decoupage with jewelry paper (or any other sparkly or diva-themed paper) or paint it hot pink. Then glue a feathery boa around the edges. Your hanger will be ready for its close-up!

RUB IT IN

Can't deal with cleaning up another craft mess? Buy some wood rub-on letters and designs, and create simple, classy, personalized wooden hangers that look great and clean up in minutes!

OLD MACDONALD

Decoupage your hanger with animal paper, grass paper, or paint it barn red. Glue a little rubber or plastic farm animal to the top of each hanger. E-I-E-I-WOW!

CAMO

Decoupage with camouflage paper and then hot glue a little plastic soldier to the top. Then send your hanger on a covert mission into your baby's closet to hang up some clothes!

IT'S A . . . HANGER!

Most craft stores and dollar stores carry teensy little plastic bottles, babies, rattles, pacis, and more for baby shower decorations. Decoupage your hanger with sweet baby paper, or paint it pink, blue, or even break the mold with lime green or neon orange! Glue some baby accents to the top and tie a little bow around the hook of the hanger for an extra dose of flair. Then go and hang up your goo-goo gorgeous hangers.

A soft and cuddly toy you'll have to wrestle her for when it's time to wash it!

SCHLEPPY

SCHLEP: (shlĕp) Slang, *v.* TO CARRY. AND THAT'S JUST WHAT *YOUR* schmoopie is going to do with this fringy little lovey. She'll carry it with her everywhere she goes—to the supermarket, to Grandma's, to the doctor, to a friend's house, and even into the (ick!) sandbox. Schleppies are soft and cozy, and their colorful fringes provide hours of entertainment. Plus, they're totally machine-washable, so after she's schlepped her Schleppy into the sandbox, you can hit the spin cycle to wash it. Wash: (wŏsh, wôsh) *v.* to cleanse, using water or other liquid, usually with soap, detergent, or bleach.

rate it:

Cost: .... $
Time: .... 🕐
Skill: .... ✂
How ga-ga they'll go: ... ♥ ♥ ♥ ♥ ♥

need it:

- ✔ ⅜ yard fleece 1 (any color or pattern)
- ✔ ⅜ yard fleece 2 (coordinating color or pattern)
- ✔ Ruler
- ✔ Marker or chalk
- ✔ Fabric scissors
- ✔ Rotary cutter (optional)
- ✔ Cutting mat (optional)
- ✔ Twenty to twenty-four ¾" x 7" multicolored fleece scraps (optional)
- ✔ Eyelet pliers
- ✔ Hot-glue gun (optional)
- ✔ Fabric glue sticks (optional)
- ✔ Computer, photo-editing software, and color ink-jet printer (optional)
- ✔ Several sheets plain paper (optional)
- ✔ Iron-on transfer paper for light-colored fabrics (optional)
- ✔ Iron (optional)
- ✔ 1 sheet light-colored felt (optional)

make it:

PREP

1 Smooth one piece of fleece out on a flat surface and use a ruler, marker, and scissors (or ruler, rotary cutter, and mat) to mark and cut out an 11" square. Repeat with the second piece of fleece.

2 Cut ¾" × 7" strips from the remaining pieces of fleece (making sure to cut the fabric so the stretch is along the ¾" edge) until you have 20 to 24 fleece strips. (Or use a variety of mismatched fleece scraps of the same size that you have on hand.)

ASSEMBLE

3 Lay the two 11" fleece squares on top of each other with the wrong sides facing, making sure the stretch of both pieces is going the same direction.

4 Use your eyelet pliers to punch (through both layers) five to six holes ½" from the edge around each of the four sides of the square.

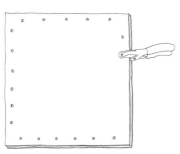

5 Fold one ¾" × 7" strip in half and push the folded loop through both layers of the first hole. Take the loose ends of the folded strip and thread them through the loop to create a cow hitch knot (see page 36). Pull it tight. Repeat until all strips are knotted in place.

6 Continue with step 7 to personalize the Schleppy, or if you like it as is, skip to step 11.

FINISH

7 Plug in your hot glue gun and insert one fabric glue stick. Plug in your iron.

8 Open up a text document on your computer and type your child's name (or the names of every baby in your

"Doing arts and crafts is so calming, especially with friends. For that short while, I'm focused on something other than how tired I am or how many loads of laundry are waiting for me!" —CRAFTY MAMA HELEN

playgroup) in a funky font at about 50 to 70 point size. Print the document in reverse at a low resolution on a scrap piece of paper before you print it on iron-on paper to make sure it's the exact size you want it to be. Adjust the dimensions on-screen and repeat as needed. Then, print your perfectly sized name onto iron-on transfer paper at the highest resolution your printer allows.

9 Read the directions on the packaging of your iron-on paper, and iron the name(s) onto the felt sheet.

10 Cut out your child's name from the felt, squeeze a line of hot glue around the perimeter of the back of the felt name, and stick it onto the Schleppy.

11 Trim the fringe along the edges. (You can make them all the same or varying lengths.)

12 Hand off the delicious little Schleppy to your snuggly little schlepper and watch him grab hold like Linus to his blanky!

personal preferences

When you're crafting with a group, create a big sheet of the alphabet so that each mama has the flexibility to decide whether she'd like to personalize with a first name, a nickname, a first and middle name, or initials. Copy the alphabet arrangement from a sheet of letter stickers (six of each vowel, four of each consonant from B to T, and three of each consonant from V to Z) and print it onto a piece of iron-on transfer paper for light colors. Iron it onto a sheet of felt, cut out the individual letters, and then hot glue them onto your Schleppy (or hat, or poncho—even a blanket or shadow box).

variation:

Schlep-over Party

If you have an older child, niece, nephew, or a neighbor who loves sleepovers but always steals your baby's blanky, use the fringe loop technique in this project to make him his very own no-sew sleeping bag! Just cut two rectangular pieces of fleece (whatever size you need to fit your special snuggler) and use eyelet pliers to make holes in three of the four sides (leaving one of the shorter sides hole-free). Cut about fifty 10" contrasting fleece strips to close up the three sides and create fringe. Popcorn anyone?

WE WELCOME WITH LOVE

LUCY ELIZABETH SCHWEITZER

JULY 9, 2006

EIGHT POUNDS, TWO OUNCES · TWENTY INCHES

AMANDA AND OLIVER SCHWEITZER

THINK INSIDE THE BOX

SO YOU HAD TWENTY-THREE HOURS OF INTENSE LABOR followed by an episiotomy, and due to your baby's insatiable hunger and the overwhelming amazement at his presence in your room, *four* days of no sleep. Now what do you do? (If you think you're about to take a nap, think again.) You pore over websites and stationery books to pick out the perfect baby announcement! And now that they're all addressed and mailed (a process that may have been more painful than your labor), don't let all your hard work and impeccable taste just sit in a scrapbook. Use that fabulous announcement—along with any other baby mementos you want to keep but don't know what to do with (the positive pregnancy test, the hospital bracelet, that engraved silver spoon from your rich aunt)—to make a shadow box you can proudly display on your wall forever. *Note:* Putting it all together takes only about two minutes, but with the number of memories and amount of storytelling that goes on, deciding how you want to put it together can take considerably longer!

rate it:

Cost: .... $ $ $
Time: .... 🕐 🕐
Skill: .... ✂ ✂
How ga-ga they'll go:... ♥ ♥ ♥ ♥ ♥

need it:

✔ 8½" x 11" sheets scrapbook paper
✔ 6" square shadow box
✔ Pencil
✔ All-purpose scissors
✔ Double-sided tape, double-sided mounting squares, or WackyTac
✔ Baby announcement or photo
✔ Scrapbook embellishments
✔ Hot-glue gun
✔ Hot-melt glue sticks
✔ Aleene's Tacky Glue
✔ Baby mementos (see sidebar, page 57)
✔ Foam dots (optional)
✔ Rhinestones (optional)
✔ Pre-cut felt shapes (optional)
✔ Letters or glass globs to create Bubble Letters (page 32) (optional)
✔ Tiny toys (optional)
✔ Acrylic paint (optional)
✔ Paintbrush (optional)

make it:

PREP

1 Choose a piece of scrapbook paper that'll look great behind your baby announcement or photo and all of your goodies.

2 Open the shadow box and remove the back (or the paper that comes inside) to use as a pattern. Lay it on the paper you picked in step 1 and trace and cut around it.

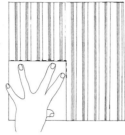

3 Take five pieces of double-sided tape (or five mounting squares), stick them onto the back of your paper (in the center and four corners), and then stick the paper onto the back piece of the shadow box.

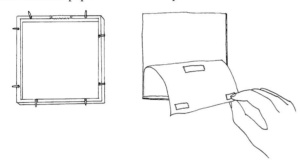

4 Lay your announcement or photo on top of the paper. If your birth announcement is too big, double-sided, or foldout style, you can still use it by cutting out the words and some of the images. Or, if the shadow box is large enough, cut up two announcements to display the front and the back next to each other.

5 Experiment with all sorts of embellishments (a soccer ball here, a pretzel there, a teensy diaper, fireflies, ducks, hot rods), leaving a 1/8" to 1/4" border around the perimeter of the paper. When you're happy with how everything looks, use double-sided tape to lightly stick it all down so that if you change your mind you can easily rearrange the pieces.

Optional: Add dimension to your shadow box by raising the announcement or embellishments with 3-D foam dots. (If an accent is tinier than the foam dot, cut a small piece off of the dot so it works with your accent.)

6 Plug in your hot-glue gun and insert one glue stick.

7 Place the top of your box carefully over your creation to check that it closes.

ASSEMBLE

8 Use Tacky Glue to permanently attach rhinestones or felt shapes.

9 Squeeze a *very* small amount of hot glue (too much hot glue will melt your items) to stick on items like the pregnancy test, silver spoon, or hospital bracelet. (*Note:* It's difficult to reposition these things once you glue them, so make sure you love the placement!) If you like your shadow box as is, skip to step 13. Otherwise, read on for more embellishing.

10 Hot glue on baby block letters for your child's initials. If you prefer your child's whole name, make and glue on Bubble Letters (page 32). If you're not feeling the letters on the inside of the box, try accenting the outside of the box with them.

FINISH

11 Change the color of your shadow box by painting a layer of acrylic paint on the outside frame of the box.

12 Hot glue a bow, rhinestones, footballs, or any other accents to the frame.

variation:

Three Times the Fun!

If you find that you're incredibly indecisive and want to cram a ton of cute things into your shadow box, try creating two or three complementary boxes to hang next to one another as a series. Try announcement and accents in one, photo with hospital bracelet in another, then booties, silver spoon, and "It's a Boy" card in the next.

13 Close it up and admire your amazingly fabulous shadow box. With all the money you saved, splurge on a babysitter so you can do something nice for yourself!

save it

Feeling super-nostalgic? This is the project you've been waiting for if you saved:

- your positive pregnancy stick (I did!)
- the hospital bracelet
- the silver spoon she'll probably never use
- the "It's a Girl" card from the hospital bassinet
- a little lock of hair
- the extra piece of belly button (my husband begged me to throw it away, but I saved that, too!)
- those teensy knit booties from Grandma, or
- all of the above!

Cool and crafty pails make organizing the nursery easy to maintain and easy on the eyes.

DECOU-PAIL

WHAT DO YOU DO WITH THE TWENTY-SIX MATCHBOX CARS, beaded necklaces, or big wooden blocks that are scattered throughout your house? Put them in a bucket! But I'm not talking about just any old plastic sand bucket. I'm talking about a fabulous mama-made decoupaged pail that looks like true room décor (as opposed to that cardboard box you've been using to store all of your kid's crap!). *Note:* Only one mama in your group should have to struggle to make the scrap paper the right size—then everyone else can just use her pattern to trace the right shape onto her scrapbook paper and get going.

rate it:

Cost: .... $ $
Time: .... 🕐 🕐 🕐
Skill: .... ✂ ✂ ✂
✂

How ga-ga they'll go:... ♥ ♥ ♥

need it:

✔ Galvanized metal bucket
✔ Large scrap paper (a big piece of newspaper or a paper grocery bag)
✔ Pencil
✔ All-purpose scissors
✔ Scotch tape
✔ Cardboard cereal box
✔ 2 pieces 10" square scrapbook paper (coordinating or contrasting)
✔ ¾ cup white glue
✔ Plastic container or paper cup
✔ Stir stick
✔ Wax paper
✔ Flat or square-edge paintbrush
✔ Brayer or plastic card
✔ Foam brush
✔ Decoupage medium (matte, semi-gloss, gloss, or sparkle)
✔ Spray bottle (optional)
✔ Hot-glue gun (optional)
✔ Hot-melt glue sticks (optional)
✔ Embellishments (optional)

make it:

PREP

1 Wrap the big piece of scrap paper gently around one side of your bucket, from one handle to the other. (It's a little tricky because the sides are angled and the bucket is narrower at the bottom.) Use your pencil to trace the actual shape of the bucket onto the paper, but stop when you have gone halfway around.

2 Cut out the shape you traced and check that it wraps snugly around half of the bucket. If it's not quite right, use your scissors to trim it or tape a thin strip of scrap paper onto the edge to make it bigger.

3 Trace the shape onto the piece of cardboard to create a durable template that everyone in your playgroup can use.

4 Lay the template on your scrapbook paper, trace it twice (once for each side), and cut out both pieces.

5 In a plastic container or paper cup, mix the white glue with ¼ cup water.

ASSEMBLE

6 Put down a sheet of wax paper. Use a paintbrush to spread a smooth, thick layer of glue solution on the back of one quarter of your paper as well as on one quarter of the bucket, starting at one of the handles.

7 Start at the gluey part of the bucket and lay the paper on from left to right. As you're slowly wrapping

the paper around the bucket, use the brayer or plastic card to smooth out air bubbles or wrinkles.

8 Paint a layer of glue onto the next quarter of your bucket and paper. Then continue wrapping the paper as you did in step 7. Repeat until your first piece of paper is entirely glued down.

9 Repeat steps 6 through 8 with the second piece of paper. If there are still any ridges or air bubbles in your paper, use the brayer or your fingernail to smooth them out. If you're happy with your decoupage (there may be imperfections, and that's okay!), clean your fingers and brayer so they're not gluey, and proceed to step 11.

☞ **BUBBLE TROUBLE** *If you're having trouble smoothing the paper, lightly mist it with a spray bottle to soften the paper and help work out kinks. If there are bubbles, pierce them with a tiny pin, then gently dab glue solution over them and try to make the bubbles smaller with your finger. Bubbles are caused when there's not enough glue coating either the paper or the pail, so be generous! If you think your wrap is a disaster, peel it off, wash your bucket, and try it again with new paper.*

FINISH

10 *Optional:* Add some decorative paper embellishments to your Decou-Pail. Use the glue solution to apply a few basketballs bouncing around, some ballerinas on their tippy-toes, rocket ships blasting off, John Wayne riding a horsey, or a big red Elmo smack dab in the center. Not only do they look cute, they're a sneaky way to hide any bubbles or imperfections you missed in step 9!

11 Wait 15 minutes for the glue to dry, and then use a foam brush to apply a thick layer of decoupage medium over the entire paper surface.

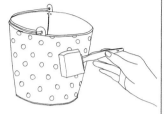

the waiting game

Take a snack break! In keeping with the theme, get a happy volunteeer to go out and buy a big *bucket* of fried chicken. If there's a mom whose little love has been a little needy during this project, this is the time to help her out with her Decou-Pail or baby. It's a nice thing to do, and it'll save you tons of calories!

12 Wait 15 to 20 minutes for the medium to dry. Add more paper embellishments or move on to step 13.

SMOOTH OPERATOR *After you've glued, if you find that there's too much paper at the edges of a Decou-Pail project, here's a tip: Use your fingernail to push it in a crevice or under a ridge along the seams of the bucket. If there're still little bits that are bugging you, use a razor or box cutter to carefully trim them off.*

13 *Optional:* Use hot glue to attach some three-dimensional accents: a thick piece of grosgrain ribbon around the middle or over any bumpy ridges, maybe some felt shapes or rhinestones.

variations:

Vincent Van Bucket

You don't *have* to cover your whole bucket with two sheets of paper. Try painting your bucket with acrylics, stenciling on shapes, painting only half the bucket, painting the inside, painting the outside, the handle, or the entire thing. Use one color or multicolors. And, if you want to decoupage *on top* of the paint, be sure to wait for the paint to dry completely before you start gluing.

Less Is More

If you like the way the metal bucket looks, don't try to hide it: Cut out images of things your child loves (poodles, aliens, tortoises) and glue them directly onto the side of the bucket. You don't have to cover the whole surface—maybe just line the bottom, the top, or the middle. But spread decoupage medium over the entire bucket when you're done, not just over the areas where you glued your pictures.

14 Put your bucket to use: Go on a scavenger hunt for all of the plastic farm animals that are hiding around your house. Can't find the horse? Look in your underwear drawer or the hamper—two popular hiding spots with the diaper-wearing set. Tuck everything in your lovely bucket and display it proudly on a shelf in your baby's room.

"I love how crafting gets me in the zone— I forget about how tired I am, and I don't worry about Theo's next diaper change. For me, the final product is the bonus!"

—CRAFTY MAMA CELIA

NO CHOKE! *If you chose to embellish in step 13, please accent with caution! Remember that anything small and 3-D is a choking hazard. You don't want your tiny tyke to pull off one of the plastic dinosaurs and eat it for a snack.*

variations:

Bottoms Up

Trim your paper so it covers only the bottom half or bottom two thirds of your bucket and paint the top with a complementary color. Use some small "themed" paper accents as a border around the top half or top one third.

Side Splitters

Decoupage one side of the bucket with a full piece of paper and leave the other half metal. Add decoupaged paper accents to the metal side.

Quilt Trip

Cut or tear out pieces of paper and overlap them on your bucket to create a patchwork background. After it's dried, lay a larger image on top.

POCKET BOOK

IF YOUR BUDDING LITTLE BOOKWORM LIKES TO READ ABOUT Paul, Judy, Harold, little caterpillars, Thomas, and Cinderella, he'll love to read all about you, Daddy, Grandma, Auntie, Cousin, and his big, furry pet dog, too. These little six-page books that you can make and take on the go will entertain your darling child, as well as prepare him for family events filled with relatives he doesn't really know. Just give him the book a few weeks in advance, have him happily interact with his faraway relatives, and—presto!—this year he might actually hug your scary Aunt Trudy rather than scream in her face and pull off her wig! *Note:* The more ornate the book, the more time it takes to make. Forsake the trim, and it can take about an hour. Otherwise you'll need the extra time I've allowed above.

make it:

PREP

1 Plug in your hot-glue gun and insert one fabric glue stick. Decide who to feature in your book: nuclear family (just the three of you and Rover), grandparents, cousins, friends, etc.

2 Sort through your photos to find the ones you want to use. Look for photos that feature big, friendly faces you can easily cut out. If you're using digital images, adjust the size on your computer and then print.

rate it:

Cost: .... $
Time: .... 🕐 🕐 🕐 🕐
Skill: .... ✂ ✂ ✂
How ga-ga they'll go: ... ♥ ♥ ♥ ♥

This is a great project to use up your fabric scraps, ribbons, extra photos, and more.

need it:

✔ Hot-glue gun
✔ Fabric glue sticks
✔ Photos (or computer, photo-editing software, and color ink-jet printer)
✔ 2 empty cardboard or cereal boxes
✔ All-purpose scissors
✔ 3 standard 9" x 11¾" felt sheets
✔ Ruler
✔ Marker or chalk
✔ Several 4¾" x 3½" pieces fabric
✔ Fabric scissors
✔ 1 roll ribbon, trim, or rickrack
✔ Embroidery needle and thread
✔ Clear contact/laminating paper
✔ 5 pieces 7¼" x ⅝" ribbon
✔ Felt letters and shapes (pre-cut, or create them yourself)
✔ Puffy fabric paint (optional)

Your little darling will delight in recognizing family and friends hidden in each pocket.

3 Cut the cardboard boxes into six 4¼" × 3¾" rectangles.

4 Place a felt sheet horizontally on a flat surface. Measure and mark the vertical and horizontal center lines on the sheet, creating four quadrants, as shown.

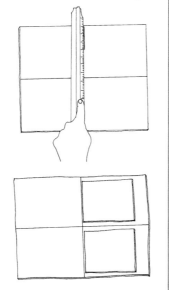

5 Position one cardboard rectangle in the upper right quadrant, flush with the left side and centered vertically. Position another cardboard rectangle in the lower right quadrant in the same way.

ASSEMBLE

6 Squeeze a thin line of hot glue onto the felt around the first cardboard piece, tracing around only the top, right, and bottom edges. (Do not squeeze glue on the felt along the left side.) Repeat with the second piece of cardboard.

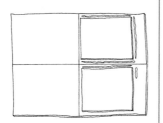

7 Fold quickly along the vertical center line, bringing the left half of the felt over the cardboard pieces to line up with the right half of

the felt. Press down firmly to secure the glue. You should have a vertical 5⅞" × 9" rectangle (with cardboard pieces sandwiched inside).

8 Cut the felt rectangle in half (between the two embedded cardboard pieces) to create two book pages.

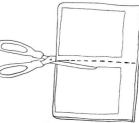

9 Create four more book pages by following steps 4 through 8 with two more sheets of felt. Lay them all out.

10 Gather together scrap material to create six pockets. If you're using a no-fray fabric like fleece or felt, cut 3" × 4¼" pockets. Then fold one in half lengthwise, cut diagonally along one of the short edges (through both layers), and unfold it to create slightly pointed pockets (like the

ones on your jeans). If you're using fabric that frays (home décor or quilting cotton), cut 3½" × 4¾" pockets, trim them to a point, and then fold the edges under ½". *Optional:* Use puffy paint to decorate your pockets and set them aside to dry.

11 Stack the pages of your book in order. (Align them so the cardboard-free margin of each page is facing left.) Fold a 2" piece of ribbon in half to create a loop, and tuck the ends between the top left corners of pages three and four (the middle).

12 Run a needle and thread up through all six pages (plus the ribbon loop) about ¼" in from the top left corner. Use a running stitch to sew down along the left side of the book, binding it together. Knot off the ends.

13 Cut the faces from your photos. Press each one, right side up, on a 2" square of contact paper and then carefully lay a second 2" square of contact paper over it. Press the layers together. Leaving a ⅛" to ¼" border, trim around the image with all-purpose scissors.

"Crafting is a way for me to relax and relieve tension. And it's great to look around my daughter's room and see the special things I've made for her."
—CRAFTY MAMA HOLLY

14 Squeeze a dot of hot glue on one end of each piece of 7¼"-long ribbon and fold it over about ¼" (to keep it from fraying). Then squeeze hot glue over the folded section, and press the back of a laminated photo face against each ribbon end.

variation:

Peek-a-Book

Show me a child who doesn't love peek-a-boo, and I'll show you a potty-trained elephant! Kids can't get enough of the game, no matter what form it takes: hands over the face, hiding behind a door, or lifting flaps in a book! Follow the Pocket Book steps 3 through 11 to create the pages, then steps 12 and 13 to sew the pages together. Print five digital photos of face close-ups (about 2½" square) onto

15 Arrange each pocket on a page of your book. Working one pocket at a time, squeeze hot glue on the wrong side of the fabric (along every edge except the top one), and press it against a page.

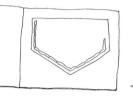
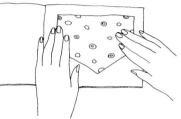

16 Hot glue the remaining end of each ribbon to the fabric page, centered inside the pocket, as shown (you're gluing the ribbon to the right side of the fabric page, not the wrong side of the fabric pocket).

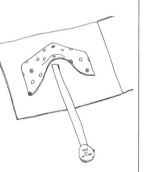

iron-on transfer paper for dark T-shirts, then iron one picture onto each page. Cut out felt pieces a bit smaller than the size of the page and create flaps by hot gluing the top of each flap to the top edge of the page, over each photo. Decorate with trim, felt letters, shapes, and iron-on words, let the glue dry, and keep your DC entertained for *hours*.

FINISH

17 Measure, cut, and hot glue ribbon, rickrack, or trim over the stitches on the front and back of your book. (If your baby is still sleeping, decorate the edges of each page.)

18 Cut and hot glue patches or trim to the pockets, arrange and hot glue the felt letters and shapes to the left side of each page spread, and decorate the cover of the book. Then go ahead and read it!

★ BABY SHOWER POWER ★

Pocket Books are a great group project because each person can add her own unique flair to a page, which makes for a very interesting final product! Just have each attendee bring a photo and give her the materials to make her own felt page. Then have the guest who's handiest with a sewing needle "bind" the book together. If there are a lot of guests, it's best to make two (or three!) books so each one lies flat when closed.

Keep pillows safe from drool—by covering them with some fun and funky fleece!

SPIT-UP LOVER PILLOW COVER

IF YOU HAVE COUCH PILLOWS, HE WILL SPIT UP ON THEM. Or smear food on them. Or chew on them. Guaranteed. You can try to protect your schmancy silk and sequined couch pillows that you bought well before you even thought of having a baby. Or, put those nice ones away until your baby is about thirteen and instead buy some cheap pillows to cover, using a technique similar to the one you used to make the No-Sew Swanky Blanky (page 41). Kids develop new interests every three months, so this is also a great way to update a room or nursery without spending a fortune. Hello Kitty, Barbie, or Transformers—take your pick.

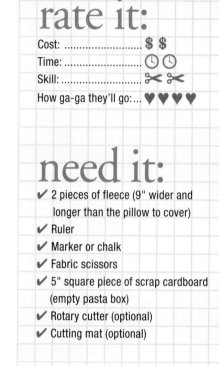

rate it:

Cost: .... $ $
Time: .... 🕐 🕐
Skill: .... ✂ ✂
How ga-ga they'll go:... ♥ ♥ ♥ ♥

need it:

✔ 2 pieces of fleece (9" wider and longer than the pillow to cover)
✔ Ruler
✔ Marker or chalk
✔ Fabric scissors
✔ 5" square piece of scrap cardboard (empty pasta box)
✔ Rotary cutter (optional)
✔ Cutting mat (optional)

make it:

PREP

1 Lay the two pieces of fleece on top of each other with the wrong sides facing. Make sure the stretchy sides are going the same way.

2 Use a ruler, marker, and scissors (or a ruler, rotary cutter, and mat) to mark and then trim the edges from both fleece pieces, making sure they're the same size (and that the rolled edges are removed to create clean, raw edges). Set the trimmed scraps aside; you'll need them for step 5.

3 Place the 5" cardboard square in one corner of the layered fleece, hold it down, and trace around it. Then use scissors to cut out the square along the marker line. Repeat on the other three corners.

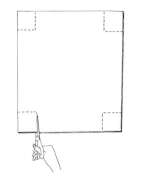

4 Take one of the long fleece strips that you trimmed off the edges in step 2 and lay it on your fabric 5" in from the edge as a guide.

ASSEMBLE

5 Decide how wide you want your fringe. (For chunky fringe, your cuts should be 1" to 1½" apart. For linguini-like fringe, make cuts ½" to ¾" apart.) Use a ruler, marker, and scissors (or a ruler, rotary cutter, and mat) to mark and begin cutting perpendicularly through both layers along one edge of the pillow cover, stopping 5" in at the fleece strip. Continue cutting fringe in this manner around the entire pillow cover perimeter.

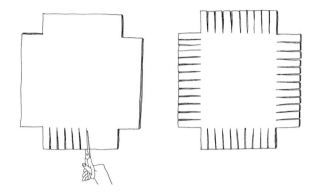

6 Tie the top layer of fringe to the bottom layer of fringe around three sides of the pillow cover, using one of the methods detailed in the Tying Tip. *Note:* You're not going crazy—due to the knit of the fleece, two of the sides *are* significantly more stretchy and easier to tie.

variation:

She Bops

Is your Boppy a little gloppy because your baby's a little sloppy? Cut a 2-yard piece of fleece in half, and lay the two pieces on top of each other with wrong sides facing. Place your Boppy on toppy of the fleece and trace around it with a marker. Make a second outline 8" outside the traced line. (Since you can't add 8" to the "inside curve," draw a line down the center, as shown in the diagram.) Cut through both layers along the outermost line and then cut 1" fringes from the

TYING TIP *When tying fringe, you have two options. For a quicker, easier knot, simply take one piece and tie it to the other. Then tie it again to make a double knot.*

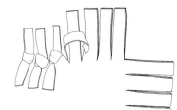

For a neater and more uniform knot, take the two pieces of fringe together, make a loop by wrapping them around your finger, and then pull the ends of both fringes through the loop.

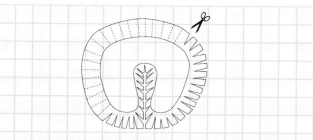

outer edge in to the inner trace line. Mark the tip of one pair (both layers) of fringe so when you separate the pieces to insert the Boppy, you can line them up again to tie them. Tie the top and bottom fringe together in double knots: a new non-gloppy Boppy!

FINISH

7 Slip your pillow into the cover through the open side, pushing it all the way into the corners. If your pillow is flat, trim some fabric from the open edge so the cover fits snugly. If your pillow is super-fluffy, pull the fringe on the last side tightly to make it fit.

8 Tie the remaining edge together in the knot of your choice and it's bye-bye spit-up! Until, of course, he spits up on the pillow cover. (If that does happen, which it probably will, untie one edge, wash the fleece cover in cold water, dry it on low, and then re-tie.)

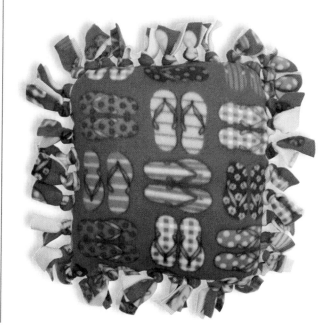

Stack your stuff
in stylish boxes
and watch your
nursery go from
drab to fab.

FOXY BOXES

LET ME GUESS: YOU DIDN'T GET ALL CLUTTERED AND disorganized after you had a baby—you've been that way ever since your wedding, when you accumulated massive amounts of cards, photos, negatives, CDs, bills, magazines, trinkets, brochures, mementos, and so on. You've managed to keep it all under control by stuffing things in random files, drawers, and boxes with little or no labeling and no true organizational principles. But the gig is up. Schmoopie is only six months old, and you already have twice the amount of extra stuff than you had before. It's about time that you add a little method to this madness. Create an easy 'n' fabulous out-on-a-shelf-worthy box for your photos and negatives, and then make another for all of the birthday and holiday cards you've been saving. And while you're at it, make one for her artwork ('cause in another seven months or so, she's going to discover crayons, and your fridge is only so big). *Note:* If you need lots of storage, use your husband's boot box. If you need just a little, use your baby's bootie box.

rate it:

Cost: .... $
Time: .... 🕐🕐
Skill: .... ✂✂
How ga-ga they'll go: ... ♥ ♥ ♥ ♥

Use an old shoe box and sale fabric, and you can make a Foxy Box for less than $5.

need it:

✔ Hot-glue gun
✔ Fabric hot-glue sticks
✔ 1 yard quilting cotton or home décor fabric (covers women's size 9 shoe box)
✔ Iron
✔ Shoe box
✔ Pen or chalk
✔ Ruler
✔ Fabric scissors
✔ Newspaper or paper bag
✔ Craft or fabric spray adhesive
✔ ⅞"- to 1½"-wide grosgrain or satin ribbon
✔ No-fray solution or decoupage medium
✔ Narrow paintbrush
✔ Iron-on transfer paper (optional)
✔ Computer, photo editing software, and color ink-jet printer (optional)

make it:

PREP

1 Plug in your hot-glue gun, and insert one fabric glue stick. If you have one with multiple nozzles, attach the "ribbon" nozzle. If your fabric is a little wrinkly, plug in your iron, let it heat up, and iron it now.

2 Lay your fabric right side down and center your box on top of it. Trace around the bottom of the box with a pen.

3 Turn the box on its side (side A) without shifting it on the fabric. Trace around side A with a pen.

4 Place the box back down on the center. Then tip the box onto the opposite side (side B), so it is flat on the fabric. Trace around side B with a pen.

5 Place the box back down on the center. Then tip it up on one end (side C). Trace around side C. Repeat for the opposite end (side D).

6 Add about 1" (or the width of your ruler) to each top edge of the shape you've traced.

7 Add 1" to both of the vertical edges of side A. Then add 1" to both vertical edges of side B.

ASSEMBLE

8 Cut out your shape along the outermost traced lines.

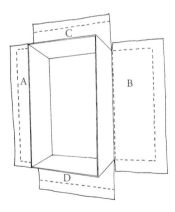

9 Mark and cut ¼" off both of the side edges of side C. Repeat on the side edges of side D.

10 Repeat steps 1 through 9 for the lid of the box. *Optional:*

Iron a picture of your cutie-patootie onto the fabric that will cover the top of the box, using the iron-on transfer method (see page 29).

11 Move all of the babies out of the room where you plan to spray your adhesive—this stuff is no good for them!—and open a window. Lay down some newspaper or a paper bag to protect the floor, and review the instructions on the spray adhesive packaging.

12 Spray the bottom of your box with adhesive, center the bottom of the box on the fabric, and push down firmly.

13 Spray all four sides of your box with adhesive, and carefully and firmly pull the fabric from side A up along the side of the box, smoothing it as you press it down. You'll have some extra fabric that wraps around to side D, and that's okay. Fold the other extra 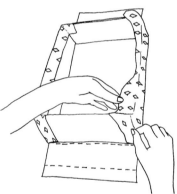 fabric over the top edge of the box. Repeat this with side B, and then sides C and D.

14 Repeat steps 11 through 13 for the lid of your box.

FINISH

15 Use your fabric hot glue to stick the four extra flaps of fabric along the inside top edge of the box to ensure a strong hold. Make sure the fabric is stretched firmly, but not so tightly that it distorts. Repeat on the box lid.

16 Measure from the edge of the fabric on the inside of the lid, over the top of the lid to the other side, and add 8". Cut two pieces of ribbon to that length.

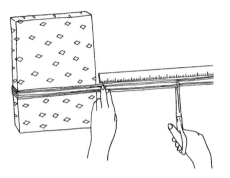

17 Measure from the edge of the fabric inside of the box, up and out around the bottom, and to the other side, and add 8". Cut two pieces of ribbon to that length.

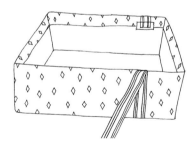

(The two ribbons from the lid and the box are going to tie together.)

18 Use your ruler and pen to lightly mark two parallel lines where you want to place the ribbon on the box. (When you're gluing it down, it's hard to tell if it's going on straight, and this line will serve as a guide.)

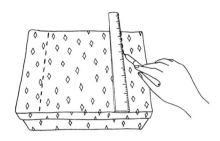

19 Use the ribbon nozzle on your hot-glue gun to squeeze about 3" of glue along the marked line on your fabric, and start attaching the ribbon to your box from where you first measured. Keep on gluing 3" at a time along the line until you reach the edge of the box.

20 Repeat steps 18 and 19 on the lid.

21 Prevent fabric fray by lightly painting the no-fray solution or decoupage medium over any exposed cut fabric along the corners of the top and bottom of your box. Let it dry for about ten minutes before you put the lid on. Tie the ribbons from the lid to the corresponding ribbons on the bottom. If you're feeling ambitious (and want your box to last longer), apply no-fray to the exposed cut fabric on the inside of your lid, too. Let dry.

22 Gather together all of your photos, negatives, CDs, and assorted picture stuff and put them in your box. Then make another box for all of your birthday cards, holiday cards, and assorted paper goods. Use a few boxes that vary in size and stack them all on top of one another.

Protect your fledgling rocker's precious CDs with a personalized case.

CD SNUGGLY

YOUR LITTLE ONE'S ADDICTED TO THIS ONE PARTICULAR Laurie Berkner CD, so of course, you take it with you wherever you go— to the mall, to the supermarket, on the three-hour trip to see your best friend's new baby. Yes, "Victor Vito" is getting old, but it really makes her happy (translation: keeps her quiet in the car). And that's why it's exceedingly important to keep it all nice and scratch-free in a mama-made, personalized CD Snuggly. Come to think of it, you might as well keep all of her CDs in there, 'cause chances are, she's going to be obsessed with a different CD in about three days. Maybe this time you'll get lucky, and she'll take to vintage Madonna. Who wouldn't mind listening to "Borderline" seventeen times in one car ride?

rate it:

Cost: .... $

Time: .... 🕐 🕐

Skill: .... ✂

How ga-ga they'll go:... ♥ ♥ ♥

The most popular color of CD cases is definitely black, but a little searching will turn up a rainbow of color options for this too-cool-for-school project.

need it:

✔ CD case or CD wallet
✔ Felt shapes and letters
✔ Opaque ribbon (not organza or nylon)
✔ Embellishments (rhinestones, little satin flowers, letters, charms, pompoms)
✔ Fabric scissors
✔ Hot-glue gun
✔ Hot-glue sticks
✔ Felt sheet (optional)
✔ Computer, photo editing software, and color ink-jet printer (optional)
✔ Iron-on transfer paper (optional)
✔ Iron (optional)

make it:

PREP

1 Lay out all of the felt shapes and letters, ribbon, and embellishments. If you're making these with your playgroup, you'll find that the vowels and popular consonants go quickly. If there aren't enough letters, cut your own out of a big piece of felt. *Optional:* Accent your snuggly with a picture of your little rocker (or one of Bon Jovi, Dan Zanes, Raffi, or any bad-to-the-bone image) by downloading a picture, printing it on iron-on transfer paper, and ironing it onto a piece of felt.

2 Plug in your hot-glue gun and insert one glue stick.

ASSEMBLE

3 Move all of your elements around on the cover of the CD case until you have the perfect arrangement.

4 Hot glue everything onto the CD case. Even if you're working with self-adhesive felt, you still need to hot glue it on, but remember to remove the paper backing first! Let dry.

FINISH

5 Dig out all of the CDs from the bottom of your diaper bag and put them in your new CD Snuggly. Keep them there forever. (Well, at least for another year, before your kid starts to like Kidzbop!)

music to *your* ears

Sick of the purple dino, the red furry soprano, and the four silly men in colored shirts? See if your little maestro will fall in love with any of these artists, all available at cdbaby.com:

- FunkeyMonkeys!
- Corey Leland
- Milkshake
- The Mudcakes
- CribRock
- Mr. David
- Lunch Money
- Daddy a Go Go

- Ralph's World
- Not Exactly Lobsters
- Laurie Berkner
- Dan Zanes
- Music for Aardvarks
- Hot Peas 'n Butter
- Rebecca Frezza
- Elizabeth Mitchell

variations:

Calling in for Backup

If you have a digital camera, you're probably uploading your pictures to your computer every once in a while. Don't let them just sit there; computers crash and you can lose your precious moments forever! Prevent that inevitable heartache by backing up your photos onto a CD every single month. Then, keep them safe and cozy in your brand-new Photo CD Snuggly.

art-schmart

Deciding what type of art you're into is a big deal, but putting up happy images in your baby's room is not. Here are some inexpensive ideas to dress up your darling's walls:

SHEET MUSIC

My friend with a son named Jude and a daughter named Simone (whom they call Mony) bought and framed the sheet music for "Hey Jude" and "Monie Monie" and hung it on the wall. She loved it so much she bought the "Michelle" and "Jeremy" sheet music (her and her husband's names) for their bedroom walls! If your kid doesn't have a name that happens to be a song title, just go for a song with meaningful lyrics.

ALBUM COVERS

Okay, so your son's name is Veikko—a wonderful name that's not in any song titles that you know of. Check out an old record store or thrift shop for some cool old album covers (the kids' stuff is neat, but if Flock of Seagulls is your thing, go with it). Frame them with album frames—you can get them at most frame stores or www.urbanoutfitters.com (and while you're there, check out their wall art—they have some cute, cheap stuff!).

KIDS' BOOKS

If you haven't already cut up that third copy of *Goodnight Moon* for decoupage, frame it! Carefully use an X-Acto knife to take the pages apart, and then frame the ones you like. Display them in separate frames (three in a row) or in one big frame (with multiple windows cut in the mat). If you have big walls, frame every page and hang them as a border around the perimeter of the room. You never know . . . all those goodnight vibes might actually make him sleep five consecutive hours!

CEREAL BOXES

Save your old cereal boxes, neatly cut them up, frame them, and then hang 'em on up. Sure, Lucky, Tony, and Franken Berry may have a little more color and pizzazz to them, but if you're not into the sugar thing, the Honey Nut bee, Cornflakes rooster, and Snap, Crackle, and Pop will do just fine! We were inspired to hang Toucan Sam and The Cap'n on Lily's wall after we saw an exhibit called "Cerealism" by Michael Albert.

FRAME IT

Your budding Da Vinci may not be ready for the Louvre just yet, but you can still make his scribbling museum-worthy by displaying them in a variety of fancy "gold" frames. It's a step up from the refrigerator gallery!

gift it

Buy or download a whole bunch of kids' CDs, create a personalized CD Snuggly, and give it to one of your musically challenged mommy friends—you know, the one who loves Celine Dion.

LITE THE NITE

OF COURSE YOUR NEWBORN ISN'T AFRAID OF THE DARK; she probably loves how very uterus-like it is. But *you* might like a little light when she sleeps so you can see her better when you check on her every seventeen minutes (just for the first few weeks, of course). As she grows, she'll start to need and appreciate your creation. At two, it might comfort her in the pure darkness. At four, she'll need it to see when she has to go to the bathroom in the middle of the night. (Yes, there will be a day when you won't have to change her diapers!)

rate it:

Cost: .... $ $
Time: .... 🕐🕑
Skill: .... ✂ ✂
How ga-ga they'll go:... ♥ ♥ ♥

Though few people will get to see it glowing in your baby's room when it's dark out, your babysitters will be very impressed.

need it:

✔ ¼ yard home décor or quilting cotton fabric
✔ Hot-glue gun
✔ Fabric hot-glue sticks
✔ Hollywood Lights™ brand self-adhesive night light
✔ Pen
✔ Fabric scissors
✔ Embellishments (grosgrain, satin, or jacquard ribbon; home décor accents; pompoms; gimp trim; fringe; beaded trim; scrapbook trim; rickrack; rhinestones; sequins; patches; letters; flowers; googly eyes; buttons; feathers; marabou trim)

make it:

PREP

1 Choose a fabric that matches your nursery (or bathroom, kitchen, or wherever you want to plug in your night light). Buy something new or use scrap fabric you have in the house. (See "What's Your Fabric Style?"sidebar, page 83 for ideas.)

2 Plug in your hot-glue gun and insert one fabric glue stick.

3 Spread out all of the stuff you have to embellish your light and think about how you want the final project to look. For example, if you love the trim with the dangling baseballs, lobster fabric might not be right.

ASSEMBLE

4 Peel off the sticky paper at the top of the night light shade to use as a pattern. Lay your fabric right side down and trace lightly around the paper with a pen.

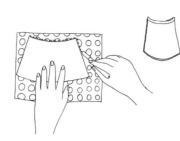

5 Cut out the fabric ½" outside your tracing mark. If you're using a thick fabric (like canvas), add the extra ½" only to the sides (too much extra fold-over fabric will look bulky).

6 Lay the fabric neatly onto the sticky night light. This might take a few tries to get everything even and centered; just peel it off and re-stick it until it's right.

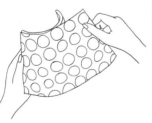

7 Squeeze a thin line of glue along the inside edge of the fabric hanging over the bottom edge of the shade. *Note:* If you're using a thick, canvaslike home décor fabric, skip to step 9.

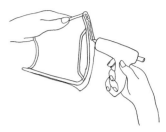

Carefully and slowly, pull the fabric up in small sections over the bottom edge of the night light. Don't stretch the fabric too much, or it will distort. Smooth out the fabric, pushing out any lumps as you go. You're not going nuts; the fabric glue is very sticky and may get on your fingers—just peel it off before you do the next part.

8 Repeat step 7 on the fabric hanging over the top edge.

variations:

Paper Moons

If you're seriously into scrapbooking and you have tons of papers and embellishments lying around, make a paper-covered night light instead (or as well!). Try creating "scenes"—sports, gardens, rock concerts, whatever you think will comfort your little love when he wakes in the night. (I'd stay away from the skull and crossbones on this one!)

I Got You Covered

Skip the fabric coating and cover the *entire* night light with something fabulous like marabou feather trim, big silk flowers, rhinestones, strips of different colored ribbon, pompoms, or feathers. The sticky tape on the night light isn't strong enough to stick everything on, so secure your stuff firmly with fabric hot glue. Trim the edges and add little accents—or leave as is. Plug it in and let it glow, let it glow, let it glow!

FINISH

9 Squeeze a thin line of glue on the extra fabric hanging over the edges on the left and right sides. Carefully pull the fabric over the edges in small sections, and press it down. If you want a plain night light, you're done!

10 Add some embellishments to your light to snazz it up. Use ribbon, rickrack, or beaded trim around the edges (especially the top and bottom) to cover up any fabric bumps or fraying. But don't stop there! Glue on a few fake flowers in full bloom, add sparkle with rhinestones or sequins, or attach some fun feathers.

11 After everything's dry, check along the edges to see if anything needs to be glued down better. Then plug the finished night light into your baby's room and light up his dreams!

TILTING TIP: *Some houses and apartments have only vertical outlets in the bedrooms and bathrooms. If that's the case for you, go to a hardware store for an outlet adapter so your night light doesn't sit sideways.*

what's your fabric style?

When picking out fabric, you're calling the shots—here are some ideas to get you inspired.

Matchy-Match: Use extra fabric from your baby's bedding or curtains for a perfectly coordinated look.

Nostalgic: Cut fabric from one of the many gorgeous dresses that your baby already grew out of (after she wore it only once, of course!). Or use the baby blanket that you used to swaddle your little snuggle puppy in.

Preppy: Use an old collared shirt to make a buttoned-up night light. Complete it by attaching the buttons and collar to the top of the shade!

Resourceful: Chop up all those pretty pillows and pillowcases that have been stained with baby goo. There's definitely an unstained chunk of fabric on one that you can use. Likewise, old sheets are fair game too!

MYOF (Make Your Own Fabric): If your baby happens to love Michael J. Fox (I know, random), download a picture of him, iron it onto cotton fabric, and your baby can dream of Alex P. Keaton every night!

The fabulous fringed quilt is worth the effort; it looks great, feels even better, and is loads of fun for your little one.

KNOT IN A HURRY QUILT

YOU COULD SPEND HUNDREDS OF DOLLARS ON A BEAUTIFUL homemade baby quilt, or . . . you could make a gorgeous, comfortable, interactive, one-of-a-kind quilt all by yourself. Now you might be thinking, "Uh, hello! I bought this book because it said that I didn't need to know how to sew!" And you don't. All you need to know how to do is make a knot—a lot of knots. So many knots that you might *knot* want to finish this project, but you will because you're *knot* a quitter! (Okay, I will *knot* waste any more of your time with my lame puns.) Go and gather together all of your fleece scraps and a season of your favorite show on DVD and knot your little love a quilt. You will *knot* regret it!

rate it:

Cost: .... $ $ $ $
Time: .... 🕐 🕐 🕐 🕐 🕐 🕐
Skill: .... ✂ ✂
How ga-ga they'll go: ... ♥ ♥ ♥ ♥ ♥ ♥ ♥ ♥ ♥

The technique is easy, but patience is the key since this project takes a long, long, long time to make! PS: Buy your fleece on sale, or use leftover fleece from other projects to make your quilt for less.

make it:

PREP

1 Lay each colored fleece piece flat and use the 9" cardboard square as a pattern to trace and then use fabric scissors to cut out forty-two quilt squares (to make a 30" × 32" quilt).

2 Use the 2" cardboard square as a pattern to trace and then cut 2" mini squares from each of the four corners on all forty-two of the 9" quilt squares.

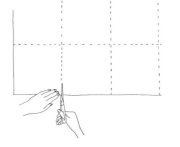

need it:

✔ 6 or more pieces of fleece ¼ to ½ yards each in coordinating and contrasting colors (for quilt squares)
✔ 1 yard fleece (for backing)
✔ 9" square piece of scrap cardboard (from an empty cereal or pasta box)
✔ 2" square piece of scrap cardboard
✔ Ruler
✔ Marker or chalk
✔ Fabric scissors
✔ Rotary cutter (optional)
✔ Cutting mat (optional)
✔ Fringe-cut slotted ruler (optional)

3 Sandwich three quilt squares together, aligning all edges, and use the ruler (or fringe-cut slotted ruler), and fabric scissors to make fringe-cuts 2" long and 1" wide on each side of the quilt squares. Repeat on the remaining quilt squares.

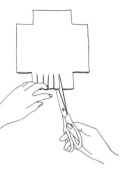

4 Arrange the squares on the floor in your desired pattern so you have seven rows of six squares each.

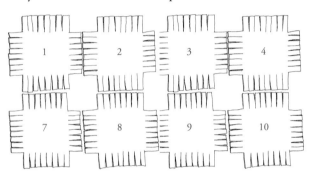

ASSEMBLE

5 Use double knots (see page 36) to tie each fringe strip along the right edge of square 1 to each corresponding fringe on the left edge of square 2. Then tie the right side of square 2 to the left side of square 3, and so on until you've tied squares 1 through 6 together.

6 Knot the squares of each of the remaining six rows together.

7 Line up rows 1 and 2 and knot the fringes on the bottom of square 1 to the fringes on the top of a square 7.

8 Knot the fringes on the bottom of square 2 to the fringes on the top of square 8.

variation:

Onesie Upon a Time

What to do with all of the cute onesies that your beefy baby grew out of? Make a quilt out of them, of course! Try using onesies instead of fleece to make a truly one-of-a-kind cuddly keepsake. If they're too small to knot, go to your local fabric store and see if someone there can help you sew them together.

9 Knot the bottom fringes of square 3 to the top fringes of square 9, the bottom fringes of square 4 to the top fringes of square 10, and so on. Continue tying in this pattern until you've tied all seven rows (forty-two squares) together.

FINISH

10 Pull all of the knotted fringe to the front of the blanket and lay it on top of the wrong side of the backing fleece piece. Smooth out the backing piece and then trim around the edges so it's the same size as the knotted top layer.

11 Arrange the outer fringes on your quilt top so they lay flat and then cut coordinating fringes into the backing piece.

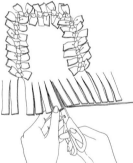

12 Double-knot the quilted top piece to the backing, one pair of fringe at a time.

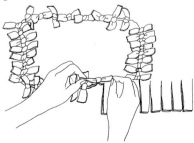

13 Lay your little squirmer on his tummy on top of your incredible creation to let him have an up-close look at his mama-made quilt!

IN ONE END AND OUT THE OTHER

From unique You-tencils to the darling Wipey Clutch, 10 mama-made essentials to keep Junior chowing down and spitting up in style.

Every mom I know (myself included) obsesses about every little morsel that passes by her baby's lips as well as every little thing that comes out the other end (yup, I'm talking about poop!). Luckily, there are thousands of books out there to give you all sorts of info and reassurances related to those eating and pooping issues. And the beautiful thing about *this* book (well, this chapter) is that it will teach you how to make some really great stuff while you discuss them. And at the end of the day, whether or not you resolve all of the issues, your child will look really cute while he's eating whatever he's eating and pooping whatever he's pooping! And isn't that what it's all about anyway?

Forget silver spoons—feed your little dumpling with her very own unforgettable flatware.

YOU-TENCILS

HOW OFTEN DO YOU LEAVE YOUR LITTLE SPOONS AND forks behind when you're chowing down on the go with your munching munchkin? Sure, baby flatware is easy to replace, but remembering to replace it is a different story. A story that, by the way, doesn't end happily when you're dealing with the tantrum your eleven-month-old is throwing as you rummage through all of your drawers to find a soft-tipped spoon. Lucky for you, there is a solution: Personalize his flatware. That way, everyone at the diner, playgroup, and gym class will know exactly who to return all of the straggling silverware to! *Note:* If your child has a long name, your production time will be cut in half. Long names mean you don't have to think as much about what other beads will go on the base of the utensil. (Samantha's, Penelope's, and Benjamin's mamas could probably make a fork and a spoon in the time that it takes Mia's or Ian's mama to make just one.)

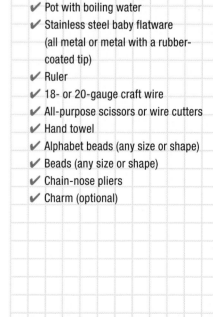

rate it:

Cost: .... $
Time: .... 🕐 🕐
Skill: .... ✂ ✂ ✂
How ga-ga they'll go: ... ♥ ♥ ♥ ♥

Professionally made personalized utensils sell in stores for $30; buy a cute little spoon at the dollar store, and you can make this for less than $3.

need it:

✔ Pot with boiling water
✔ Stainless steel baby flatware (all metal or metal with a rubber-coated tip)
✔ Ruler
✔ 18- or 20-gauge craft wire
✔ All-purpose scissors or wire cutters
✔ Hand towel
✔ Alphabet beads (any size or shape)
✔ Beads (any size or shape)
✔ Chain-nose pliers
✔ Charm (optional)

make it:

PREP

1 Boil your flatware utensils to sterilize them.

2 Measure and cut a piece of wire seven times the length of the handle of your utensil.

3 Spread out a hand towel or bead board in front of you, so your beads don't roll all over the place.

4 Pick out letter beads to spell your child's name as well as some decorative beads for accents. Lay your beads beside the handle of your utensil to measure how many you need. If your child's name has only three letters, you'll probably need four to six extra beads; if your little Rumpelstiltskin has a long name, you might not need any. *Note:* You don't want to completely cover the handle with beads; leave 1" to 1¼" of the handle free to have room to start and finish off the You-tencil.

★ BABY SHOWER POWER ★

A whole set of beautiful, hand-decorated flatware makes a wonderful gift for an expectant mama. Each shower guest can make a spoon or tiny fork emblazoned with the baby's name (if it's been chosen already), or they can just choose letter beads that spell out fun words like "YUMMY," "BURP," or "PEAS!"

ASSEMBLE

5 Grab one end of your wire with your pliers, bend it about ⅛", and then curl it around itself three to six times, creating a flat coil.

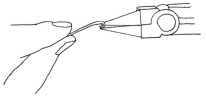

6 Use one hand to hold the coil in place on the front or back of the base of the handle. Use your other hand to wrap the loose end of wire around the handle tightly two or three times to anchor the wire in place.

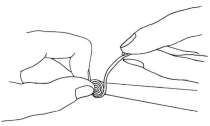

---

variations:

All About You
If you love the way your You-tencils came out, get ready to wrap beads around other items for your little "Asher," "Suri," or "Brooklyn." (None of the stickers, necklaces, key chains, or mugs at the mall bear his or her name, after all.) Here are just a few of my faves:

- The YOUthbrush: Wrap beads around the handle of a solid-colored kiddie toothbrush. They're sold in multipacks at the dollar store.

- The YOUttle: Decorate a rattle that has a thin handle. A metal rattle works best—try to avoid the plastic ones.

"Crafty Mamas inspired me to make party favors for my son's first birthday. People couldn't believe I made them!" —CRAFTY MAMA STACEY

7 Slide on your first bead. Tightly wrap the wire around the handle once or twice. Slide on the next bead and wrap again. Continue wrapping all of your beads onto the handle.

8 When you're done, wrap the wire around the handle two or three more times to secure your beads on the end, then trim just enough wire off to allow for a coil.

- The YOUmb: I know it sounds like I'm asking you to wrap beads around your womb, but no. This is about wrapping beads around the top of a comb (or the handle of a hairbrush).

FINISH

9 Make the second coil at the end of the spoon, as in step 5, and twist it into place on the front or back of the spoon. *Optional:* Hang a little charm (pages 34–35) off the spoon's top.

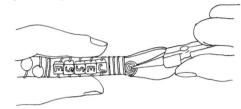

10 Feed your hungry little caterpillar and don't worry if you leave his spoon behind—now that it's a swanky personalized You-tencil, you'll surely get it back!

☞ **CLEAN UP, CLEAN UP** *These embellished utensils are not dishwasher safe. Wash them by hand in warm water and then dry immediately to avoid tarnishing.*

talk amongst yourselves

Chew on this conversation topic while you craft: that little phase they call teething. A painful process—or an excuse for why my baby's crying? After all, babies *do* have incoming teeth along the upper or lower gum lines for the first two years of their lives, but sometimes a bad mood is just a bad mood.

The ultimate accessory for your puréed-squash-eater: a fashionable, easy-clean bib.

VINYL DINER BIB

YOU DON'T WANT YOUR BABY TO BE A WALKING BILLBOARD FOR one big name brand. Which is why you painstakingly shop at many a store to pull together a killer outfit for your kid that's affordable, comfy, and hip. But let's face it: Between bottles, jarred food, soups, yogurts, and snacks, your darling child spends two thirds of his day wearing a bib (aka "outfit spoiler"). Lucky for you, no outfit need be spoiled nor soiled thanks to this fabulous-looking, easy-clean, mama-made bib. (Though the bib takes an hour to make, it takes only thirty seconds to clean!)

rate it:

Cost: .... $
Time: .... 🕐 🕐
Skill: .... ✂ ✂
How ga-ga they'll go: ... ♥ ♥ ♥ ♥

need it:

✔ Photocopier and paper
    (or 8" x 14" bib to trace)
✔ All-purpose scissors
✔ Iron
✔ Hot-glue gun
✔ Fabric hot-glue sticks
✔ ⅜ yard quilting cotton or home
    décor fabric (or an old sheet,
    pillowcase, or T-shirt)
✔ Ruler
✔ Pen
✔ Fabric scissors
✔ 10" x 15" sheet clear iron-on
    flexible vinyl
✔ 3 yards ⅜"-wide ribbon or
    1¾ yards gimp trim or
    braided cord
✔ Eyelet pliers
✔ Transparent tape
✔ Hook-and-loop tape
✔ Needle and thread

make it:

PREP

1 Photocopy the pattern (see page 101) at 200 percent. Use the all-purpose scissors to cut it out. As an alternative, use a clean 8" × 14" bib as your pattern.

2 Plug in your iron. Plug in your hot-glue gun, and insert one fabric glue stick. Review instructions for using the iron-on vinyl.

3 Lay your quilting cotton (or home décor fabric, old sheet, pillowcase, or T-shirt) flat, right side up, and iron out any wrinkles or creases.

ASSEMBLE

4 Use ruler, pen, and fabric scissors to measure and trim the fabric to a 10" × 15" piece and smooth it out flat.

5 Put the iron-on flexible vinyl over your fabric. Lay the protective wax sheet (it comes with the vinyl) over the vinyl and iron over it to fuse the fabric and vinyl together.

6 Lay your paper pattern on the wrong side of the fabric (non-vinyl side) and trace around it with the pen. Follow the trace lines to cut out the bib shape, using fabric scissors.

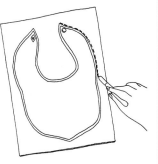

7 Cut a length of ribbon two and a half times the circumference of your bib shape, or cut a length of gimp trim or braided cord equal to the circumference of your bib. If using ribbon, skip to step 9. If using gimp trim or braided cord, go on to step 8.

8 Squeeze hot glue along the edges of the bib (on the vinyl side) and press the gimp trim or braided cord down, 2" at a time. Let it dry and skip to step 13.

9 Flip your bib over, wrong side up, and use a pen to mark little dots about ¼" in from the edge and ½" to 1" apart around the perimeter. Punch holes with your eyelet pliers over each dot. Snip off any excess unpunched fabric circles with scissors.

10 Iron the back (non-vinyl) side to smooth out any puckers that might have developed.

11 Wrap one end of your ribbon with a little bit of transparent tape (so it looks like the tip of a shoelace). Starting at one of the tips of the bib, thread the ribbon through one hole, around the edge, and through the next hole. Tape the end of the ribbon to the bib so it doesn't slide through the first hole as you continue threading. Continue wrapping the ribbon in that manner until you reach the hole where you started.

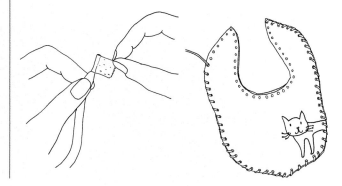

12 Use a little dab of hot glue to attach the loose ends of ribbon to the back of the bib.

FINISH

13 Cut a 1" square of hook-and-loop tape.

14 Use a running stitch to sew the rough piece of hook-and-loop tape to one tip of the bib (on the wrong side of the fabric) and the soft piece of the hook-and-loop tape to the other tip (on the right side of the fabric) so they line up. If you can't bear to sew them on, go ahead and use fabric hot glue.

★ BABY SHOWER POWER ★

Every mother needs a bevy of bibs—so get the mama-to-be started with a bunch of these easy vinyl numbers! At the baby shower, the hostess can provide the materials and the guests can choose the themes and color schemes. By the end of the party, the guest of honor (you know, the one with the big belly) will have a whole mealtime wardrobe for her messy little muncher.

15 Give any small fly-away strings a little trim with your scissors, and then turn your bib over and iron it once more on the non-vinyl side to make it nice and flat.

16 Go and grab some grub—and don't hesitate to put your baby in his chic, mess-free eating vest!

variation:

Save the World, One Placemat at a Time!

Serve up some Cheerios, noodles, or cut-up cantaloupe on a placemat to go with your baby's vinyl bib. Cut out an 11" x 17" sheet of cute quilting cotton or home décor fabric and "vinylize" it with your iron-on vinyl (step 5 of the bib instructions, above) and use fabric hot glue to stick grosgrain ribbon or gimp trim around the perimeter of the mat to create a nice border. Roll it up and take it to go!

A pair of scissors and some old faded denim make the ultimate dream team at mealtimes.

I DREAM OF JEANY BIB

DO YOU DREAM OF GETTING A FULL NIGHT'S SLEEP? OF having a meal where everyone sits contented in their seats, appreciatively eating what's being served? Of the time when the words "No, you can't have that right now!" are not followed by whining or a tantrum? Yeah, me too. But I'm not so sure all of those are going to happen anytime soon, so I've found some new dreams. Now I dream of the bib that I can make out of my old jeans that'll look really cute on my wonderful little early-rising, picky-eating, tantrum-throwing kid. And whaddaya know? It's a dream come true!

make it:

PREP

1 Photocopy the pattern on page 101 at 200 percent and cut it out using all-purpose scissors. As an alternative, use a clean 8" × 14" bib as your pattern.

2 Cut up the inseam of your pair of jeans to "open" the leg and lay it out flat. Lay the paper pattern (or bib) flat over a seam or pocket on your jeans, and trace it with a pen. Continue to trace as many bibs as you can on the same

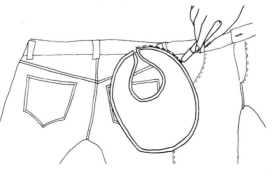

rate it:

Cost: .... $

Time: .... 🕐 🕐

Skill: .... ✂

How ga-ga they'll go: ... ♥ ♥ ♥

If you don't want to sacrifice your perfectly broken-in jeans, there's an enormous selection of denim at rock-bottom prices at your local thrift store.

need it:

- ✔ Photocopier and paper (or 8" x 14" bib to trace)
- ✔ All-purpose scissors
- ✔ Iron
- ✔ Old pair of jeans (or jean jacket, jean skirt, jean shorts)
- ✔ Pen
- ✔ Fabric scissors
- ✔ Hook-and-loop tape
- ✔ Needle and thread
- ✔ Patches
- ✔ Hot-glue gun (optional)
- ✔ Fabric hot-glue sticks (optional)
- ✔ Patch Attach or fusible webbing adhesives (optional)
- ✔ Faux suede lacing (optional)
- ✔ Iron-on metal studs or gems (optional)

pair of jeans in order to make them for the whole group. *Note:* Maternity jeans give you more bang for your buck!

3 Plug in your iron or your hot-glue gun (insert one glue stick), depending on how you plan to attach your patches.

ASSEMBLE

4 Cut out your traced shape using fabric scissors. Pull the strings that hang off the edges to fray the denim. (For maximum fraying, machine wash and dry the denim after you cut it.)

5 Cut a 1" square of hook-and-loop tape.

6 Use a running stitch to sew the rough piece of hook-and-loop tape to one tip of the bib (on the right side of the fabric) and the soft piece of hook-and-loop tape to the other tip (on the wrong side of the fabric) so they line up. If you can't bear to sew them on, use fabric hot glue.

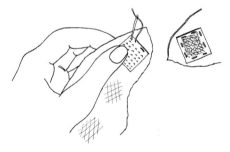

FINISH

7 Hot glue your patches onto the bib or use a needle and thread to sew them on. If you were inspired and bought Patch Attach or fusible webbing, go ahead and iron them on. *Optional:* Accent your bib with some faux suede lacing around the edges, iron-on metal studs, or gems.

8 Put the fabulous I Dream of Jeany Bib on your little mischief-maker, get out your best jar of puréed pasta dinner, and make a wish.

talk amongst yourselves

Here's a good topic for food-obsessed mamas: Talk about that tremendous mess you made that time you tried to whip up your own puréed baby food. Does anyone do that on a regular basis? Do kids actually eat it? For those moms who forgo the jar, which purées has baby liked best? Was it the peas, spinach, and carrot combo meal, or that oh-so-inspired rice and apple mash?

variations:

Viva la '80s
If patches bring back bad Brownie troop memories, like the time Margaret McConner threw up all over you on the bus ride to the senior center, try accenting your bib with something else. Splatter bleach or acrylic paints on your bib. Any stains he gets will blend right in.

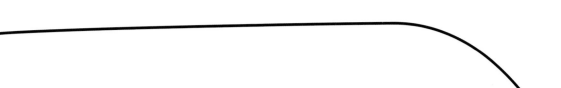

*Photocopy this pattern at
200" × 17" paper.
Cut out your paper pattern
and use it as a template
for the I Dream of Jeany
Bib—and the Vinyl Diner
Bib, too (page 95).*

*Photocopy this pattern at
200% onto 11" × 17" paper.
Cut out your paper pattern
and use it as a template
for the I Dream of Jeany
Bib—and the Vinyl Diner
Bib, too (page 95).*

Viva la '60s

Your hippie babe already has great experience in political activism, seeing as the first two weeks of his life were a sit-in. Now it's time for him to express his radical beliefs on his bib. Stencil or use puffy paints to get across such important global messages as "Give PEAS a chance!"

Scissor Happy

Want to cut up more and more things and convert them into bibs? Try chopping up old terry cloth bath towels. Just trace a bib onto the back of your towel, cut it out, and add hook-and-loop tape to the neck. Terry is great for absorbing your baby's many spits and spills.

It's a mealtime miracle! These plates make your little muncher a member of the clean plate club.

MIRACLE PLATE

MEALTIME IS EASY FOR SOME PARENTS; YOU PUT FOOD IN front of your hungry little dinosaur, and she eats and eats and eats. But for other parents (like me), it's a circus; in order to get her to eat, you need to entertain, excite, trick, surprise, and do everything in your power to get that food into her mouth. I lost all of *my* baby weight trying to get my little darling to down just a quarter of a jar of applesauce. But one day, I took a chance and put her soy chick'n nuggets on this special plate at mealtime. It went something like this:

MOM: Where's Greg? [Mom picks up strategically placed nugget piece to reveal Greg Wiggle.] There he is!

LILY: Greg! Greg!

MOM: Let's eat this bite for Greg!

LILY: (chewing) Mmmm.

MOM: Uh-oh! Where did Grandma Susan go? [Picks up another strategically placed nugget chunk over Grandma's smiling face.] There she is!

LILY: Me-ma!
And so on.

Lily ate a lifetime record that day. Two chicken nuggets, three bites of spinach, and seven grape halves—the first of many mealtime miracles!

So you see, these plates turn eating chopped-up meatballs with a side of broccoli into a thrilling game! Your child might even ask for . . . *more*.

rate it:

Cost: .... $

Time: ....

Skill: ....

How ga-ga they'll go: ...

These customized plates are an inexpensive way to add both fun and focus to mealtimes.

need it:

- ✔ Decoupage images (images or photos from the Internet, magazines, comic books, wallpaper, wrapping paper, catalogs, scrapbook paper— see page 31 for more ideas)
- ✔ All-purpose scissors
- ✔ Clear plastic plates (or bowls)
- ✔ Wax paper
- ✔ Decoupage medium
- ✔ Straight-edge or flat paintbrush
- ✔ Brayer or plastic card
- ✔ Acrylic paint (any color)
- ✔ Clear acrylic finish spray or sealant

make it:

PREP

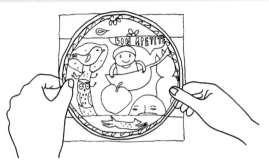

1 Print from the Internet or your digital photos or cut out from magazines a few pictures of people or things your baby loves: balls, furry red monsters, your smiling face, bananas, and so on. Arrange the images on a flat surface. Place a clear plate on top of the images to see if you like the design. *Note:* You're going to be decoupaging on the back of your plate—not on the front where the food goes.

2 Paint an even coat of decoupage medium onto the *front* of one image and stick it in place on the *back* of the plate. Push down the paper and use your finger, a brayer, or a plastic card to make it as smooth as possible. Repeat this process until all of the images are glued to the plate. (If any of the images overlap, the ones you glue down first will be visible.) Wait 15 to 20 minutes for the glue to dry.

3 When it is dry, move the plate onto a piece of wax paper and paint a coat of decoupage medium over the back of it, covering only the back of the images. Let it dry for 15 to 20 minutes. (If you left some of the plate blank, don't paint it with the decoupage medium.)

FINISH

4 Paint the back of your plate gently with a generous coat of acrylic paint (if you push down too hard on the brush, the paint may seep under the edges and onto the images). Wait about 15 minutes for the paint to dry and paint a second coat. If you want the plate to be completely

variations:

Mr. Big Face

Cut out a big face the size of the center circle in the plate. It could be your grandma or someone else like Dora or David Hasselhoff. Leave the rim of the plate clear, paint it, or decorate it with smaller faces, hearts, motorcycles, or other designs. Your child will love to lift his hunka, chunka meatloaf to reveal his friend!

opaque, apply a third coat of acrylic paint. Wait for the last coat to dry.

5 Go outside, or someplace far away from the kids, and spray a coat of finishing spray or acrylic sealant onto the back of your plate. (This will seal the plate so you can wash it again and again.) Let dry and then spray a second coat. Let your plate dry overnight.

6 Make your child something delicious for dinner and watch as he miraculously scarfs down his brussels sprouts, just so he can see a nice photo of you! Mom always said, "Don't play with your food." But she never said anything about playing with your plate!

CLEAN UP, CLEAN UP *While these Miracle Plates are fabulous and adorable, they're not so dishwasher-safe. Wash them by hand in warm water with soap, and they'll get just as clean as they would in the washer—plus, they'll stay intact.*

★ **BABY SHOWER POWER** ★

Experienced moms know that mealtime can be a little less than fun, so why not prepare the new mommy for future dinner disasters by making her a set of Miracle Plates? Choose a theme, or let everyone do their own thing. Either way, the guest of honor will end up with enough dishware to keep her baby entertained (as she tries to coax peas into his mouth) for years!

talk amongst yourselves

While you wait for the glue to dry, discuss: Picky eaters—nature or nurture? Who among you has the pickiest eater of all? And which tricks actually work to get the food eaten?!

Ha-Ha
Feature a comic strip in the center of the plate, with scrapbook paper behind it. This one's really for Mom since we could all use a little humor at mealtime.

Family Tree
Draw, trace, or cut out a tree. Stick photos of family faces in the branches. At mealtime, strategically cover the faces, and watch as he delights in picking a yummy berry off the tree that reveals . . . Daddy!

Alphaplate
Rip out a page from a book with tons of big, colorful alphabet letters on it, decoupage it on, and attempt to teach him the alphabet while he chows down. "Look what was behind that piece of eggie. An E. E is for eggie." Do the same with numbers.

Bowl o' Fun
Follow the same instructions using a bowl as your base instead.

Wherever,
whenever, a
stylish bib
clip instantly
transforms
any napkin
or dishcloth.

INSTA-BIB

THERE'S NOTHING YUMMIER THAN GOING ON A LUNCH DATE with your messy little munchkin. There's also nothing grosser than sticking a macaroni-, chicken soup–, and sweet potato–encrusted bib into your diaper bag at the end of that date. As soon as you leave the restaurant, the crumpled mess starts to bounce around your bag, and next thing you know, there's a hard string of chicken stuck to your new cell phone. Ew! But rather than stop dining out, simply *start* bringing your mama-made Insta-Bibs with you. Clip one onto a cloth or paper napkin, feed your Messy Madeline all the soupy peas and pureed pasta she wants, and let her drool and drip to her heart's content. Unclip the napkin when she's had her fill and leave the restaurant happily with a scum-free bag!

rate it:

Cost: .... $
Time: .... 🕐
Skill: .... ✂
How ga-ga they'll go:... ♥ ♥ ♥

It's easy to make a couple of backups— not just in case you lose one, but for all your lunch bunch mom friends who'll think it's brilliant.

need it:

✔ Hot-glue gun
✔ Fabric hot-glue sticks
✔ 1 pair mitten clips (makes 2 Insta-Bibs)
✔ Fabric scissors
✔ ¾"- to 1¼"-wide grosgrain or jacquard ribbon
✔ Ruler or tape measure
✔ Embellishments (rhinestones, silk or satin flowers, small patches)

make it:

PREP

1 Plug in your hot-glue gun and insert one glue stick.

2 Cut off the elastic from one of the mitten clips, leaving just two metal clips.

ASSEMBLE

3 Measure the ribbon by placing one end on your baby's left collarbone and running it around the back of her neck to her right collarbone. Pinch the ribbon at that point, add an extra 2", and cut it.

4 Thread one end of the ribbon through the metal slit in one clip. Squeeze a small dab of hot glue to the underside of the end of the ribbon and fold it over to meet the back of the ribbon. Repeat, using the other end of the ribbon and the second clip.

FINISH

5 Hot glue accents to the ribbon or on top of the metal clips. (Not too many, since you will have to wash it from time to time.)

6 Go to a restaurant, attach each clip to a corner of *their* cloth or paper napkin (no laundry for you tonight!), and relax as your child chows on that spaghetti with red sauce.

variations:

Sassy Paci

How the heck do you keep baby from spitting her paci onto the floor every three minutes? Make a Sassy Paci! It's a ribbon strap that easily attaches to any pacifier and then clips onto a garment. Start by folding each end of a 10" piece of ribbon ½" and hot gluing to prevent fraying. Slide one end of the ribbon 1" through the slot on a mitten clip, fold it over, and hot glue it. Hot glue a ½" piece of hook-and-loop tape ¼" in from the edge on the opposite end of the ribbon. Then hot glue the matching ½" piece of hook-and-loop tape 1" farther. Snap the mitten clip onto your baby's shirt, jacket or stroller strap, attach the other end around the handle of your baby's paci, and happily go to the mall, the playground, or even the waste and recycling center . . . knowing that your paci is safe and sassy!

got crap?

Does your child love to collect lots of little things? When his toys aren't tagging along with him, organize them by theme in a set of Decou-Pails (page 59). Decorate a bucket for each type of toy: action figures in one bucket, musical instruments in another, Matchbox cars, tiaras, and so on. Install a special shelf (low or high) in your nursery to display all of your buckets. Then, when your little babe is in a hot-rod mood, bring down that bucket, dump out the cars, and have yourselves a good old-fashioned drag race!

La Leash

You *could* buy seventeen identical versions of your child's favorite toy/animal/doll so that when it falls or gets launched out of her stroller onto the sticky floor at the food court, you have sixteen more on deck. Or, you could strap one to the stroller with La Leash, and walk away from the pizza shop with the toy you brought.

Stitch or hot glue a ½" rough piece of hook-and-loop tape ¼" in from one end of a 26" piece of ribbon. Attach a soft piece of hook-and-loop tape 3¾" farther, and then another soft piece 2½" beyond that. Sew a rough piece ¼" in from the opposite end, and then sew a soft piece 3¾" farther, followed by another soft piece 3" beyond that.

Strap one end around a toy and the other to the stroller. Then treat your eyes to something other than the ground. Ah, so this is what your neighborhood looks like!

Linger a little
longer at meal-
time with a
collage of friends
at the feast!

FOTO-MAT

YOU COULD BUY YOUR CHILD ONE OF THOSE PLACEMATS with shapes, letters, maps, numbers, or presidents on it so he can keep his mind active and his brain sharp while he nibbles his nuggets. Or, you could make him a placemat with all of his favorite people on it so he'll look at them and talk to them and smile while he chows. These days, not everything needs to be about making your kid smarter; sometimes, you just want her to know that she's loved. (That said, you can always place some letters, numbers, and shapes next to the people who love her to sneak in some of that learning!)

rate it:

Cost: .... $
Time: .... 🕐
Skill: .... ✂ ✂ ✂
How ga-ga they'll go: ... ♥ ♥ ♥ ♥

Very simple to make, but the contact paper can present a *sticky* situation, to be sure. They're much easier to make when you have a second pair of hands helping you.

need it:

✔ Computer, photo editing software, and color ink-jet printer
✔ Photos
✔ All-purpose scissors
✔ Vinyl placemat
✔ Double-sided tape or photo mounting squares
✔ Stickers (letters and/or images)
✔ Scrapbook paper
✔ Ruler
✔ Contact paper (enough to cover the vinyl placemat)
✔ Decorative-edge scissors (optional)

make it:

PREP

1 Print some photos, any size. You can have one big 8" × 10" picture, three 4" × 6" pictures, or ten 3" × 5" pictures. Or, collage a bunch together in your photo editing program. If you don't want to limit yourself to photos of grandma and grandpa, go online and search for copyright-free pictures of Elvis, a cupcake, a NYC subway map, or that big purplesaurus.

ASSEMBLE

2 Cut out the images, either with all-purpose scissors or decorative-edge scissors, and stick your images onto your vinyl placemat with double-sided tape or photo mounting squares. Accent your design with text, scrapbook paper, or stickers (but nothing 3-D or puffy). *Note:* Leave a 1" to 2" border free and clear of pictures around the edges of the mat.

3 Cut a piece of clear contact paper that's at least ½" bigger than your placemat (vertically and horizontally).

4 Review the instructions that come with your contact paper, so you don't end up with a wrinkled mess. Carefully lay the contact paper on top of your placemat and then smooth out any bubbles or bumps with your fingers.

HANDY TIP *Ask for help when you apply the contact paper. Four hands are way better than two!*

FINISH

5 Trim the extra contact paper from around the sides of your mat.

6 Put it on the table and watch as she says "Grandma!" and then spells out G-R-A-N-D-M-A! Harvard, here she comes!

stuck on you

To stop your creation from slipping and sliding, stick a roll of double-sided tape in your diaper bag and kitchen drawer, and apply it to the back of the mat before you press it to the table. Or, buy some inexpensive little suction cups at the hardware or craft store, and hot glue them to each corner on the underside of the mat. Now let's see if Junior can pull a Houdini on his bologna.

variations:

Chalky-Mats

Want to keep your table clean *and* keep your child occupied for at least seven minutes of a meal? Coat the top of a vinyl placemat with chalkboard paint (follow the steps on the back of the jar). Decorate the edges using stencils and acrylics, or create a border using masking tape. While you're waiting for the chalkboard paint to cure, run out and buy some chalk. Make yourself a really decadent dinner as he draws squiggles galore—oh, wait, I think those are dinosaurs.

snack attack

Is your baby tired of Cheerios? Even if he's not, you probably are. (Admit it, you always munch a handful when you bust them out for him!) Here are some alternative, healthy finger foods for kids. (But just in case your child has any allergies, please read the labels and ask your physician before serving any of these to your baby.)

Soy chips: Made in tons of different flavors and packed with protein. Most munchers like the lightly salted or apple cinnamon ones, but surprisingly the BBQ and onion-flavored chips are popular among tots, too!

Spelt pretzels: Regular butterfly-shaped pretzels are great, but for a healthier treat, try spelt. It packs more protein than most pretzels and tastes the same.

Peas: Sounds crazy, right? But warm up some frozen peas, put them in a little snack box, go for a stroll, and stare in amazement as your baby munches away! If he doesn't go for the peas, try green beans.

Space food: Okay, so he didn't go for the peas or the green beans (see above). But maybe he'll eat them if they're freeze-dried—you know, like the astronauts eat! Gerber now makes freeze-dried finger food veggies and fruits that are tasty, crunchy, and fun to eat. They're 100 percent natural (always a plus) and it's the only way my daughters will consume vegetables.

Cereal: There's more than one O on the block. Kashi makes a great O cereal called Heart to Heart. It's a little sweeter, and the Os come with cute little hearts! Try organic Os, too; they come in fruity and chocolaty flavors without all the refined sugar!

Rice cakes: I used to get away with feeding my kids the unsalted ones, then they graduated to the lightly salted treats, then to the white cheddar ones, and now we're onto caramel and chocolate. Whatever the flavor, they're very entertaining to eat (and watch be eaten), and healthy, too. You might even get away with calling them "big cookies!" (I do!)

Bars: Once your baby is about a year old, you can give him soft granola or cereal bars. Try organic varieties for kids; they're smaller, healthier, and (bonus!) sometimes have Elmo and Grover on the box.

Puffs: Stay away from the crappy orange doodles for now, and treat your baby to some cheesy or fruity baked puffs. Look for puffy wheels, stars, and teddy-shaped puffs, too.

Fruit leather: Once he's five (really, two), all he's going to want to eat is fruit by the foot and gummy fruit snacks. So take advantage of his non-sugared system and start him out with natural fruit leather bars. They're yummy, all natural, and available at grocery stores. If you're ambitious, you can even find out online how to make your own.

Blueberries: Kids love "bluebs," fresh or dried, and they're great on the go.

Wipe baby's cheeks (both kinds!) in style with this classy clutch.

WIPEY CLUTCH

WHO IN THE WORLD ACTUALLY WANTS TO CHANGE A DIAPER?
You! Well, you do once you have this amazingly gorgeous Wipey Clutch in
your tool kit (handbag). Even the squirmiest kid with the smelliest diaper is a
pleasure to change when you have this dazzling diaper wipe case on hand. It
is so fantastic and inspiring, you'll find that you want to take it out and wipe
everything you see—runny noses, tables, toys, dusty TV sets, car windows,
muddy shoes. And the best thing is, it also doubles as a formal clutch. Judith
Leiber, eat your heart out!

rate it:

Cost: .... $
Time: .... 🕐 🕐
Skill: .... ✂ ✂
How ga-ga they'll go: ... ♥ ♥ ♥ ♥ ♥

need it:

✔ Hot-glue gun
✔ Fabric hot-glue sticks
✔ ⅜ yard cotton quilting or
   home décor fabric (or a 10" x 14"
   piece of leftover fabric is perfect
   for a standard travel-size wipe box)
✔ Travel-size wipe box
✔ Ruler
✔ Pen
✔ Fabric scissors
✔ 1½ yards gimp trim
✔ No-fray solution, clear hot-melt
   glue, or clear nail polish
✔ Iron-on transfer paper (optional)
✔ Computer, photo-editing software,
   and color ink-jet printer (optional)
✔ Iron (optional)
✔ Embellishments (optional: rhine-
   stones, googly eyes, letter beads,
   felt shapes)

make it:

PREP

1 Plug in your iron and hot-glue gun, and insert one fabric glue stick.

2 Lay the fabric flat, wrong side
up. Open up your wipe box all the
way, lay it on the fabric, and trace ¼"
outside the edges of the box.

ASSEMBLE

3 Cut fabric along the traced lines.

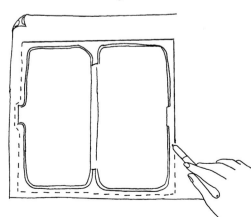

4 Wrap the cut piece of fabric around the wipe box. About ¼" of the wipe box should be showing along its edges. Mark and trim any excess fabric. (Don't worry if the fabric isn't perfectly even;

you'll hide it when you add trim along the sides of the box.) *Optional:* Print your little diaper dude's name, nickname, or photo on iron-on transfer paper for dark-colored fabrics. Wrap the fabric around your box to figure out where to place the iron-on. Carefully unwrap the fabric so you maintain proper placement and iron the decal into place. *Note:* Do not iron on after you glue the fabric onto the box. You'll warp the plastic!

5 Apply hot glue around the perimeter of the top side of the wipe box and carefully press half of your fabric in place over it. The fabric glue is malleable, so make any adjustments while it's still wet.

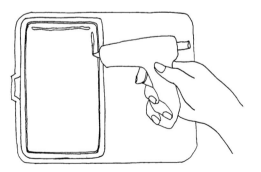

6 Apply hot glue around the perimeter of the other side of your wipe box, then carefully pull the fabric around the box

and press it into place. Make sure you pull the fabric tight, so it's smooth and unbuckled, but not so tight that you can't open and close the box.

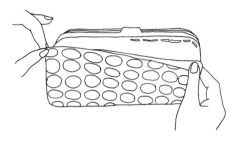

7 Check that there's ¼" of the wipe box showing along the sides of the box and trim excess fabric if needed. Then apply hot glue around the perimeter of the wrong side of the fabric and carefully stick it down along the sides of the box.

variations:

Distracta-Box

In a greased pig contest, a farmer takes a little pig, smears oil all over him, and then sends some innocent person into the pen to try to catch the slimy porker. If this reminds you of changing your little squealer's diaper, then you need a Distracta-Box! Hot glue a variety of foam shapes and letters to your wipe box. Pick a theme (dinosaurs), create a scene (transportation), or just go with shapes and letters. Hand it over to your slippery squirmer at changing time

FINISH

8 Take your gimp trim and wrap it tightly around the edge of the box to measure the length; add ¾" to the length, and cut it. Then cut a second piece of gimp trim the exact same length.

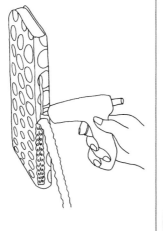

9 Start at the back of your box, squeezing 3" of glue at a time, and press the wrong side of the gimp trim around the perimeter of the upper lip of the box. (Fabric glue dries white, so try not to put on too much.) Continue 3" at a time, and pull the gimp trim tightly as you go. Repeat with the second piece of gimp trim on the lower lip of the box.

and he'll stare, point, and gurgle in amazement! Get in on the brainy baby bandwagon by pointing to things and making comments like, "Look honey, a D for distraction." And, "Oooh! A plane! That's what Mom and Dad are going to ride in when we go on a fantastic vacation—sixteen years from now!" (Just don't get too distracted yourself, since the foam shapes could become a choking hazard if pulled off.)

10 Apply a dab of no-fray solution or clear hot-melt glue (or clear nail polish!) to the end of your gimp trim so it doesn't unravel.

11 Jazz up the Wipey Clutch with some rhinestones, googly eyes, letter beads, or felt shapes if your baby isn't a crazy puller. But if he loves to pull, pick, and tug, you should probably stick to the iron-ons in step 4.

Snack in a Box

Obsessed with fabric-coating things? Gather a round plastic snack case with a hinge (better than one where the top and bottom separate), trace the top and bottom onto fabric, cut them out, and hot glue them to the snack box. Wrap a piece of fabric around the sides of the box. Cover the lip of the top of the box lid with thin gimp trim. Hot glue gimp trim around the base of the box to cover the fabric seams. If your child is older than three (and not likely to pick things off and eat them with his pretzels!), embellish to your heart's desire.

Take his nursery to the next level by covering that boring plastic case with just a little bit of fantastic fabric.

THE BETTER BOLDER WIPEY HOLDER

YOU KEEP YOUR VALUABLE JEWELRY IN A NICE JEWELRY BOX, so why would you keep your wipes in anything less? (Face it, you use wipes way more than your pearls or diamond studs these days!) Give that big hunk of plastic some fabric love and transform it into the glorious accessory it deserves to be. And new mommies love these: A friend who had a baby before I started making them told me she was considering having another child just so she could get one as a shower gift! (The perfect finishing touch is a note inside that says, "You are now officially on mommy doodie!")

rate it:

Cost: .... $ $
Time: .... ⏰ ⏰ ⏰
Skill: .... ✂ ✂
How ga-ga they'll go: ... ♥ ♥ ♥ ♥

need it:

- ✔ Hot-glue gun
- ✔ Fabric hot-glue sticks
- ✔ Large plastic wipe box
- ✔ ½ yard* quilting cotton or home décor fabric
- ✔ Pen
- ✔ Ruler or tape measure
- ✔ Fabric scissors
- ✔ 2 yards gimp trim
- ✔ No-fray solution, clear hot-melt glue, or clear nail polish
- ✔ Embellishments
- ✔ Iron-on transfer paper (optional)
- ✔ Computer, photo-editing software, and color ink-jet printer (optional)
- ✔ Iron (optional)

*If you already have some leftover fabric on hand, an 18" x 20" piece will suffice for covering a standard plastic wipe box.

make it:

PREP

1 Plug in the hot-glue gun and insert one glue stick.

ASSEMBLE

2 Center the box on top of your piece of fabric (facing wrong side up) and trace around the bottom of the box (A).

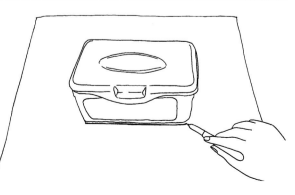

3 Turn the box up on its back carefully and trace around the side (B). Turn the box again to trace the lid of the box (C).

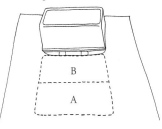

4 Place the box back in the center (A), and turn it up on its front. Trace around the side of the box (D). Then bring the box back to the center (A) and onto the other two sides (E and F) and trace around them, too.

5 Remove your box from the fabric and add about 1" to the end of sides D, E, and F, as shown.

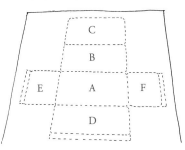

6 Cut the fabric along the outside perimeter of the shape you traced. *Optional:* Print an image onto iron-on transfer paper for dark-colored fabrics. Wrap the fabric around your box to figure out where to place the iron-on. Carefully unwrap the fabric so you maintain proper placement and iron the decal into place.

7 Squeeze a line of hot glue on the perimeter of the bottom of the box, and press it onto the wrong side of fabric section

A. Pull and smooth out the fabric to make sure there are no buckles or creases.

8 Squeeze a line of hot glue along the perimeter of the box side that corresponds to fabric section E. Pull fabric section E up to meet the side of the box and press it in place, tucking the top of the fabric under the top edge of the box. Repeat on the opposite side of the box (corresponding to fabric section F) and then the front side (corresponding to fabric section D).

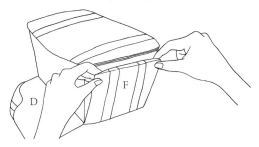

9 Squeeze a line of hot glue around the perimeters of the side and top of the box (which should correspond to fabric sections B and C), one side at a time. Pull the fabric up along the back and top of the box and press it down, making sure it is smooth and tight.

FINISH

10 Measure and cut a piece of gimp trim 1" longer than the distance around the base of the wipe box. Then measure and cut a piece of trim 1" longer than the distance around the top of the box. Lastly, measure and cut four pieces of trim to run along the vertical edges of the wipe box (without adding additional length).

11 Squeeze a line of glue along one vertical edge and press one of the short pieces of gimp trim against it, covering up the fabric seams. Repeat on each remaining vertical edge. (The fabric glue dries white, so try not to add too much.)

12 Apply a dab of no-fray solution or clear hot-melt glue (or clear nail polish!) to the end of your gimp trim so it doesn't unravel.

13 Using the same technique as in step 11, start at the back corner and hot glue the gimp trim around the bottom and top of the box.

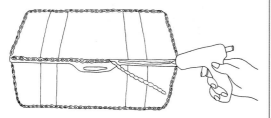

14 Accent the box with embellishments that complement your fabric. If you used a floral print, hot glue on a big silk flower. If you used an animal print, hot glue on a few plastic pigs. And if you used a snazzy graphic design, bling it up with some sparkly rhinestones or bows.

15 Now go ahead and decorate another as a jewelry box!

myow (make your own wipes!)

If you're the type of person who realizes she has no more toilet paper *while* she's on the toilet, then you're probably someone who runs out of baby wipes as you're changing your little pooper. Next time that happens, try whipping up some of your own! (Of course, that means you need to have paper towels in stock!)

1. Cut a roll of paper towels in half with a sharp knife or electric knife to get two mini rolls.

2. Remove the cardboard center from the inside of one half and place the paper towels in an empty wipe box. (Save the other half for spills or the next time you run out of wipes!)

3. Mix together 1½ cups water, 1½ tablespoons baby oil, and 1½ tablespoons baby shampoo.

4. Pour the mixture over the paper towels. Turn the towels over to make sure the mixture gets on both sides, close the wipe box, and shake it a bit.

5. Wait 10 minutes for the liquid to totally absorb. Now go and change that diaper; it's starting to stink up your house!

Keep diapers clean and fresh—stack them in a handy-dandy Diaperlope!

DIAPERLOPE

JUST BECAUSE YOU ALREADY MADE THE INSTA-BIB (PAGE 107) doesn't mean that the diapers at the bottom of your bag are 100 percent protected from occasional crumbs-in-the-crease syndrome. Be honest: How many times have you reached for a diaper from the bottom of your bag and found a stale graham cracker nesting inside it? Problem solved: With some easy folding and gluing, one of those colorful bandanas that's been nesting in the back of your drawer for years can become the perfect safe envelope for a few clean diapers. The handy Diaperlope keeps your little rugrat protected from getting crackers in his crack.

rate it:

Cost: .... $
Time: .... 🕐 🕐
Skill: .... ✂ ✂
How ga-ga they'll go: ... ♥ ♥ ♥

need it:

✔ Iron
✔ Hot-glue gun
✔ Fabric hot-glue sticks
✔ Bandana (or 21" square quilting cotton or home décor fabric)
✔ Ruler
✔ Pen
✔ Fabric scissors
✔ Needle and thread
✔ 1" hook-and-loop tape tab
✔ Trim (gimp trim, pompom trim, braided cord trim)
✔ Iron-on transfer paper (optional)
✔ Computer, photo editing software, and color ink-jet printer (optional)

make it:

PREP

1 Plug in your iron and set it to cotton. Plug in your hot-glue gun and insert one fabric glue stick.

2 When the iron is heated, iron your bandana or piece of fabric.

ASSEMBLE

3 One side at a time, squeeze hot glue 1" in from the edges of two adjacent sides of the wrong side of your bandana or fabric and fold over each side (A and B) 1½".

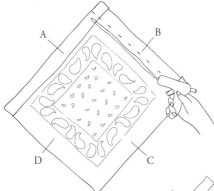

4 Take the corner between A and D and fold it in to the center of the fabric, making an 8" triangle. Repeat, using the corner between B and C. Squeeze a small dab of hot glue on the underside of each corner and press it into the center.

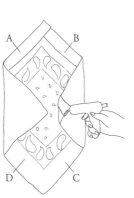

5 Fold up the bottom triangle (between C and D) about 8¼" to 8½" until it meets the section you just glued. Carefully glue the top corner and edges of the triangle down to secure it.

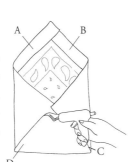

6 Fold up the bottom edge until it reaches the bottom of the "roof" of your house-shape to create the envelope-shape. Squeeze hot glue between the layers of the two vertical sides of the envelope. Use small dabs of glue as needed to seal any remaining gaps.

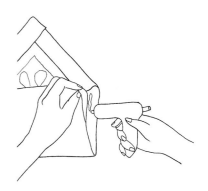

FINISH

7 Use a running stitch (hot glue won't hold!) to sew the soft piece of hook-and-loop tape to the inside of the pointy flap of your envelope. Sew the coordinating rough piece of hook-and-loop tape to the main body of the envelope so it lines up with the first piece.

8 Hot glue decorative trim along the outside edges of the "flap" of your Diaperlope, as shown.

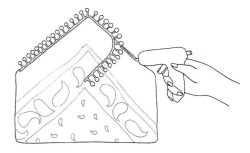

Optional: Make an iron-on of your baby's name, photo, or favorite thing (garbage truck, bowl of oatmeal, or that cute little builder who likes to fix things) and iron it onto your Diaperlope.

9 Stuff a few diapers, along with your snazzy new Wipey Clutch (page 115), into your Diaperlope. Heck, if you have room, put a tube of A+D in there, too!

"It's cool to be a mom and still have time to whip out these projects and work out my creative inner crafter!"
—CRAFTY MAMA HALEY

mini makeover

Most people decorate their nursery—cute critters, clouds, teddies, and pastels or plaids galore—with a delicious little baby in mind. But before you start stenciling puppies onto the walls, remember that your little one is going to have a big opinion sometime soon. By the time your infant is about eighteen months old, he or she is going to be passionate about trains, princesses, fish, flowers, dinosaurs, ballerinas, outer space, horses, fast cars, guitars, or mice with falsetto voices.

To avoid a costly extreme makeover, design a nursery that can be easily converted into a big-kid room. Use wall decals, rather than permanent paint for wall accents. Buy inexpensive sheets, curtains, and decorative pillows that you can swap out later on. Put up a shelf 8" to 12" below the ceiling to display your big kid's favorite things of the moment. And as for colors, try to go one shade darker than your baby impulse.

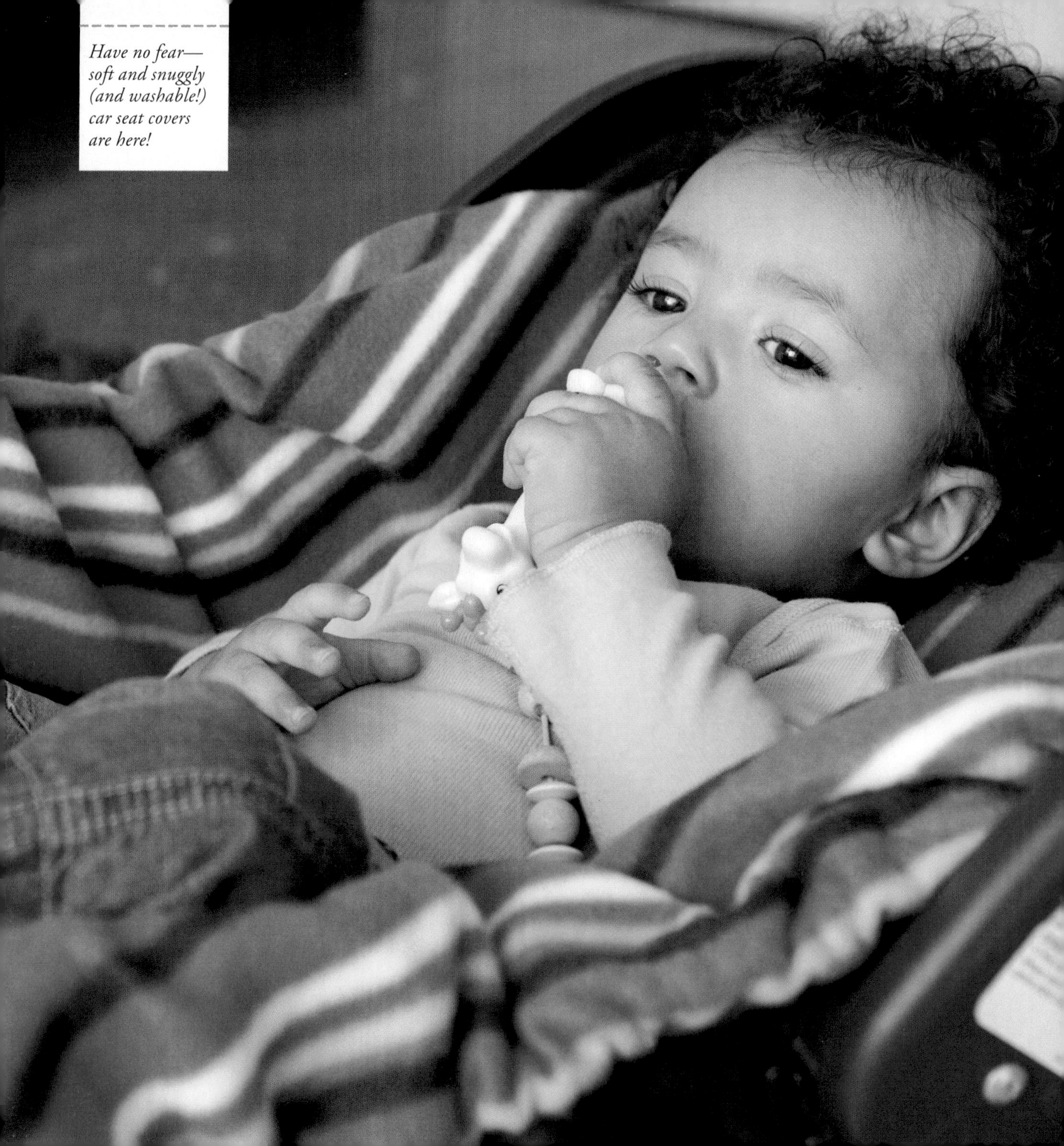

Have no fear—soft and snuggly (and washable!) car seat covers are here!

PIMP MY RIDE

YOU'RE MEETING YOUR OLD COLLEGE ROOMMATE IN TEN minutes and the restaurant is fifteen minutes away. Your baby is screaming bloody hunger and with negative five minutes on your side, you know you need to feed her on the go. So you fill up a bottle, rush to the car, strap her safely into the five-point harness, and step on it. She sucks her baba down in three minutes flat as you drive with a smile. And then you hear a sound. A sound that's all too familiar to you (and your old college roommate). It's the sound of . . . barf. In the back of your mind you knew a bottle on the go wasn't such a good idea, but it's okay, because Super You remembered to cover your trusty Graco with your mama-made pimped-out seat cover. You arrive at the restaurant, change her clothes, take off the barfy seat cover, throw it in a baggie, and run in to meet your child-free friend, who, it turns out, is even later than you.

rate it:

Cost: .... $ $
Time: .... 🕐 🕐
Skill: .... ✂
How ga-ga they'll go: .... ♥ ♥ ♥ ♥

These sell for $30 to $65 in fancy boutiques!

need it:

- ✔ Hot-glue gun
- ✔ Fabric hot-glue sticks
- ✔ 1 yard stretch fabric (fleece, cotton jersey, washable faux fur)
- ✔ Infant car seat
- ✔ Tape measure
- ✔ Fabric scissors
- ✔ Safety pin
- ✔ 2 yards ¼"- to ½"-wide elastic
- ✔ Marker
- ✔ ⅝"- to 1"-wide grosgrain ribbon
- ✔ No-fray solution

make it:

PREP

1 Plug in your hot-glue gun and insert one glue stick.

2 Lay the fabric over your infant seat to determine whether a 45" × 30" piece is enough fabric to cover your car seat. Use the tape measure to roughly estimate the length. (If you have a Graco or Peg Perego infant car seat, skip this step, because it will definitely be enough fabric.) If the length is more then 30", you'll need to modify the measurements in steps 3 and 4.

③ Cut your fabric into a 45" × 30" rectangle. (The stretchy part of the fabric should be the 30" side.)

④ Round off the corners and sides of your rectangle to create a 45" × 30" oval.

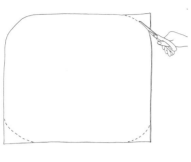

ASSEMBLE

⑤ Squeeze a 5" line of hot glue about 2" away from the edge of your fabric, parallel to its edge, to begin making the casing for the elastic. Take the edge of the fabric and fold it over so it meets the glue, and then press down firmly.

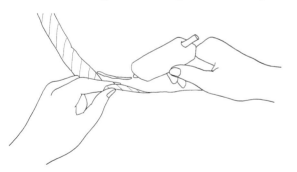

⑥ Continue gluing down the edge, 5" at a time. Because you're gluing an oval shape, you need to make little pleats in the fabric as you glue and fold. Leave 5" open at the end.

⑦ After the glue has dried completely (about 10 minutes) hook the safety pin onto one end of the elastic and insert it into the opening left in the casing. Thread the elastic all the way through the casing (in the same way you threaded the drawstring that came out of the comfy velour sweats you wore five days a week while you were preggo).

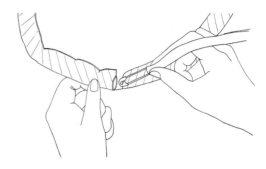

leather lover

You probably weren't thinking about a baby when you picked out leather seats for your new car. You relished the beautiful smell, until they made you ill because you had morning sickness. Then, when the stench was tolerable, the thought of your fine leather being wrecked by a car seat made you want to puke. But hold on to your lunch! You can buy a "seat saver" at most baby stores, or you can also just make one: Put a towel, piece of fleece, or padded vinyl tablecloth under your car seat to prevent dents, scratches, or bottle spills on your leather seats. Or search online for a "car seat protector." Whatever you do, though, please make sure that your seat is installed correctly, because a broken baby is a lot worse than a broken seat.

8 Hold the two ends of elastic together and slip your project onto the car seat. If the elastic is the right length, tie the two ends together in a double knot. If it needs to be looser or tighter, adjust it, and then double-knot the two ends together. Trim off any of the extra elastic and glue down the final 5" that you left open in step 7.

9 Slip the seat cover onto your car seat. Push it all the way back against the seat so you can feel where the straps are.

FINISH

10 Use a marker to mark exactly where the straps are on the seat. Then cut slits into the seat cover along those lines.

11 Cut two pieces of ribbon for each slit, each piece the same length as its slit. Use no-fray solution on both ends of each ribbon piece and let dry for about ten minutes.

12 Squeeze a line of hot glue along the back of the ribbon. Fold one ribbon around each side of each slit so that half of the ribbon appears on the front of the seat cover and half is hidden on its back.

13 Rethread the car seat straps through the new seat cover and catch a ride!

the diaper diaries

Tips from the depths of the diaper bag . . .

Reduce, reuse, recycle, reswim: Swim diapers ain't cheap. If you take one off, and it's not brown inside, stick it in the washer and dryer, and it'll be as good as new!

Got mommybrain? Keep a laminated card with your important phone numbers on it (yours, your spouse's, your pediatrician's, your neighbor's) in your diaper bag just in case you (or your babysitter) accidentally leave it in the park, a class, or at Starbucks.

A+D rash cream: Got some extra on your fingers? Don't waste it on a wipe, smear it on your face! Seriously! Nothing fights flaky skin better than the zinc and aloe in this miraculous bum cream.

One more disposable: I know you're all hooked up with your camera phone and tricked-out PDA. But even the most wired mom has a short circuit every once in a while. Keep a disposable camera in your diaper bag; you never want to miss a Kodak moment!

HIGH STYLIN'

Barrettes and booties, T-shirts and tutus—20 fashion projects to deck out your mini model from top to toe.

With all the squirming and protesting, it can take a good twenty minutes to get your little dude dressed in the morning, but when it's all said and done, he looks so fantastically cute in his little army pants and rock star T-shirt that you don't mind the hassle. You excitedly rush out the door to show him off to everyone in your Mommy 'n' Me class, where you soon realize that two other moms just went through the exact same thing with the *exact same outfit*. There are two ways to dress your little fashion plate like an individual these days: (1) Buy really expensive one-of-a-kind threads at trendy chic boutiques. (2) Make them! And since this book is called *Crafty Mama,* I'm going to try to help you out with the latter.

I Love Lucy

DAILY DOSE OF IRON

WHAT T-SHIRT COULDN'T USE A PICTURE OF FERRIS BUELLER on it? An iron-on instantly transforms a plain old toddler tee that comes in a three-pack into an incredibly hip piece of baby couture! Buy a few triple-packs, and make a different one for every day of the week: Liza Minnelli Monday, Mr. T Tuesday, Dwayne Wayne Wednesday, John Travolta Thursday, Farrah Fawcett Friday, Squiggy Saturday, and Suzanne Somers Sunday! (Be forewarned: With all the food spills and other messes, you may go through all seven in a single day.)

rate it:

Cost: .... $ $
Time: .... 🕐 🕐
Skill: .... ✂ ✂ ✂
How ga-ga they'll go: ... ♥ ♥ ♥ ♥

Cheap tees or onesies, borrowed iron, free downloaded designs and fonts: Talk about bang for your buck! They sell funky graphic tees everywhere these days for $15 to $40!

make it:

PREP

1 Brainstorm your weekly theme, be it '80s icons, third-world revolutionaries, or obscure vegetables. See "the ABCs of iron-ons" (page 135) for ideas. Choose a specific image for each of the seven days.

2 Log onto a major search engine online to conduct a copyright-free "image" search by typing in the name or a description of each image you're looking for.

☞ PHOTO TIP *If you can't find your image online, but you have a hard copy, use a scanner or a digital camera to capture the image, and then upload it to your computer.*

need it:

✔ Computer, photo editing software, and color ink-jet printer
✔ Images, photos, text (digital or hard copy)
✔ Computer scanner or digital camera (optional)
✔ Several sheets 8½" x 11" plain paper
✔ Iron-on transfer paper for light or dark colors
✔ 7 cotton baby's T-shirts (or onesies)
✔ Iron
✔ Iron-on letters (optional)

3 Save the images to your computer and arrange them all in a Word document (see page 24 for tips on organizing your electronic "craft files"). Size the images and print them at a low resolution on computer paper before you print them at high resolution on the iron-on paper to make sure each image is the exact size you want. Adjust the dimensions on-screen, and repeat as needed.

ASSEMBLE

4 Note which days of the week will be ironed onto what color T-shirt, and print the image accordingly: regular printing for dark-colored clothing and in reverse for light-colored clothing. Then print your perfectly sized image onto the transfer paper at the highest resolution your printer allows. (Consult pages 28–30 for an iron-on refresher course.)

5 Read the instructions on the packaging of your iron-on paper, and iron the image or images onto each tee, Monday through Sunday. *Optional:* Use iron-on letters to add the days of the week, or other fun statements to each tee.

☞ **IRON-ON TIP** *When it comes to iron-ons, it's all about experience. Like your baby, every iron is different, so the more you get to know how your iron works, the better your iron-ons will be. Try a few practice ones before your masterpiece. (That said, please don't try any "practice" babies!)*

FINISH

6 Why wait till Monday rolls around? Dress your kid in the onesie that's designed for today, and let him enjoy all the attention and fun comments.

variations:

Iron-Enriched

Once you master the iron-on tee or onesie, the sky's the limit. Try pants, canvas shoes, burp cloths, blankets, socks, diaper covers, bibs—you name it!

Personal Trainers

Fast-forward a couple of years: Your child has long outgrown his days-of-the-week onesies, but he's getting ready for his big-boy undies. Pick new themes—chances are, he has his own opinions now—and iron them on seven plain pairs, just below the waistband.

the ABCs of iron-ons

Don't know what to iron on? Try out any of these alphabetical ideas:

A IS FOR ANIMALS

The fabulousness of the T-shirt depends on the animal you iron on. Sure, a shirt would look cute with a golden retriever puppy on it, but a child wearing a chicken, a manatee, or a sea monkey will really get noticed.

B IS FOR BANDS

Iron on current bands, retro bands; heck, you can even make an iron-on with your wedding band on it! Prefer solo artists with just one name? You've got Madonna, Prince, Cher, Seal, Liberace, Ludacris, or Raffi!

C IS FOR CANDY

Having sweet memories of BB Bats, Necco Wafers, and Big League Chew? Don't just sit there salivating, go online and search "retro candy." Download wrapper images for shirts—all without getting a single cavity! And what little girl wouldn't want a Sugar Daddy . . . on her T-shirt?

D IS FOR DRESS-UP

Tired of listening to your mom say things like, "When you were little, kids didn't wear blue jeans all the time. They wore dresses or slacks with a nice shirt"? Why not make Grandma happy by putting your little man in a tie onesie? Iron on a picture of a bow tie or straight tie to the front of his onesie. Or try a frilly-looking collar, buttons, or even a photo of a dress for your little lady's tee.

E IS FOR EXQUISITE BUILDINGS OR WORKS OF ART

If you're lucky enough to remember all of the beautiful art and architecture you studied in college, why not strut your artsy knowledge on his T-shirt? Look in your old textbooks, find stuff you loved, and reminisce about the college days . . . when pulling an all-nighter was a voluntary act!

F IS FOR FAMILIES FROM TV

Why not put your "model child" in a shirt sporting a "model family" like the Keatons, the Cosbys, or the Carringtons? Just think of your favorite fam, download some copyright-free photos, and then iron them on the latest member of *your* dramatic family!

G IS FOR GADGETS

Get retro with a device of your day like a tape recorder, Atari 2600, or a rotary phone. (How did we ever make a call that wasn't cordless?) Or, go mod and put a BlackBerry, iPod, or Digi-cam on your kid's shirt. Come to think of it, it's all retro to him, 'cause by the time he's a teen, he's gonna be watching TV on the palm of his own hand!

H IS FOR HOT FOODS

Spice up your baby's wardrobe with images of your favorite hot 'n' fiery foods like Tabasco sauce, chili peppers, or a basket of buffalo wings. It's the best way to give your baby some flavah, without having to deal with the diaper explosions latah!

I IS FOR INVENTORS

You *could* put Ben Franklin, Marie Curie, or good ol' Tommy Edison on a onesie, but don't be so predictable! Dress your baby Einstein in a onesie celebrating inventors like Dr. D. C. Fleet (who gave us Chapstick), Ruth Wakefield (the inventor of chocolate chip cookies), Chester Greenwood (earmuffs), Mary Phelps Jacob (the bra), or Ray Tomlinson (e-mail).

J IS FOR JUNK FOOD

I don't really recommend feeding your pure little baby anything with a shelf life of more than one week, but that doesn't mean you can't put a Twinkie, Devil Dog, or some Cheetos on her shirt!

K IS FOR KARTOON KARACTERS

I know, I already used "C," but I really wanted to get cartoons and comics in there, so whether you're into the Wondertwins or Wonder Pets, Pepé Le Pew or Pikachu, Li'l Abner or the Little Mermaid, download a copyright-free image and make your super-kid into a super-dresser!

L IS FOR LETTERS

Download a cool font or get yourself some iron-on letters to make words, sentences, phrases, or paragraphs out of them. Write names, nicknames, funny phrases (check out tees you see on the web for inspiration), quotes, jokes, paragraphs, or even your wedding vows. (See page 25 on font finding.)

M IS FOR MOVIE STARS

You might not get away with wearing Johnny Depp or Angelina Jolie on your shirt these days, but your kid can totally pull it off! Download your current favorites or revisit the past with Scott Baio, Heather Locklear, Ricky Schroder, or old-school Alyssa Milano from *Who's the Boss*.

N IS FOR NATURE

Does your little Buddha love flowers, mountains, and lakes? Download pretty pictures, iron them on, and try meditating with your big-bellied babe.

O IS FOR OBSCURE OBJECTS

Everything doesn't need to have so much meaning. Stick a picture of a big toe, a lawn mower, a Q-tip, or a cashew nut on your edgy little cutie! Enjoy the comments and stares.

P IS FOR PLANES, TRAINS, AND AUTOMOBILES

I'm not talking about Scoop, Thomas, or Jay-Jay here. I'm talking about real-mobiles like a '65 Ford Mustang, the Japanese Bullet Train, a hang glider, a paddle boat, a DeLorean, or Leonardo's original sketch of an airplane!

Q IS FOR QUEENS, KINGS, PRINCESSES, AND OTHER ROYAL TREATS

Does your *petit prince* love all things regal? Bedeck his clothing with images of kingdoms, knights, dragons, jesters, and gnomes. If it's all glitter and ball gowns for your royal wonder, scan in the pages of fairytale books to surround her with fairies, castles, horses, and every princess imaginable.

R IS FOR RETRO

In second grade, you didn't even know long division, let alone how cool and valuable your iron-on T-shirts would become. So apologize to your mom for yelling at her because she threw away your favorite "Braces Are Beautiful" tee, and head online to search for "retro iron-ons." The images you'll find are perfect for your little Charlie's Angel.

S IS FOR SPORTS STARS

The last sports legend that I really loved was Mean Joe Greene. (Remember that cute Coke commercial?) Download images of Mean Joe, or the latest hot skier, basketball player, football star, snowboarder, tennis pro, skateboarder, pitcher, swimmer, or diver to land him or her a sweet endorsement deal.

T IS FOR TOOLS

Your little budding builder probably likes tools and big construction equipment. A quick online search of John Deere, CAT trucks, and construction websites yields all sorts of powerful results.

U IS FOR UNICORNS (OR OTHER NOSTALGIC ICONS)

Beyond unicorns (was there anything beyond unicorns?), go for Legos, rainbows, Pound Puppies, G.I. Joe, Rubik's Cubes, Transformers, Dressy Bessy, Betsy Wetsy, or 2-XL Robots. Share your treasured toys with your little tyke, and watch every twenty- to forty-something who sees it shed a tear of joy upon seeing those toys on her tee.

V IS FOR VEGGIES

Your child might not like to eat them, but that doesn't mean that he can't wear his veggies with a cute pair of camo pants once in a while. *Note:* Some veggies are more humorous than others. Stay away from the carrots and corn, and go for the funnier polysyllabic veggies like cauliflower, brussels sprouts, or asparagus.

W IS FOR WORLD LEADERS

Gandhi and Che: Love 'em, but they're everywhere! Dress *your* little Napoleon in the likes of Cleopatra, Louis XIV, Sonny Bono, or Joan of Arc. Pick your favorite pacifist, revolutionary, socialist, tyrant, or president and iron on!

X IS FOR XYLOPHONES AND OTHER INSTRUMENTS

What kid doesn't like to make some noise? Download pictures of maracas, Fender guitars, bongos, flutes, banjos, or the good ol' didgeridoo, and iron them on without all the noise!

★ BABY SHOWER POWER ★

What do you give the mom-to-be who's had her nursery decorated and fully stocked since day one of her second trimester? A slew of Crafty Mama–made iron-on onesies! Along with the R.S.V.P., have each guest email a link to an image she'd like to iron on. The hostess prints out all of the iron-ons beforehand, borrows a few irons from party guests or neighbors, and the fun begins! If the new mama is a serious foodie, make her little dish some onesies featuring Chicken Marabella or Eggs Florentine. If she has a secret crush on Captain Kirk, deck out her soon-to-be trekkie with a head shot of Shatner himself. The possibilities are endless!

Y IS FOR YOU

Sending your precious cargo on a weekend trip to Grandma's? Pack him with a mom-and-dad onesie, so he can cuddle with it when he misses you. Wait, who are we kidding? His grandparents are going to spoil him rotten with treats and toys, and he's not even going to remember you're gone! Scratch that—pack him with a onesie to remind him that you exist!

Z IS FOR ZODIAC SIGNS

Let potential playmates know if they're compatible with your star child by proudly displaying her sign on her chest! Virgos and Cancers, Aquarius and Gemini, Pisces and Scorpios—you all make perfect pairs! But if you mix a Capricorn with a Libra, an Aries with a Cancer, and an Aquarius with a Taurus, you're in for one heckuva playdate!

Bell bottoms and tie-dye may not work at thirty—but a three-year-old hippie couldn't be cuter!

TO DYE FOR

BY THE TIME YOUR BABY'S SEVEN MONTHS OLD, THERE'S going to be a stain on everything from her cute little onesie to your luxurious 500-thread count white Italian sheets that you got as a wedding gift from your rich uncle. Whether she's breastfed or bottle-fed, eats organic or generic, wears cloth or disposable—when your baby leaks (from either end), *stains happen*. Thankfully, they don't need to stay. You could try rubbing that spinach mush out with some magic elixir (good luck!), or you could transform your stained little onesie into a trendy and wearable work of art. (And those 500-thread count sheets? Just let 'em go.)

The more people you dye with and the more stuff you dye (white or light-colored baby tees, onesies, socks, hats, burp cloths, blankets, etc.), the cheaper this project will be. *Note:* In planning for this project, the tie-dyeing itself is quick. It's the set-up and clean-up that take time. Plus, the dyes need a day to set! But people sure flip for this stuff. The colors are amazing, and the designs come out great. I gave one to my sister-in-law as a gift and ended up with orders from eleven of her friends the day that her son wore it.

make it:

PREP: THE NIGHT BEFORE

Although you can do it the same day, I like to prepare the dyes the night before because it's a little messy to do with a group and also very meditative to do alone!

rate it:

Cost: .... $ $ $
Time: 🕐🕐🕐🕐🕐🕐🕐
Skill: .... ✂
How ga-ga they'll go: ... ♥ ♥ ♥ ♥ ♥

need it:

✔ Dyeable items
✔ 8-ounce plastic squirt bottles (one for each color dye)
✔ Permanent marker
✔ Latex gloves
✔ Tap water
✔ Liquid measuring cup
✔ 1-quart or larger pitcher
✔ 3 to 5 containers of Procion Mx Fiber Reactive Cold Water Dye* (in a variety of colors)
✔ Tablespoon measure
✔ Stirring spoon or stick
✔ 4 buckets (11 gallons each)
✔ Soda ash
✔ 5 to 10 plastic 1-pint bowls
✔ Plastic tablecloth
✔ Rubber bands
✔ Ruler or clothespin
✔ Plastic wrap

*Don't use Rit or Tintex for this project.

❶ Pre-wash and dry your garments in order to make the dye stay better. Then change into clothing you don't mind getting messy in and remove any nice rings.

❷ Label each squirt bottle (with a marker) according to what color dye will go in it, and put on latex gloves.

❸ Pour two cups of warm water into your pitcher, add four tablespoons of dye powder, and stir well. Then pour the liquid dye into the appropriate squirt bottle. Rinse out the pitcher and mix each of your colors, one at a time, pouring them into their respective squirt bottles as you go.

PREP: THE DAY OF

When your playgroup is all together, fill one or two 11-gallon buckets three-quarters full with warm water. (The number of buckets you need depends on how many projects you're dyeing. Plan on one bucket for seven to ten baby items.)

❶ Follow the guide on the soda ash packaging in order to get the correct water–to–soda ash ratio. Measure and pour it in.

❷ Remove the tags from your dyeable items and submerge them in the buckets to soak for at least thirty minutes.

❸ Set up your dyeing area by covering the table with a plastic tablecloth, taking the caps off the dye bottles, and lining them up. Place a plastic bowl in front of every other bottle, making sure to leave some table space clear so you can fold each dyeable item. Also fill the remaining large

★ BABY SHOWER POWER ★

What's more fun than tie-dyeing duds with your pals? Not much, and that's why it's the perfect activity for an afternoon baby shower! The host should prepare the dyes the night before, and guests can bring their own dyeables to the shower—white onesies, burp cloths, or even tiny socks—so the expecting mom has a whole slew of creative and one-of-a-kind, colorful baby gear. (Alternatively, triple-packs of white onesies—in different sizes—or multipacks of white socks are relatively inexpensive for the host to purchase and make available for each guest.)

buckets with clean, warm water so you can rinse your hands in between each color (otherwise, your dyeable items will become messy).

❹ Remove the items from the bucket(s) after thirty minutes and wring them out really, really well. (Your shirt should not be dripping at all; too much water will weaken the vibrancy of the colors.)

❺ Choose one of the following tie-dye design projects, follow the instructions, and then proceed to "Finish It" (page 146).

practice makes perfect

Afraid to commit to a design or color combo? Try it out first! Just take a baby wipe, wet it a teensy bit, and then wring it out. Wrap the rubber bands around it in whatever pattern you want to experiment with. Then take some washable markers and color in the different sections. Make sure you color both sides and really try to get the marker in all of the cracks. Unwrap it and—voilà!—a little mini version of what might be your next big thing! (If you really want to see how this design would look on your item, cut the wipe in the shape of the item, wrap it, color it, and reveal!)

bull's-eye

ASSEMBLE

1 Lay your dyeable item flat on the table, and pinch the material between your fingers at the spot you'd like to be the center of the bull's-eye.

2 Lift it off the table, and tightly wrap one rubber band approximately ½" to 1" from the tip of the pinched section.

variations:

Seeing Multiple
Try making several little bull's-eyes all over the item to create mini bull's-eye bursts.

No Bull
Wrap your dyeable item, using extra rubber bands placed very close together. Then dip it in just one color to create squiggly lines that will resemble a batik effect.

3 Wrap another rubber band 1" to 3" down from the first, and continue moving down the pinched fabric, adding rubber bands. (The more you use, the more white you'll have on your finished project.)

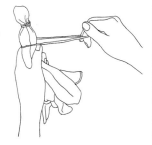

4 Use a dye bottle to squirt color between the rubber bands, making sure the dye gets on all sides.

5 Squeeze out the excess dye and rinse your hands before applying each color. Use as many, or as few, dye colors as you want.

FINISH

6 Wrap the rubber-banded project in plastic wrap after you've finished applying color and let it sit for 24 hours. Then proceed to "Finish It" (page 146).

stripes and stripes forever

ASSEMBLE

1 Lay the tee flat on the table, and accordion-fold it lengthwise or widthwise (lengthwise folds will produce horizontal stripes; widthwise folds will produce vertical stripes) to create a long bundle of fabric.

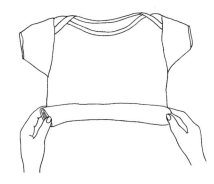

variations:

Target Practice
Rather than bull's-eye the whole shirt, just rubber band one third to one half of the front of the shirt and dye (or leave) the rest a solid color. For pants, make a cute splotch on your little bull's bum!

Sleevers
Using a long-sleeve shirt, wrap a rubber band tightly at each shoulder. Dye the body of the shirt one color, and the sleeves another.

Belle Bottoms
Using a pair of pants, wrap a few rubber bands tightly around the bottom one fifth of the legs (you can wrap them together or separately). Dye the larger top section one color and go crazy on the ends.

2 Fold the fabric "fan" in half and wrap rubber bands lightly 1" to 3" apart all along the bundle. The rubber bands will serve as a guideline for your dyeing. The more you put on, the more stripes you'll have.

3 Use a squirt bottle to apply dye between two of the rubber bands, all the way around the segmented section of the bundled tee. 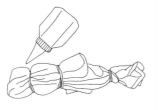 Squeeze the excess dye into a bowl, and rinse your hands in the clean water bucket.

4 Apply more colors in the same manner, squeezing out the excess dye and rinsing your hands between applications. Use as many, or as few, colors as you want.

FINISH

5 Wrap the rubber-banded project in plastic wrap after you've finished applying color and let it sit for 24 hours. Then proceed to "Finish It" (page 146).

give yourself a break

Are you at the point where you're not quite ready to leave your baby alone with a sitter, but would give your right arm for a few hours of "me" time? Hire a babysitter for a couple of hours to come and watch the kid while you get things done around the house, catch up on your TiVo recordings, or take a long, luxurious bath! Let her (or him) do the changing, burping, and cooing for a bit—you've earned it!

Go Halfsies

For a simpler take on the stripes, go sectional. Wrap a rubber band tightly one third to one half of the way down your bundle fabric. Dye one section one color and the other section another. You can also use the rubber bands to split your dyeable thingy into thirds or quarters.

Tie-dyeing isn't just for tees—try onesies, socks, hats, and more!

the swirly-gig

ASSEMBLE

1 Lay your dyeable item flat on the table, place a ruler end down in the center (or about one third of the way down the front) of it, and then turn it clockwise, pressing it into the center, so the fabric twists around it. *Note:* You can also use a clothespin to twist the fabric.

2 Keep turning the ruler or clothespin until all of the material is wrapped around it to form a circular disc that looks like a cinnamon bun. Gently remove the ruler or clothespin.

3 Wrap three or four rubber bands carefully around the cinnamon bun shape, so it's sectioned off into triangles (like a pizza pie). *Note:* When rubber banding, don't pick up your material or it will unfold. Instead, slip half of the rubber band under the fabric to get it on. Also, the rubber bands should be wrapped loosely; don't double wrap them.

4 Use a bottle of dye to apply horizontal stripes of color to your cinnamon bun shape. Flip it over to make sure the dye goes through to the other side, and if it doesn't, squirt on some more. Use as many, or as few, colors as you want. Rinse your hands between each color.

5 Squeeze out any excess dye carefully into a bowl and rinse your hands in the clean water bucket.

FINISH

6 Wrap the rubber-banded project in plastic wrap after you've finished applying color and let it sit for 24 hours. Then proceed to "Finish It" (page 146).

variations:

How Radiant

Your swirl will radiate from wherever you place your clothespin. Try halfway down, at the lower right, or at the upper left.

Seeing Double

Fold your dyeable item in half or quarters and then do the swirl. The result will have multiple swirls. Dude, it's like, trippy!

finish it:

Wait 24 hours to bring your dyeables to term. (That's nothing compared to the nine months you just waited.) If you find that you just can't wait that long, you can take them out after 18 hours, and you probably won't notice the difference in color.

1 Put on a pair of rubber gloves, unwrap your dyed item from the plastic wrap, and with the rubber bands still on, rinse and squeeze out the item under running cold water, until the water runs clear.

2 Turn off the water and remove the rubber bands.

3 Rinse and squeeze out the dyed item in cold water again until the water is relatively free of color. (Yes, your forearms are going to be sore tomorrow!)

dyeing to be neat

Want to dye without all of the fuss? Try *dye strings*. Wrap them around your shirt in whatever pattern you like and then drop them into a bucket of hot water. Poof! A tie-dye appears! You can't control the designs as much, and the strings don't come in colors like salmon or robin's egg, but there's no dye prep, no waiting, and best of all, virtually no mess!

"It's a really amazing feeling: Anytime anyone asks me where I bought my baby's T-shirt, I'm able to say proudly, 'I made it myself.'"
—CRAFTY MAMA SUSAN G.

4 Lay the dyed item flat on a plastic-covered area on the floor or table. Don't hang it over a chair or clothesline, or the colors may run and ruin the design.

5 Repeat steps 1 through 4 with the rest of your items.

6 Wash items with blues, purples, greens, and browns together in one cold-water cycle in your washing machine, using your normal detergent. Wash your reds, yellows, pinks, and oranges together in a different cold-water cycle. If you have a rainbow tie-dye that mixes the two color groups, wash it separately, or with other similar items. *Note:* The dye will not stain your machine! I tie-dye all the time in my building's shared washing machines, and I've never gotten any complaints from my neighbors. You don't even have to run an empty wash afterward.

7 Dry your items on low to prevent shrinkage—unless, of course, you want them to shrink! *Note:* Although some people recommend ironing them to help set the color, it doesn't work. *Optional:* Not that your amazingly fabulous tie-dyes need any sprucing, but if you want to take it to the next level, iron an image, name, or phrase onto your colorful tee! (For iron-on ideas, check out page 135.)

8 Strut her stuff! Put one of your gorgeous garments on your baby to wear to a Mommy 'n' Me Yoga class (all that rinsing and squeezing has made you stiff!) and delight in your babe's one-of-a-kind creation!

☞ **WASHING TIP:** *Remember, for the first few washes, combine your tie-dyed items with like colors. Blue-based items work with jeans and other dark clothing, and pink-based ones go with pinks and other lighter colors.*

savvy savers

I've never met a mom who didn't love a bargain. And if you're a mom-to-be, it's the perfect time for you to start learning the ropes.

I Love the Dollar Store Buy your solid onesies and baby T-shirts for dyeing and ironing on at the dollar store. While you're there, see if they have any cute socks, hats, or sweats.

Everybody Loves a Sale Of course you want to keep your little diva au courant. But, honestly, do tiny little bikinis, snowsuits, boots, or mittens really go out of style? Save cash on next year's summer or winter wear by shopping the end-of-season sales. Buy everything a size bigger than your little fish or snow angel wears now.

Swap 'Til You Drop Some people like to dress their little one like a fancy French enfant, and some go for the skater look. To each his (mom's) own! But no matter what you like to buy, gift givers will buy what they like, which results in the every-mom's pile of "cute, but he'll never wear it" clothing! Plan a clothing swap for your playgroup, so everything can get to its rightful owner; prepsters take the polos, sportos get the jerseys, skaters get the baggy stuff, and hipsters get the funky tees and brown cords.

A funky fleece hat is the perfect frame for his funny little face!

HATS OFF TO MAMA

IS IT TIME TO SAY GOOD-BYE TO THE HOT 'N' SWEATY DAYS of chasing your little Speedy Gonzalez around the playground for his thrice-daily sunblock application? Then say hello to the fresh 'n' chilly days of chasing your Speedy Gonzalez around the playground for his thrice-daily hat application! Maybe if you tell him this year that you labored for hours (well, an hour) on his very special hat, he'll keep it on his head for more than seventeen seconds . . .

Maybe not. But at least you'll make up for it with the compliments you'll receive every time you plunk this hat on his noggin at the park or playground. Of course, how much gushing you get depends on the fleece. A chocolate brown with pink polka-dots hat is going to attract way more ogling than a simple navy blue number.

make it:

PREP

1 Measure and cut a 15" × 22" piece and a 12" × ¾" strip from fleece 1. (The fabric should stretch along the 22" side of the large piece.) *Note:* This hat is sized for infants to two-year-olds.

2 Measure and cut two 24" × ¾" strips from fleece 2. (The fabric should stretch along the ¾" sides.) *Optional:* If you have enough extra material from fleece 1, use it for these two strips, and make the entire hat in the same fleece pattern.

rate it:

Cost: .... $

Time: .... 🕐🕐🕐

Skill: .... ✂✂✂

How ga-ga they'll go: ... ♥♥♥♥

If you find cute, cheap fleece, and you make your hats with some crafty friends, they can cost less than $4 each.

need it:

✔ ⅜ yard fleece (fleece 1)*

✔ ⅛ yard matching or contrasting fleece (fleece 2)*

✔ Ruler

✔ Fabric scissors

✔ Tape measure (or hat that fits your child)

✔ 4 to 6 safety pins

✔ Eyelet pliers

✔ Marker or chalk

✔ Rotary cutter (optional)

✔ Cutting mat (optional)

*If you already have some leftover fleece on hand, a 15" x 22" piece along with a 12" x ¾" strip will suffice for fleece 1, and two 24" x ¾" strips are needed for fleece 2.

ASSEMBLE

3 Fold the 15" × 22" rectangle in half lengthwise, with the fold at the left.

4 Measure around the widest part of your baby's head, divide by two, and then add ½". Mark that width measurement across the bottom of the folded fleece, and trim the excess material on the right. As an alternative, if your baby's squirmy or his head's particularly wobbly, use a baby hat that you already own as a template, adding ½" to the right side.

5 Lay the rectangle flat again and fold up the bottom of the front of the hat about 1½". Fold it again 1½" to create a double band of fabric and attach safety pins to hold it in place. Then fold the hat in half lengthwise (with the fold at the left).

6 Use your eyelet pliers to punch a hole about ⅛" from the bottom and ¼" from the side edges through all layers of the folded band.

7 Punch a second hole through both layers ¼" from the side edge and about ½" up from your first hole.

> *"Pre–Crafty Mamas, I had loads of unfinished projects cluttering my house. Now, with the support to actually complete something, I leave class accomplished and proud!"*
>
> —CRAFTY MAMA MICHELLE

8 Measure from the bottom of your baby's ear up to the center of his head. Mark that length, up from the bottom, along both sides of the hat. If you're using a baby hat as a template, mark 2" from the top of it.

9 Continue punching holes about ¾" to 1" apart up from the bottom, along the open vertical edges of your fabric. Stop when you reach the mark you made in step 8.

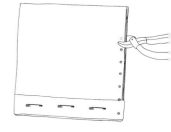

10 Repeat steps 6 through 9 on the opposite (folded) side of the hat. *Optional:* Punch holes in only the open right side (leaving just one seam in the back of the hat).

FINISH

11 Start at the bottom of the hat band and thread one 24" × ¾" fleece strip through the first set of holes. Leave 4" trailing at the end.

12 Wrap the long end of the fleece strip around the edge and through the next hole, and repeat as if you were sewing a whipstitch, all the way up the top of the hat, as shown.

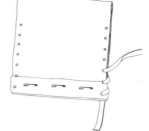

13 Tie the fleece strip in an overhand knot at the top of the hat to finish it off. Tie a double knot with the excess strip at the bottom of the band, and trim the end.

14 Repeat steps 11 through 13 on the opposite side of the hat.

15 Cut vertical fringe into the top edge of the hat down to the marks you made in step 9, as shown. *Note:* Thick strips— about 1" wide—will stand up. Thin strips—about ¼" to ½" wide—will flop over.

16 Gather the fleece fringe at the top of your hat (just above your last stitch), and wrap and knot the 12"-long fleece strip around it. Leave the strings of the tie long or trim them short. Remove safety pins and wear!

talk amongst yourselves

While you loop your fleece, discuss playgrounds: Though you may be totally in love with the newfangled, fancy playgrounds your kids enjoy, reminisce about those metal-and-concrete ones of your childhood . . . the time you chipped a tooth when you fell off the monkey bars onto the concrete (not that foamy, padded stuff they use now) . . . or the time your arm got crushed by the heavy metal bar on the baby swing (not the nice rubber baby swings they have these days).

Babies look cute
in everything—
but they look
utterly adorable
in this goofy
square hat.

SPONGEBOB SQUAREHAT

TIRED OF SQUINTING TO FIGURE OUT WHICH ONE OF THE kids hidden under a round hat in a puffy coat on the playground is yours? Thought so! That crazy yellow cartoon sponge has got it right—it's definitely hip to be square these days. Make this fringy, square hat (no sewing required) so you can pick her out of a crowded sandbox in seconds (unless, of course, she's in the sandbox with all of the kids from your Crafty Mamas playgroup)! If that's the case, you can go back to the squinting.

rate it:

Cost: .... $
Time: .... 🕐 🕐 🕐
Skill: .... ✂ ✂
How ga-ga they'll go: ... ♥ ♥ ♥ ♥

need it:

✔ ⅜ yard fleece (fleece 1)*
✔ ⅛ yard matching or contrasting fleece (fleece 2)*
✔ Ruler
✔ Fabric scissors
✔ Permanent marker or chalk
✔ Tape measure (or hat that fits your child)
✔ Eyelet pliers
✔ 8 to 12 safety pins
✔ Rotary cutter (optional)
✔ Cutting mat (optional)
✔ Embellishments (optional: sequin appliqués or patches)
✔ Hot-glue gun (optional)
✔ Fabric hot-glue sticks (optional)
✔ Embroidery thread and needle (optional)

*If you already have some leftover fleece on hand, a 10" x 22" piece will suffice for fleece 1, and twenty-four 8" x ½" strips are needed for fleece 2.

make it:

PREP

1 Measure and cut a 10" × 22" piece from fleece 1. (The fabric should stretch along the 10" side.) *Note:* This hat is sized for infants to two-year-olds.

2 Measure and cut twenty-four 8" × ½" strips from fleece 2. (The fabric should stretch along the ½" sides.)

ASSEMBLE

3 Fold the 10" × 22" fleece rectangle in half lengthwise, so the two short edges match up.

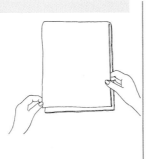

4 Measure around the widest part of your baby's head, divide by two, and then add ½". Mark that width measurement across the bottom of the folded fleece, and trim the excess. As an alternative, if your baby's squirmy or her head's particularly wobbly, use a cotton baby hat that you already own as a template, adding ¼" to both sides.

variation:

For the Big Kids

For an older child (or yourself), buy ½ yard of fabric and use measurements (or a hat that fits you or your kid) to modify the pattern.

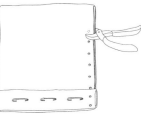

"Crafty Mamas helps me make time to be human again while having my baby at my side."

—CRAFTY MAMA SUSAN B.

5 Fold up the bottom of the front side of the hat about 1½". Fold it again 1½" to create a double band of fabric and use safety pins to hold it in place.

6 Repeat step 4, folding up the back of the hat, making sure that the bottom edges are even on the front and back.

7 Insert two or three safety pins carefully through both sides of the hat brim without shifting the fabric to temporarily keep it together. Place more safety pins up the sides of your hat to keep it in place.

8 Use your eyelet pliers to punch a hole about ⅛" from the bottom and ¼" from the side edges through all layers of the folded band, as shown.

9 Punch a second hole through all layers about ¼" from the side edge and about ½" up from your first hole.

10 Continue punching about 9 or 10 holes ¾" to 1" apart through all layers along this side edge all the way up to the top of the hat.

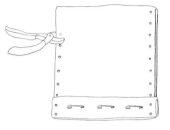

11 Repeat steps 8 through 10 on the opposite side of the hat.

animal planet

Have a cotton or wool solid color hat that's just too blah to cover your brilliant baby's brain? Unroll the brim a little and stuff the top with a few cotton balls or a small wad of fiber fill, creating a little knob on the top of the hat. Wrap a small elastic band or a length of embroidery string around the fabric at the base of the knob and then tie a ribbon around it. Hot glue or sew on little animal eyes, nose, and mouth. Top off your snuggly friend by attaching felt ears, hair, or whiskers.

FINISH

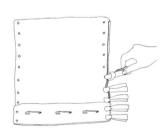

12 Fold one of the 8" × ½" strips in half lengthwise and push the folded part through the first hole you made in the band of the hat. Insert the two loose ends of the strip through the loop and pull them tight to create a cow hitch knot. Repeat with the remaining strips, until all of the holes are filled. Remove the safety pins. *Optional:* Leave the strips long and floppy, or give your fleece strips a short 'n' spiky haircut.

13 If you choose, embellish your hat by hot gluing or stitching on a snazzy appliqué or patch, or by embroidering your child's name.

*A little bit warm
'n' cozy plus a
little bit rock 'n'
roll equals 100%
fabulous.*

THE NO-SEW MOHAWK

IF YOUR BABY LIKES THE RAMONES MORE THAN THE WIGGLES, try this hat on for size. Your little Kid Vicious will love it. And if he's just beginning to take a walk on the wild side, this hat is the perfect first step. In just less than an hour, you can transform your little prepster into an edgy rocker babe (without ponying up the extra cash for the actual haircut, which might not go over so well with Grandma!). If you and your child like to keep a low profile, this is *not* the hat for you. People can't help but point and stare. Heck, you might even have a brush with the paparazzi.

rate it:

Cost: .... $
Time: .... 🕐 🕐
Skill: .... ✂ ✂
How ga-ga they'll go: ... ♥ ♥ ♥ ♥

If you really want to take it to the next level, sew a Sex Pistols, the Clash, or Children of Reagan patch onto the side of the hat before heading to the playground.

need it:

✔ ⅜ yard solid or patterned (fleece 1*)
✔ ⅛ yard solid or patterned (fleece 2*)
✔ Ruler
✔ Fabric scissors
✔ Permanent marker or chalk
✔ Tape measure (or hat that fits your child)
✔ Eyelet pliers
✔ Rotary cutter (optional)
✔ Cutting mat (optional)
✔ Patches (optional)

*If you already have some leftover fleece on hand, a 10" x 20" piece will suffice for fleece 1, and twenty-four 8" x ½" strips are needed for fleece 2.

make it:

PREP

1 Measure and cut a 10" × 20" piece from fleece 1. (The fabric should stretch along the 10" side.) *Note:* This hat is sized for infants to two-year-olds.

2 Measure and cut twenty-four 8" × ½" strips from fleece 2. (The fabric should stretch along the ½" sides.)

ASSEMBLE

3 Fold the 10" × 20" piece of fleece in half with the folded part on the top.

4 Measure around the widest part of your baby's head, divide by two, and add ¾". Mark a horizontal line equal to that measurement 3" up from the bottom (A).

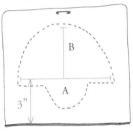

5 Mark a vertical line (B) equal to length A that extends up from the midpoint of A. Draw an arc connecting the ends of A and the top of B, as shown. *Note:* As an alternative, use a child's rounded knit cap as a template, and trace ¼" to ½" wider than its perimeter. Add an upside-down half-moon shape for the bottom of the hat, as shown (to create ear flaps). Refer to step 4 diagram.

6 Cut along the lines, through both layers.

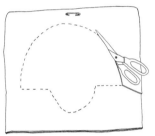

variation:

Scarf It Up

With your leftover fleece, make a matching scarf for your petit punk. Cut a 36" x 5" rectangle of fleece (so it stretches the long way) and punch holes along the edge of both short ends with your eyelet pliers. Using a cow hitch knot, loop strips of fabric through the holes to create fringe.

7 Use the eyelet pliers to punch twenty to twenty-four holes evenly spaced, through both layers ¼" in from the long arc of the hat.

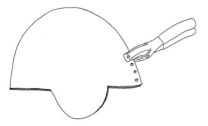

FINISH

8 Fold one strip in half and push the folded loop through both layers of the first holes. Take the two loose ends of the folded strip and thread them through the loop to create a cow hitch knot. Pull it tight. Repeat until all strips are looped in place.

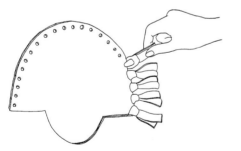

9 Give your mohawk a trim. Keep the ends longer for a floppy look, or cut them short for a spikier, edgier look. Then put it on your little wild child and watch him rock the sandbox.

cradle cap

While one of these mama-made hats will cover up your baby's cradle cap, it won't cure it. If you're looking to get rid of the little, yellow, harmless scaly things on your cutie's cranium, my doctor (the fabulous Dr. Kosme) recommends rubbing in a little olive oil before bed. *Note:* The oil might stain your baby's sheets, so don't use her fine linens when marinating her scalp. When she wakes up (a full eight hours later, if you're lucky!) comb her scalp—even if there's little to no hair there—and then wash her hair with a mild baby shampoo. Try this for a day or two, and if you don't see any changes, consult your pediatrician.

Finally, all of
those tights
with just one
pesky run can
be put to good
use—decking out
her sweet little
noggin!

TUTTI BELLA FONTANELLA

YOU KNOW THOSE MUSHY SPOTS ON YOUR BABY'S HEAD? Those are the fontanels. The bones in her head didn't fully form before she was born so her noggin could squish its way through the birth canal. Why not whip up a hip headband to femme up her sweet little soft spots?

make it:

PREP

1 Plug in your hot-glue gun and insert one fabric glue stick.

2 Lay one knee-high stocking flat, and cut off the foot.

ASSEMBLE

3 Overlap the two ends about 1" and use a running stitch to sew them together. Pull the thread tight to gather the layer. Sew through the gathered material two times to secure the gather. Knot and trim the thread.

4 Stretch your headband around something about the size of your baby's head. (I use my leg, a 2-liter soda bottle, or a full paper towel roll.)

FINISH

5 Use hot glue to attach embellishments over the gathered seam. (If using your leg as a form, insert a dishtowel or wash cloth under the headband to prevent burning!)

6 Let the glue dry, and try it on your soft-headed little love.

rate it:

Cost: .... $
Time: .... ⏱
Skill: .... ✂ ✂
How ga-ga they'll go: ... ♥ ♥ ♥ ♥

I got the most colorful, soft knee-highs for 33 cents a pair. If you find the right source, you can make four headbands (with embellishments) for less than $3!

need it:

✔ 1 pair knee-highs or nylon stockings, each leg cut off at the knee
✔ Fabric scissors
✔ Hot-glue gun
✔ Fabric hot-glue sticks
✔ Needle and thread to match knee-highs
✔ Embellishments (big silk flowers, small satin rosettes, buttons, rhinestones, felt shapes)
✔ 2-liter soda bottle or full paper towel roll (optional)

A bevy of beautiful barrettes for your budding fashion plate!

RIBBON WRAPPUCCINO

GROWN WOMEN CAN ADD A FEW EXCITING AND SPARKLY PINS, earrings, rings, necklaces, bangles, bags, and belts to any not-so-hot outfit to transform it into one sizzling number. We call it accessorizing. But kids, they don't have it so good: Pins are pointy, earrings are for the pierced, necklaces get tangled, rings never stay on, and a bag is fairly useless unless it's big enough for diapers. The only real accessory that can convert your little love's dorky bunny jumper into a hip ensemble is a fabulous mama-made barrette! (And, of course, a great pair of booties—but more on that later.)

You can make scads of fantastic barrettes that will take her outfits to the next level for less than the cost of one new T-shirt. And the nice thing about this project is that you can stop and interact with your cutie after each barrette. Make one, feed her, make another, read a book, make a third, change a diaper, make another!

P.S. One very unscientific survey shows that the "Pebbles" style (a few hairs up in the middle of her head) garners a lot more attention than the classy side sweep.

rate it:

Cost: .... $
Time: .... 🕐
Skill: .... ✂ ✂ ✂
How ga-ga they'll go:... ♥ ♥ ♥ ♥

These barrettes are small, making them a little harder to hot glue. Go into this project knowing that you might burn a fingertip or two!

need it:

✔ Hot-glue gun
✔ Fabric hot-glue sticks
✔ Embellishments (fake flowers, rhinestones, beads, charms, buttons)
✔ ¼"- to 1"-wide grosgrain, jacquard, or satin ribbon
✔ Fabric scissors
✔ Metal alligator clip barrettes

make it:

PREP

1 Plug in your hot-glue gun and insert one glue stick.

2 Pick out a cute embellishment to be the "subject" of your barrette and then cut a 5"-long piece of ribbon that matches it.

ASSEMBLE

3 Pinch the clip open and slip one end of your ribbon, wrong side up, all the way inside. Release the clip, so it closes on your ribbon.

4 Squeeze a thin line of hot glue along the entire top of the barrette. Wrap the ribbon around the tip and over the top of the barrette. Then, press it down firmly into the glue. (The top "jaw" of the barrette should be sandwiched between two layers of ribbon.)

5 Squeeze a thin line of hot glue on the remaining length of ribbon and carefully wrap it around the top part of the barrette "handle." Trim any excess ribbon to fit.

FINISH

6 Pinch the clip open to check that the ribbon on the underside is secure. If not, squeeze small dabs of glue as needed and firmly press down on the ribbon.

7 Hot glue your embellishments onto the ribbon on the outside of the barrette, careful not to overdo it with the glue since it dries white. Let it dry for 5 minutes.

8 Clip it into her hair to transform that stained jumper into an awesome outfit. *Note:* Always supervise your child when she has a barrette in her hair. (See page 168.)

variations:

'Tis the Season

This Christmas, skip the reindeer sweaters and simply stitch a cute little jingle bell or glue a felt Christmas tree on top of a red velvet–covered barrette! Glue decorative egg buttons in the middle of a bow for Easter; red, white, and blue star-shaped rhinestones on top of silver ribbon for the Fourth of July. Heck, you can even glue a felt tree to your barrette in honor of Arbor Day! Spray candy corn or message hearts with polyurethane spray (to protect them from rotting) and hot glue them onto a barrette for Halloween and Valentine's Day! The possibilities are both endless—and low-budget!

Kung Fu Grip Clip

If the pincher clip keeps on slipping out of your baby's hair, try putting a strip of hook-and-loop tape (the soft side) along the length of the inside of the clip. Or, make this style barrette with a snap clip since they hold the hair a little bit tighter.

embellish me, please

There is no doubt that simple ribbon barrettes are great (especially if your ribbon is already decorative), but up the cute factor with a few well-placed embellishments like these.

RHINESTONES

Line them up in a row, biggest to smallest, or put a large heart-shaped one in the middle of your barrette and surround it with two little hearts. Or create a gem flower with one stone in the middle surrounded by five or six smaller ones.

FELT SHAPES

Cut small flowers out of felt and layer them on top of one another using a rhinestone for the center. Or, cut out hearts or stars and use embroidery thread to make some thick decorative stitching along the edges.

BEADS OR CHARMS

Use little letter beads to spell out names, nicknames, initials, or personality traits. Stitch them or hot glue them onto your barrette. Cute charms look extra-great when sewn onto the ribbon or dangling off your baby's barrette.

RIBBON FLOWERS

Craft stores sell satin ribbon rosettes in all sorts of shapes and sizes. Arrange them on your barrette and hot glue them in place. Add gems or some glitter glue for sparkle.

TRIM

Most fabric stores sell beautiful trim by the yard, but it can get a little expensive. Buy ¼ or ½ yard, cut it to the size of your little barrette, and hot glue it on. (Save the rest to make dozens more barrettes!)

SCRAPBOOK ACCENTS

Wander down the scrapbooking aisle or rummage through your scrapping box. There are tons of great embellishments that'll transform a plain barrette into a conversation piece. Hot glue on mini picture frames with photos of your child's grandparents or siblings; fun words like "princess" or "tantrum" in metal; fuzzy trim; sticky ribbon; or pre-cut and bedazzled felt flowers, hearts, or animals. Just try to stay away from the paper stuff, because it can tear easily!

SEQUINS

Sequin trim comes in every color, or you can attach individual sequin flowers and hearts to your barrette.

BUTTONS

Sew a few to the ribbon *before* you glue it on, or if you have a button with a little loop on the back, trim it off and hot glue the flat button onto your barrette. Buttons come in every shape these days: seahorses, blow dryers, lawn mowers, and more!

POMPOMS . . .

. . . Feather boas, googly eyes, mini dollhouse accessories, doll clothing, and more. Basically, if it's small, cute, light, and won't break easily (no glass or paper!), glue it on.

With their long, flowing ribbons, these awesomely retro barrettes have timelessly pretty appeal.

I LOVE THE '80S BARRETTES

FOR ME, EIGHTH GRADE WAS ALL ABOUT SECRETLY WATCHING R-rated movies, going to boy-girl parties, and making ribbon barrettes! I'm not looking forward to my daughters experiencing the first two things *ever*, but the moment Lily had enough hair to use a real barrette, I clipped an old-school ribbon number onto her cute little head, and it sent me right back to 1983! That night, my husband and I secretly rented *Porky's* and then locked ourselves in the closet for seven whole minutes. And nine months later we had our second daughter, Sasha. (Kidding!)

Even though these barrettes are super-duper-girly, they'll also appeal to those die-hard sports-obsessed dads. That's because you can make them in his favorite team colors! Whip up a pair, clip 'em in her hair, and sit her on the couch next to Dad for the big game. Rah!

rate it:

Cost: .... $
Time: .... 🕐 🕐
Skill: .... ✂ ✂
How ga-ga they'll go: ... ♥ ♥ ♥ ♥

Make a pair of barrettes today for less than you paid for the ones you bought twenty-five years ago.

need it:

✔ Two 64" lengths ⅛"-wide ribbon in different colors
✔ Fabric scissors
✔ 2 double-bar barrettes
✔ Beads (optional)

make it:

PREP

1 Cut the two 64" pieces of ribbon in half. Place one of each of the two colored ribbons side by side so they line up. Set the other two aside.

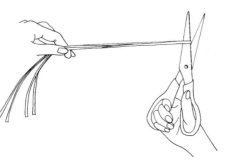

ASSEMBLE

2 Thread the two ribbons halfway through the fulcrum of the barrette, as shown.

3 Take one half of the ribbons (A ribbons) and run them over the first bar (bar 1), down through the center of the barrette, and underneath the second bar (bar 2). Hold them in place with your left hand.

4 Run the second half of the ribbons (B ribbons) over bar 2, down through the center of the barrette, and underneath bar 1. (The same color ribbon should appear on top of the barrette.)

5 Run the B ribbons over bar 1, down through the center of the barrette, and underneath bar 2 without twisting them. (The B ribbons should now reveal a different color showing on top of the barrette.)

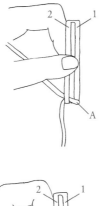

6 Run the A ribbons over bar 2, through the center of the barrette, and underneath bar 1 without twisting them. (Ribbons A and B should now have the same color showing on top of the barrette.)

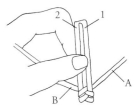

7 Continue this process until you've filled the length of the barrette.

FINISH

8 Double-knot the A and B ribbons together, and let the ends hang from both sides. Or, thread the ends over to one side before knotting them so they all hang together from one place. Repeat with the ribbons you set aside in step 1 to complete the pair! *Optional:* Knot beads onto the ends of the ribbons.

no choke!

Barrettes are small—and so are the things that you're gluing or tying onto them. Please don't leave your child alone with a barrette in her hair. Anything that can fit through a toilet paper roll is a choking hazard for kids younger than three.

OH SO BOW-TIFUL

BEFORE YOU HAD A BALD LITTLE GIRL, YOU MIGHT NOT HAVE considered sticking a bow in your baby's hair. But by the seventeenth time some idiot calls your darling diva all dressed in pink "a handsome feller," you start becoming painfully conscious of the frilly ways to hammer her femininity home. Here's a really simple and classic bow to try out (not to mention, a much less expensive and painful alternative to getting her ears pierced—the next and ultimate step in girlifying your bald babe!). It's a lot easier to simply clip on this bow than to gather together her fine, silky, sparse hair and struggle to tie an actual piece of ribbon around it.

If the bow doesn't work, just whack the dummies who can't tell a boy from a girl over the head with your diaper bag. (Do I sound bitter? I am!)

rate it:

Cost: .... $
Time: .... 🕐 🕐
Skill: .... ✂ ✂
How ga-ga they'll go: ... ♥ ♥ ♥ ♥ ♥

They're simple to make, but because of their size, do involve some technique with the hot gluing.

need it:

✔ Hot-glue gun
✔ Fabric hot-glue sticks
✔ Ribbon (as wide or wider than your barrette)
✔ Ruler or tape measure
✔ Fabric scissors
✔ Metal barrette or snap clip
✔ Embellishments (rhinestones, jewels, ribbon rosettes)

make it:

PREP

1 Plug in your hot-glue gun and insert one glue stick.

2 Cut one piece of ribbon 1" longer than the length of your barrette. Cut a second piece of ribbon 4" long, and cut a third piece of ribbon 3" long. (The 4" and 3" pieces will create your bow.)

Add fab
feminine flair
to your little
lady with this
classic clip-on
hair bow.

ASSEMBLE

3 Open your barrette and squeeze a thin line of glue along the top of it. Center the first piece of ribbon over the glue and press it down. Trim the excess ribbon to ½" on each end.

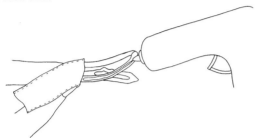

4 Squeeze a thin line of glue on the extra ½" ribbon at each end of the barrette and wrap it around the tips of the barrette.

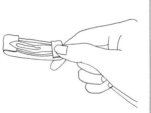

5 Wrap the 4" ribbon into a loop and hot glue the ends together. Squeeze a dab of hot glue on the inside of the loop seam and pinch the loop in half, as shown.

FINISH

6 Take the 3" piece of ribbon and gently wrap it (without bunching) around the pinched center of the loop. Use a dab of hot glue to secure it.

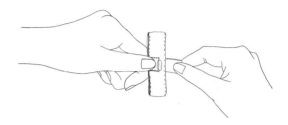

7 Squeeze a dab of hot glue on the center underside of your bow and stick it on your ribbon barrette. Accent with small rhinestones, jewels, flowers, or buttons for more pizzazz.

8 Fasten it on your sweet girl's pretty little head and let her strut her stuff.

variation:

The Bald-rette

When your baby's really, really bald, most barrettes just won't stick. But have no fear. We'll get her on the accessory bandwagon yet! Cut a piece of hook-and-loop tape (both sides) 1" x ¼". Sandwich the pieces, rough sides in, and stitch them together along one edge. Cover the outside with ribbon, rhinestones, or a bow. Pull apart the hook-and-loop tape barbs, opening it like a barrette, and gently attach it around the few hairs on cutie's bald head.

Keep him warm on a cool day at the stadium in a sporty poncho—he'll be hassling referees in no time!

THE PONCHERELLO

"PULL OVER! AND KEEP BOTH HANDS ON THE EXERSAUCER where I can see them!" This poncho, named after *CHiPs* officer extraordinaire, Frank "Ponch" Poncherello, will look incredibly stylish on your little sidewalk patrol kid. Plus, it's warm, practical, and fun—just like "Ponch" himself.

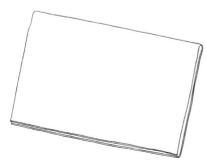

make it:

PREP

1 Lay the fleece flat vertically and then fold it in half lengthwise so the fold is at the top and the stretchy part stretches horizontally).

2 Lay your little one's tee flat on top of the folded fabric. The end of one sleeve should line up with the left side of the fabric.

ASSEMBLE

3 Mark the point where the other sleeve ends, and cut a straight vertical line down from that point to the bottom of the fabric through both layers.

4 Lay the T-shirt down diagonally across the top left corner of your fabric. Trace the arc of the neckline. Remove the tee and modify the arc so its midpoint plunges about 1" deeper, but the endpoints remain the same. Cut along the arcing line through both layers to create the neck hole.

5 Check the size before continuing by fastening a safety pin through both layers at the top left side and slipping the poncho on over your nugget's noggin. Trim the neck hole if it needs to be wider; trim the body if it needs to be smaller.

6 Use your eyelet pliers to punch holes ¼" to ½" away from the edge of the fabric and ¾" apart through both layers of fabric along the top left side of your poncho.

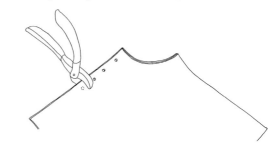

7 Cut a 40" × ½" strip from the extra fleece from this project (so the fabric stretches along the ½" side). Or, use a strip of fleece in a contrasting color or pattern so it stands out.

FINISH

8 Start at the neck hole and thread the strip of fleece through both layers of the first hole. Tie a knot around the edges of the fabric to secure the end.

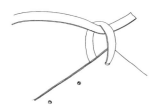

9 Loop the strip around the fabric edges and through each of the holes. At the end, tie the strip to the fabric and trim the excess.

10 Punch holes about ¼" from the bottom of the poncho and ¾" to 1¼" apart for your fringe.

11 Cut thirty to forty 8" × ½" strips of coordinating or contrasting fleece for the fringe. *Note:* You need to fringe each layer individually, so if you made twenty holes, you need forty strips of fleece—one for each hole on the front of the poncho and one for each hole on the back.

12 Fold one of the 8" × ½" strips in half lengthwise and push the folded part through the first hole. Insert the two loose ends of the strip through the loop and pull them tight to create a cow hitch knot (see page 36). Repeat with the remaining strips until all of the holes are filled. *Optional:* Use fabric hot glue to attach rhinestones, flowers, or trim to the poncho.

13 Dress your little officer and go. Just make sure not to exceed the speed limit, or your kid might give you a ticket!

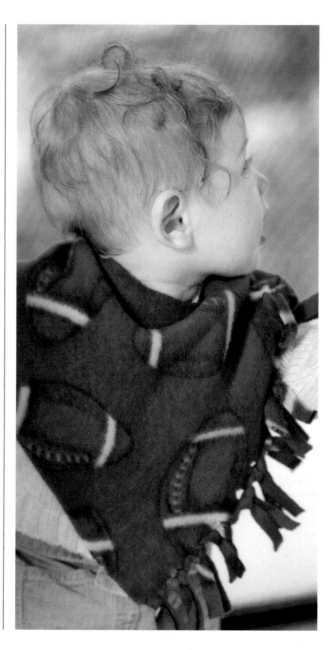

She's positively precious in a poncho trimmed with pompoms— and it's a snap to make!

HASTA LA PONCHO

REMEMBER WHEN YOU USED TO SWADDLE YOUR LITTLE LOVE into a sweet little baby burrito? Well, now that she's older, and spicier, wrap her like a quesadilla in a mama-made poncho! She'll stay warm as a tamale and look as sweet as dulce de leche. This poncho is perfect for those transitional seasons and climates when the temperature jumps from *¡caliente!* to *¡muy frío!* in a matter of minutes. (*¡Dios mio!*)

rate it:

Cost: .... $ $
Time: .... 🕐 🕐
Skill: .... ✂ ✂ ✂
How ga-ga they'll go: ... ♥ ♥ ♥ ♥

Check out the decorative trim that's on sale at fabric stores— you'll find some wild, funky choices that are just perfect for this poncho.

need it:

✔ Hot-glue gun
✔ Fabric hot-glue sticks
✔ 1 yard patterned or solid fleece
✔ Tape measure
✔ Marker or chalk
✔ Fabric scissors
✔ Baby's T-shirt (for sizing)
✔ 2 yards decorative trim (need 1½ yards for bottom)
✔ Baby's coat or sweatshirt (optional)
✔ Embellishments (optional: rhinestones, patches, pompoms, tassel)

make it:

PREP

1 Plug in your hot-glue gun and insert one glue stick.

2 Lay your fleece vertically, and then fold it in half lengthwise so the fold is at the top and the stretchy side of the fabric is running horizontally.

ASSEMBLE

3 Use the tape measure to find the length of your child's arm span from wrist to wrist. If she's sleeping, measure her coat or sweatshirt. Mark that measurement across the width of the folded fabric and cut off any excess fabric.

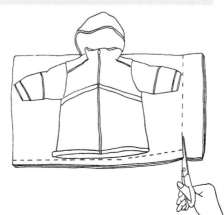

4 Decide how long you want the poncho to be (hold the folded fabric up against your child, with the fold at the top), and mark the desired length. Draw a straight line horizontally through the mark (parallel to the top fold) and cut off the fabric below it.

5 Fold the already folded fabric in half widthwise, and mark a diagonal line from the top right corner of the fabric to the bottom left corner, creating a triangle. Cut along the line, removing the bottom right half.

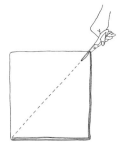

6 Take the baby tee, fold it in half widthwise (to get a measurement of half your baby's neck size) and place it in the top left corner where your fabric is folded. Mark around the neckline, and cut the fleece along the line.

7 Unfold the fleece completely to see the diamond shape of your poncho. Trim the neckline as desired, keeping in mind that you can always make a small hole bigger, but you can't reverse it.

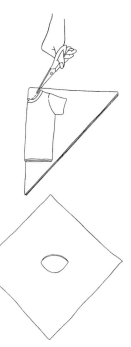

"I look forward to my weekly Crafty Mamas session like a kid looks forward to going to a candy store." —CRAFTY MAMA PRIYA

FINISH

8 Squeeze hot glue, 5" at a time, along the decorative trim and press it onto the bottom edge of the entire poncho as you go. *Optional:* Use hot glue to add even more embellishments to the body of the poncho or glue more decorative trim around the neck.

9 Try your Hasta la Poncho on your little hot tamale and say "Hasta la vista" to the playground and "Hola" to your nearest Chipotle.

variation:

Bottle Warmer

If your babe (and your boobs!) are kinda cold from nursing in the fall or winter, make a poncho for yourself and let him sip warmly and discreetly underneath your mama-made boobie blanky.

THE TEN-MINUTE TUTU

A GIRL CAN NEVER HAVE TOO MANY SHOES—OR TUTUS! And lucky for you, tutus are far less expensive (never mind the ballet classes that follow)—especially if you make them yourself. These tutus are pretty and floaty enough to inspire even the littlest Sugar Plum Fairy to dance around on the tips of her toes. But the best thing I've found about these tutus is that they adjust in size. Now when my prima ballerina, Lily, insists that daddy wear a tutu while he twirls around with her to "Sing-Along Princess Songs," Mike can slip one of these on (no matter what size pants he's wearing these days), and pirouette in comfort and style!

rate it:

Cost: .... $
Time: .... 🕐 🕐
Skill: .... ✂
How ga-ga they'll go: ... ♥ ♥ ♥

This project definitely elicits more "wow!" when your little darling is able to stand up and twirl around the room. But don't let that stop you from making one for your little rolling or crawling prima ballerina.

make it:

PREP

1 Measure and cut twenty-eight 24"-long strips of organza ribbon. Cut both ends of each piece of ribbon into an inverted V or on a diagonal, as shown.

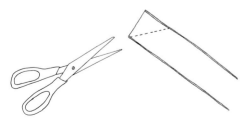

need it:

✔ 15 yards 1½"- to 2"-wide sheer organza ribbon
✔ Ruler or tape measure
✔ Fabric scissors
✔ Elastic headband (looks like an oversize ponytail holder)

Ten minutes and a few yards of ribbon can bring hours (days! years!) of tutu-twirling fun.

ASSEMBLE

2 Wrap each ribbon at its halfway point around the elastic headband and gently tie it in a double-knot. *Note: Tying the knots too tight will stretch out the headband. The ribbon should be able to—with a little push—move around the headband.*

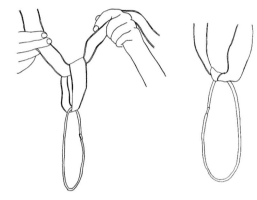

FINISH

3 Suit up your little ballerina, put on some classical music, and spend the next two hours of playgroup watching your tiny dancers plié, jeté, and arabesque around the room!

variations:

Plié with Pizzazz

Use hot glue to stick a rhinestone, silk flower, chunky piece of feather boa, or button to *both sides* of the bottom tips of the ribbons. (You need to glue to both sides of the ribbon because it's so thin that one side will stick to the work surface if you don't.) If you don't want to use two of everything, coat the other side with a small piece of satin or grosgrain ribbon. If you can tie the accents on (a bead or a bell), do it! The embellishments help weigh down the ends of the ribbons.

Puff Up the Jam

For a fuller, fluffier, more swanlike tutu, cut forty 6" x 14" pieces of tulle (instead of ribbon) and tie each one onto the elastic. You don't need any embellishments to weigh down the ends because the beauty of this tutu is that it's fabulously pouffy. On the other hand, you might want to accent the knots on the band with silk or satin flowers or tie on colored ribbons for flair.

With diamonds on the tips of her toes, she'll be taking her first wobbly steps in style.

BOOTIE-LICIOUS

BABY FEET ARE JUST SO CUTE AND DELICIOUS. HOW ELSE CAN you explain your willingness to play "This Little Piggy" for hours on end? Or the ink footprints you made for the birth announcement? Or the fact that you gobble up those teensy toes at least once a diaper change? And as much as you'd like to show off your baby's scrumptious bare tootsies 24-7, there are times when they simply must be covered (like when it's below 60° outside!). For those instances, a pair of absolutely adorable booties fits the bill. So break out the rhinestones and ribbon (or baseball patches and buttons) and deck out those footsies with the most darling, daring, and dashing shoes they'll ever sport (that is unless the little one acquires Mama's grown-up shoe addiction!).

rate it:

Cost: .... $ $
Time: .... 🕐 🕐
Skill: .... ✂ ✂
How ga-ga they'll go: ... ♥ ♥ ♥ ♥

The cost really depends on how much you pay for the shoes. Most dollar stores sell tiny little canvas booties for a buck.

need it:

✔ 1 pair canvas sneakers
✔ ¼"- to ½"-wide ribbon
✔ Fabric scissors
✔ Transparent tape
✔ Hot-glue gun
✔ Fabric hot-glue sticks
✔ Embellishments (buttons, rhinestones, silk or satin flowers, chunky foam beads, sequins, trim, ribbon, rickrack, beads, patches, pompoms, feathers)
✔ Computer, photo editing software, and color ink-jet printer (optional)
✔ Iron-on transfer paper (optional)
✔ Iron (optional)
✔ Embroidery needle and thread (optional)
✔ Felt (optional)
✔ Fabric pens (optional)

make it:

PREP

1 Remove the laces from the shoes and hold one up against a length of ribbon. Cut two pieces of ribbon to match that length.

2 Wrap a piece of transparent tape around each end of each ribbon, sealing them off to make them look like official laces (and making them easier to lace).

ASSEMBLE

3 Choose a shoe décor theme from the list on the opposite page and follow the instructions to create personalized shoes.

👉 **WHITE-OUT!** *What are you to do when your baby's born right after Labor Day and it's oh-so-very-gauche to wear white shoes? Get a fabric marker and color the canvas red, green, blue, citron, deep aubergine, camel, endive, geranium, glacier, graphite, or blush—and then accent away!*

FINISH

4 Lace up the new pair of booties and hit the town!

★ **BABY SHOWER POWER** ★

Women love shoes, and while little canvas baby booties aren't exactly Manolo Blahniks, they still get us really excited! At a baby shower, have each guest decorate a pair of baby booties in an array of sizes, from the tiniest infant bootie to one that will fit a 12-month-old. This way the new mom can keep her growing little darling properly outfitted for the year to come with funky, one-of-a-kind kicks!

sock it to me!

Sometimes, when buying a baby gift for your hairdresser, dry cleaner, or friend of a friend, you don't have the time to go all-out with a pair of personalized, Bootie-licious shoes. Those little baby feet still need attention, so here's an idea: Buy twelve pairs of inexpensive, colored baby socks. Roll up each pair (tie a thin satin ribbon around each if you want to), and stick the whole dozen into an egg carton. Wrap some pretty organza ribbon around the box and—voilà!—a token gift that is creative, practical, and (best of all) inexpensive!

one, two, make a fab shoe

Whether Junior's a hippie or a preppy, here are a few fun ideas to soup up your baby's booties:

TRÈS SHOE

Hot glue a sweet ¼"- to 1"-wide ribbon across the front top of your shoe (about ½" down from the tip). Make a bow and hot glue it off to the side, along the ribbon. Look at her fancy French feet!

FLOWER POWER

Hot glue six small feathers (or felt petals) into the shape of a flower on the front of her shoe. Glue a pompom or a big gem in the center. Or keep it simple and glue a giant, colorful silk flower. Don't forget to stop and smell those cute feet!

NOT SO MONO-GRAM

Use rhinestones to create baby's initials—on the front, side, or back of each shoe.

NAME THAT SHOE

Use little white letter beads to spell out his name, nickname, or favorite things on the top, sides, or back of the shoe. Embellish by hot gluing patches, felt letters or shapes, pompoms, chunky foam beads, or silk/satin flowers on the front, sides, or back of the shoes.

FANTASTIC FABRIC FEET

Using a fabric pen, trace the top front piece of each shoe onto a patterned piece of fabric (any weight)—camo or stripes for boys, flowers or dots for girls, or keep it unisex! Cut out the fabric and use hot fabric glue to adhere it to each shoe top.

WRAP 'N' STROLL

Wrap some cute ribbon around the sides of the soles of the shoes and secure it with hot fabric glue. Don't feel left out if you have a boy—they sell cool "sports" ribbon, plaid ribbon, car ribbon, and camouflage ribbon.

QUICK DRAW McGRAW

Make designs on each shoe with your fabric pens or puffy paints. Use small stencils if you're afraid to draw!

HOT STUFF

Iron on small images to the front or sides of the shoes. (For image ideas, see page 135.)

JACKSON SHOELOCK

Splatter-paint the shoes as an homage to Jackson Pollock . . . as well as to your entire wardrobe in the '80s, and your baby's shirt after you attempt to feed him peas!

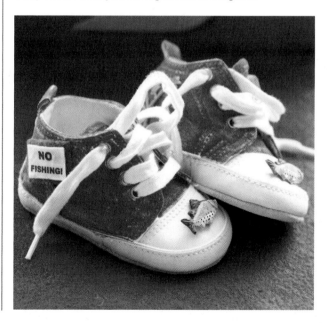

Plain old flip-flops just won't cut it for a special big sis, so tie up a fringed, funky pair just for her!

FRINGE 'FLOPS

WHILE FLIP-FLOPS MIGHT FLOP RIGHT OFF THE TEENY tootsies of your seven-month-old, they are perfectly suited for big sibling or cousin feet! Kids from three to ten will love traipsing around town in these silly, funky flip-flops. Spice up a plain old dollar store pair with ribbon, fleece, or feathery fringe and your (bigger) little loves will have the coolest, comfiest feet in town. Not to mention that a soft, fleecy pair can double as slippers for padding around the house—we moms do think of everything, don't we?

rate it:

Cost: .... $

Time: .... ⏱

Skill: .... ✂

How ga-ga they'll go: ... ♥ ♥ ♥

To keep costs down, never spend more than $2 on flip-flops, and use the fleece scraps left over from the poncho and hat projects. You'll be your niece's favorite aunt, guaranteed.

need it:

- ✔ Ruler
- ✔ Fabric scissors
- ✔ ¼ yard no-fray fabric (cotton jersey, fleece, or furry fleece) or ribbon
- ✔ 1 pair plastic flip-flops
- ✔ Embellishments (optional: silk flowers, rhinestones)
- ✔ Hot-glue gun (optional)
- ✔ Fabric hot-glue sticks (optional)

make it:

PREP

1 Cut forty 5" × 1" strips of fabric or ribbon.

ASSEMBLE

2 Tie each piece of fabric in a double knot around the rubber straps of your flip-flops.

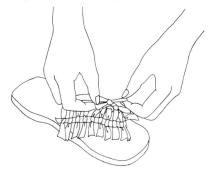

FINISH

3 Push each knot close to the next to create a furry fringe effect. If you decide you want shorter fringe, give them a haircut. *Optional:* Glue a silk flower or a rhinestone at the center of the straps where the toes divide.

> *"With Crafty Mamas there is no pressure to be all perfect. You can cut outside the lines, smudge the paint, and, sure, you'll burn your fingers on the glue gun from time to time."* —CRAFTY MAMA RAQUEL

variations:

Everybody Cut Footloose

Not feeling the fringe? Dig into your treasure trove of embellishments for some great alternatives:

- Hot glue ribbon or decorative trim along the straps. Glue a race car, flower, or other little trinket at the strap intersection.
- Wrap ribbon or embroidery thread around and around and around the straps and then tie at the ends. This is a fun activity for kids ages six and up.

- If you just can't decide between the pink rickrack or the purple pompom trim—buy some hook-and-loop tape fashion trim (like regular hook-and-loop tape, but thinner, softer, and comes in great colors), hot glue strips of the hook-and-loop tape onto your flip-flop straps and your embellishments, and then change it up daily!

TRANSFORMA-TEE

HOW MANY TIMES HAVE YOU RECEIVED A BOXY KID'S T-SHIRT two sizes too big with a shark, a taxi, or a "My Grandma Loves Me!" on it? The answer is: as many times as your mom or mother-in-law has bought your child a T-shirt! It's about time you learned how to transform the latest souvenir from Grandma's cruise to Aruba into a wearable, hip piece of couture. Seriously, did you ever think a "Someone Who Went to Atlantic City Loves Me!" tee could ever look so good? (And if you don't think your little macho man will want to wear a slashy fashion tee—make some for yourself. Chop and refashion your maternity wear to fit your newly bounced-back bod.)

make it:

PREP

1 Spread out your T-shirt on a flat work surface.

2 Decide which of the designs on the next four pages you'd like to make first.

rate it:

Cost: .... $

Time: .... 🕐

Skill: .... ✂

How ga-ga they'll go: ... ♥ ♥ ♥

A little scissors-snipping goes a long way in chopping up an old T-shirt. Cheap and easy, these projects are for one of those playgroups when everyone can only come for a little bit before rushing off to the dentist's, to lunch with an old coworker, or to drop the kids with Mom and get that much-needed cut and color.

need it:

✔ Old T-shirt
✔ Fabric scissors
✔ Chalk (optional)

Transform a boxy tee into a hip top in mere minutes—crafting never looked so cool!

shredded melody

Does your baby love to blare her Beethoven really loud? Then this is the T-shirt for her!

ASSEMBLE

1 Cut off the sleeves of the T-shirt to make it a tank.

2 Cut horizontal slashes about 1" to 2" apart from one side of the shirt to the other, through only the back layer.

3 Make a straight vertical cut down the center back of the shirt, cutting each of your slashes in half.

FINISH

4 Try the T-shirt on your little rocker (slashes in the back) and double-knot the ends of the strips together to get a really great fit. If that's not a reality (most little rockers like to squirm a lot), double-knot the ends together while the shirt's still on the floor, and tighten or loosen the knots when she tries it on later.

5 Blast your Beethoven and rock out to the beat!

le shrug

What do you do with all of your baby's plain tees that have formula stains on the chest and snack smears on the belly? Cut out those well-placed stains and turn those tees into shrugs!

ASSEMBLE

1 Lay the T-shirt flat and cut off approximately ½" of each sleeve to create cap sleeves. (For an alternate look, use a long-sleeve shirt and keep the sleeves full length.)

2 Cut out the neckband.

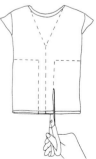

3 Cut through only the top layer (the front of the shirt) to create a V-neck and ties, as shown. *Note:* Use a piece of chalk to mark first, if you prefer.

FINISH

4 Cut a straight line across the back layer to meet the horizontal cuts from the front of the shirt.

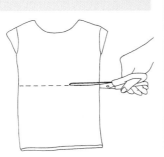

5 Try your mama-made fashion piece over a little dress or tee! Or, put her in a leotard and her Ten-Minute Tutu (page 179), add the shrug on top, and sashay off to ballet class!

million-dollar halter

Carrying baby around is a great way to get your arms all toned for summer. Make a halter to show off your new buff biceps, and make your million-dollar baby one, too!

ASSEMBLE

1 Lay the T-shirt flat and cut off the neckband and sleeves.

2 Flip the shirt over and cut across, armpit to armpit, going through *only* the back layer.

3 Make a vertical cut from the center of the cut you made in step 2, up the back of your shirt (through only the back layer) to the neckline, creating two flaps.

4 Trim the two flaps to match the width of the shoulder fabric as it is on the front of your shirt.

FINISH

5 Tie the two flaps behind the neck.

6 Cut a vertical slit or a V out of the front neckline to make a V-neck.

knotty and nice

The Gap, Children's Place, Fruit of the Loom: Everybody seems to be making fitted tees for kids. (Everybody except the people who mass-produce tourist tees, that is.) But fear not! With a few snips and knots, you can easily make an "I ♥ NY" tee go from boxy to foxy!

ASSEMBLE

1 Cut along the sides of the shirt from the hem all the way up to the sleeve. If the shirt has side seams, cut them off.

2 Cut 1" to 3" horizontal slits each about ½" to 1" apart into the right side of the shirt, through both layers. (The length of the slits depends on how tapered you want your tee.) Repeat on the left side of the shirt.

FINISH

3 Double-knot the corresponding strips together down each side. You know what they say: If the shirt fits, wear it!

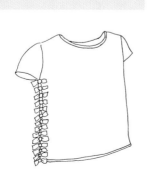

bahama-mama

Want to add a little island flair to any tee? Simply cut off any bands or cuffs. Cut vertical 3" to 5" slits ½" apart along the sleeves and/or the bottom to create fringe. Slip a bead onto every (or every other) strip, knot the fabric at the end to keep the beads on, and—voilà!—pretend you're on a tropical vacation!

BRAGGING RIGHTS

For the fridge or on-the-go, 8 photo projects to show off those dimpled cheeks, gummy grins, and fabulous firsts.

Of course your kids are fantastic, and you could talk about their amazing feats and personalities all day long, but let's pause for a moment. Would *you* want to hear about someone else's kid nonstop? Didn't think so! Thankfully, there are a whole slew of crafts you can make that can do the talking for you. Between the magnets, purses, mini photo albums, charm bracelets, puzzles, and picture frames, everyone you come upon will know how adorably wonderful your baby is without you ever having to say a word! It's okay to tell a cute story once in a while, but try to avoid turning into one of *those* moms by leaving the real bragging to your innocent accessories.

LOVE MOM

HAVE AN

AMAZING NEW YEAR

❤ the PECORIELLO FAMILY CIRCUS

Featuring

SASHA
The Bearded Baby

LILY
The Tattooed Girl

TO DO:
- p.v. drycleaning
- yoga
- Lily's b-day
- hugs for Sasha!

Fancy up your fridge with a cluster of magnets so you can gaze at your darling baby as you sneak a scoop of ice cream from the carton!

PHOTO BRAGNETS

WHAT DO YOU GIVE A MOTHER-IN-LAW WHO HAS EVERYTHING but a Sub-Zero fridge? Not a Sub-Zero, of course—those things are ridiculously expensive! Instead, give her a set of eight Photo Bragnets that she can proudly display on her good ol' 1973 Kenmore! Her mah-jongg club will be so impressed when they come over on Tuesday night. And while you're hot gluing, make a set for your mom, your brother, your sister, and yourself!

They're so easy to make, you can practically craft a set *while* in labor. Okay, early labor. Well, maybe while you have those Braxton-Hicks contractions.

rate it:

Cost: .... $
Time: .... 🕐
Skill: .... ✂
How ga-ga they'll go: ... ♥ ♥ ♥

You absolutely can't beat the three minutes each magnet takes to make—talk about instant gratification.

make it:

PREP

1 Plug in your mini hot-glue gun and insert one glue stick. (If the whole playgroup is making them together, plug in two or three mini guns—far away from the babies, of course!)

2 Look through your printed photos for images in which the subject is small enough to fit under the glass glob (about 1½" diameter). Or, resize your photos on the computer, or print a contact sheet full of thumbnail images. Before you print your resized photos in high-resolution on nice photo paper, set your printer at its lowest resolution and do a test print on plain printer paper. When you've confirmed that the size and color are right, print the images onto photo paper. *Note:* If you don't have photo paper, it is okay to use regular white computer paper for this project.

need it:

- ✔ Mini hot-glue gun
- ✔ Mini clear hot-melt glue sticks (one per magnet)
- ✔ Photos (where the subject is the size of a quarter)
- ✔ Large or jumbo glass globs (1" to 2⅓", one per magnet)
- ✔ All-purpose scissors
- ✔ ¾" circular magnet buttons
- ✔ Embellishments (optional: rhinestones, glitter, pompoms, ribbon)
- ✔ Computer, photo editing software, and color ink-jet printer (optional)
- ✔ Several sheets plain paper (optional)
- ✔ Several sheets digital print photo paper (optional)

3 Arrange some glass globs on your pictures to see which ones work best. Rotate them and swap them out until there's a glob for every image.

ASSEMBLE

4 Hold one glass glob, flat side up, and squeeze a generous blob of hot glue (about six squeezes with your mini hot glue gun) onto the flat side.

5 Turn the glob over *very* quickly (clear hot glue dries in 3 to 5 seconds!) and place it flat side down onto your photo. Press down firmly to get out all the air bubbles. Let the glue dry for 1 to 2 minutes. (Don't worry if glue blobs over the edges; you'll fix it in the next steps.)

6 Repeat steps 4 and 5 until all your glass globs are glued onto a photo.

FINISH

7 Use scissors to trim the excess photo paper and glue from around the glass glob. *Note:* If the photo separates from the glass glob, just squeeze more glue onto the glass glob—enough to melt the glue beneath it—and carefully re-press the picture in place.

8 Squeeze a small blob of hot glue (about one squeeze from your mini glue gun) onto the back of a magnet button and press it quickly and firmly onto the back of the photo on the glass glob. Attach all of your magnet backings to the glass glob/photos in this manner. *Optional:* Bling it up! Put rhinestones or glitter all around the circumference of the magnet or add just one small, flower-shaped rhinestone on top of the glass glob to make it look like it's in her hair. Or, glue a piece (or two) of ribbon dangling down from the back of the photo for a streamer-like effect!

9 Start your own book club, feed your guests salty foods (so they have to go to your fridge for water), and observe the oohs and ahhs as they check out your magnets!

variations:

Collage University

Instead of using just one photo per magnet, make a mini collage on colored paper the same size as your glass glob with the teeny little "index" pictures you get when you have your photos developed.

How Ornamental

Forsake the magnet on the back, and, instead, hot glue a little loop of ribbon at the top of your glass glob to make an ornament.

Stuck On You

Now that all of your pictures, coupons, and invites are firmly magnetized to your fridge, how about pinning down the other 300 random papers on your desk with a personalized paperweight? Find a big blank glass paperweight, and follow the same instructions.

NO-TIME FRAME

NOW THAT YOUR BABY IS FIVE MONTHS OLD, YOU PROBABLY have about 1,253 pictures of him (unless, of course, he's your second or third, and then you have about seven). Your computer stores them all, your albums and brag books are filled with the cute ones, but those super-precious ones need to be prominently displayed so everyone can plainly see how adorable your child is! And, since you have a captive audience, you might as well make the frame yourself, so everyone can plainly see how talented *you* are! While you're at it, make a few as gifts. Make nine of these fine frames and your own mind frame will be in fine form in no time. (Try saying that five times fast!)

rate it:

Cost: .... $
Time: .... 🕐 🕐
Skill: .... ✂ ✂
How ga-ga they'll go: ... ♥ ♥ ♥ ♥

Cheap frames and one perfect piece of paper—you can make two frames for less than $5.

need it:

✔ Plain, unfinished wooden picture frame (any size or shape)
✔ Decoupage paper, bigger than your frame
✔ Pen
✔ All-purpose scissors
✔ ¾ cup white glue
✔ Plastic container or paper cup
✔ Stir stick
✔ Flat paintbrush
✔ Brayer or plastic card
✔ Foam brush
✔ Decoupage medium or clear acrylic finish spray
✔ Hot-glue gun (optional)
✔ Hot-glue sticks (optional)
✔ Embellishments (optional: letters, trinkets, sparkly things)

make it:

PREP

1 Open the back of your frame and remove the glass. (You can use any frame for this project, but frames with thick borders work best.) Lay your frame facedown onto a piece of decoupage paper, trace around the inside and outside edges, and cut it out. Check that the cut piece is the right size and trim if needed.

2 In a plastic container or paper cup, mix the white glue with ¼ cup water.

*Your kids' pictures
deserve better
than a boring old
wooden frame—
it's time for some
decoupage!*

ASSEMBLE

3 Paint the white glue solution onto the front of the frame *and* onto the back of your decoupage paper.

4 Start on the left side and carefully lay the paper onto the frame, smoothing out any bubbles or bumps as you go from left to right. (If you have a brayer, run it along the paper; if not, smooth out the paper with a plastic card.)

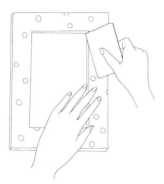

5 Let the glue dry for about 10 minutes. While you wait, plug in your hot-glue gun and insert one glue stick if you plan to add any embellishments to your frame.

FINISH

6 Brush a coat (or two if you have time) of decoupage medium over the whole frame with a foam brush, or spray on a coat of clear acrylic finish. Let the first coat of decoupage medium dry 10 to 15 minutes before adding a second coat.

7 Use hot glue and embellishments to accent the frame with rhinestones, googly eyes, trinkets, or letters—whatever works!

8 Insert a photo and display it. And then try to catch up on the million things you never have time to do!

HANG IT UP *If your frame can't be hung on the wall, but you want to do so, hot glue on or screw in some saw-tooth hangers (available at most craft and hardware stores) to the back.*

variations:

Half and Half

Are you a little bit country and a little bit rock 'n' roll? Find two complementary pieces of decoupage or scrapbook paper. Trace the top half of your frame onto one piece, and the bottom half onto the other. Cut them out, trim them, and decoupage them onto the frame. Hot glue a length of ribbon to cover the seam where the papers meet. Accent the top or bottom with a metal word plate, book plate, or metal letters that spell out your baby's name.

Getting Scrappy

If you're feeling indecisive about just one or two themes, then this is the frame for you! Cut 5" squares out of a few different papers. Rip them into ¾" to 1½" pieces. Use white glue solution to stick one piece on, then another, and another, slightly overlapping as you go. (Use this technique on the whole frame or just the top, bottom, or sides.) Wait for the glue to dry, then brush a few coats of decoupage medium over the top. Very country quilt-ish!

the right frame of mine

A fabulous frame can really bring a picture to life. Try one of these themes or cook up one of your own.

THE NAME GAME

There are tons of frames out there with "My Baby," "Mama's Boy," or "Princess" on them. There are even many with "Sarah," "Jake," or "Kayla" on them. But how many frames have you seen with "Suri" or "Pax" or "Apple" on them? None! (Unless Katie, Angelina, or Gwyneth made them.) So go ahead and make a frame for your little hipster with the unique name! Don't just write it once, spell it out several times in a bunch of

different mediums. Hot glue on glass globs, blocks, or letter beads, or use decoupage. Hey, even if your little darling's named David, he deserves a super-personalized frame.

LE PLASTIQUE MYSTIQUE

Stroll the aisles of the dollar store and pick up a few bags of small plastic toys—pigs, army men, rings, race cars, lizards, bowling pins, bananas, frying pans, maracas—whatever catches your eye. Hot glue them in the corners, on the top, or anywhere else on your frame. Top it off with a little name personalization in any medium you dig—

Paint & Paste

Is your nursery all themed and fabulous? Choose the images that'll go best with your décor. Paint your frame or leave it natural. Cut up a whole bunch of paper dolls, retro airplane images, or scenes from Archie comic strips, and decoupage them around your frame. (If the images are too big for the frame, it's okay to chop them up.) Accent with a decoupaged, glass glob–lettered name. Add rhinestones or other embellishments for a little 3-D action. (While you're at it, make a Decou-Pail, shadow box, stool, and coat rack to match.)

Barrette Parking

After you finish your fantastic frame, hot glue three ½"- to 1"-wide x 8"-long ribbons to the back of its base. Then clip your baby's budding barrette collection (mama-made, of course; see page 167) on the ribbons for easy storage and access. If she doesn't have any barrettes, well, hurry up and make her some!

decoupage, glass globs, plastic scrapbook letters, or beads—and you've got yourself one faboo frame.

FLOWER POWER

Every girly girl (and girly granny) loves a flowerful frame. Distress it with white or cream-colored crackle medium and then hot glue silk flowers, dried flowers, or felt flowers all around your frame. For a simple, sweet look, hot glue three flowers in a row to the top front of the frame. Spray a dash of your favorite floral perfume on them so when people stop to admire your baby's adorable photo, they can smell the flowers, too! P.S. If you're not into floral, add a pretty bow (a thick gold or pink organza ribbon) instead. Personalize the bottom with a name or a phrase.

FIRSTS

First smile, first shoes, first haircut, first tooth, first birthday! In your baby's first year, the famous firsts come fast. Capture each one on camera and then make a frame to celebrate them. Use pre-made scrapbook embellishments or make your own Bubble Letters (page 32) to spell out each special moment. Skip the mantle display and hang them all in a cluster on a wall. For an impressive wall piece, string together small square frames with ribbon and decorate each with a "My First . . ." plaque.

THE FAST AND THE FABULOUS

In a hurry? Thought so. Simply hot glue some cute rickrack or trim around the front of your frame and then accent it a little bit here and there. Try some little satin flowers, rhinestones, or cutesy baby trinkets in the corners or along the trim. Or, hot glue a little piece of Lego, a small plastic ball, a dinosaur foam bead, or a metal stud along the frame. Use letters that match to spell his or her name for a personal touch.

feng baby

Feng shui is the ancient Chinese art of positioning things, inside and outside of your home, to create harmony and balance in your life and environment. When Lily was about six months old and having some sleep "issues," I combed the Internet, looking for any answers and advice I could get. One feng shui solution for restless sleep was to put wooden framed pictures of your family and pets in your baby's nursery. These wooden frames filled with loved ones are meant to comfort your baby as she's falling asleep and after she wakes up. Desperate for some sleep myself (her sleep issues gave me sleep issues), I framed a few photos of her cousins, hung them up, and, miraculously, Lily slept well that night. (Of course, she didn't sleep well the night after that, or the one after that, but she *did* sleep the one after that, and for two weeks more . . .)

Take a regular old Saturday-afternoon outfit to the next level and show off your beautiful babies with an über-hip purse for your hip.

HIP PURSE

FANNY PACKS WERE NEVER THE MOST GLAMOROUS FASHION statement, but you have to admit that it was a heckuva lot easier to get your Bonne Bell, Erasermates, and Hubba Bubba out of your fanny pack than out of your backpack. And that's why Gucci, Louis Vuitton, and Prada have brought them back, post-millennium style, as "belt bags" or "waist packs."

These oh-so-chic and oh-so-practical bags come in all sorts of newfangled shapes and sizes. And thanks to their reinvention, moms no longer need to schlep the entire heavy diaper bag around the playground just to keep their essentials safe. Simply throw your wallet, cell, and digital camera into your "hip purse" and run your fanny off chasing your kid around the playground. You'll be the envy of every bulky-pocketed or diaper bag–toting mom.

rate it:

Cost: .... $ $
Time: .... 🕐 🕐 🕐 🕐
Skill: .... ✂ ✂ ✂
How ga-ga they'll go: ... ♥ ♥ ♥ ♥ ♥

need it:

✔ Digital photos
✔ Computer, photo editing software, and color ink-jet printer
✔ Canvas, denim, or cotton hanging wallet purse
✔ Several sheets plain paper
✔ All-purpose scissors
✔ Iron-on transfer paper (for dark-colored fabrics)
✔ Iron
✔ Hot-glue gun (ideally with a ribbon nozzle)
✔ Fabric hot-glue sticks
✔ Ribbon or trim (different widths, colors, and textures)
✔ No-fray solution (optional)
✔ Embellishments (optional: rhinestones, buttons, beads, patches)
✔ 1"- to 1½"-wide grosgrain ribbon
✔ Needle and thread

make it:

PREP

1 Sort through your digital pictures to find the one(s) you want to use to decorate your purse. Use as many or as few as you want and make the images any size you want. Collage a few together, spread them out, or create one big image. Just make sure they all fit onto the front of your pack (the back will be hidden) and make sure you leave at least 1" around the edge for decorative ribbon or trim.

2 Juice up those images in your photo editing program and then save them to your "Bragging Rights" folder. When you're ready to print, import them into a text document to size them (see page 24 for a refresher).

3 Test-print your photo(s) at a low resolution on plain paper before you print them on your iron-on transfer paper. Cut out the image(s) and check the size. Then adjust the dimensions on-screen and repeat as needed until it's the right size.

4 Print your perfectly sized photo on iron-on transfer paper at the highest resolution your printer allows. *Note:* To save iron-on paper, see if there's one willing mama in the group who can print everyone's pictures together. If nobody's brave enough to step up, you're it, and it's time to consult page 29. Also, if you're planning on making any

variation:

Brag Bag

If you *need* to carry around a big purse but you still want to fashionably show off your little love, decorate a zippered change purse instead. Just attach the change purse zipper to key ring hardware on your big bag and fling it over the side of the bag for all to see! (Now the next time your baby decides to throw a fit while you're in line at the grocery store, your brag bag will be in full view to tell a different story of just how cute your little tomato is when he's not totally freaking out.)

iron-on onesies, tees, or booties later on, print those images now, too, to save paper!

5 Plug in your iron. Plug in your hot-glue gun, and insert one fabric glue stick.

ASSEMBLE

6 Carefully cut off the hanging strap from the purse. Follow the instructions on the transfer paper packaging to iron your images onto the *front* of the purse.

☞ **NYLON FIX** *If you can't find a canvas hanging wallet/passport purse, you can buy a nylon one but don't iron directly onto it! Instead, iron your photo(s) onto a piece of fabric, trim it to the appropriate size, glue it on, and proceed.*

7 Spread out your ribbons and trimmings to choose which ones you'd like to use. Try a few different arrangements, and draw inspiration from the other mamas before you settle on your design.

8 Measure the length of each ribbon you need by laying it around your photo like a frame; add an extra 1" to the length, and then cut it.

9 Squeeze a dab of hot glue at one end of the ribbon, fold it over ½", and press firmly. Repeat on the other end. *Note:* If you plan to use no-fray solution, cut the ribbon to the exact length you want, apply the solution to each end, and skip the hot glue in this step. Wait 10 to 15 minutes for the no-fray solution to dry.

10 Squeeze a thin line of hot glue around the perimeter of the back of the ribbon (not just in a line down the middle) to ensure that it stays put, but don't overdo it (the glue dries white and will show up). Then press it into place on your purse. Continue gluing all of your ribbons and trim in place. *Optional:* Add some oomph by hot gluing on some embellishments (rhinestones, patches, beads). Wait a few minutes for all the pieces to dry and then gently pull on the items to make sure they're secure.

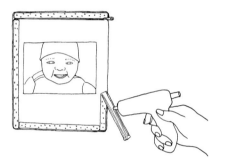

the crop shop

Did you ever notice that the digital photos you develop don't always look like the ones stored on your computer? Hands, feet, and heads are often cropped out. That's because the dimensions of your digital camera pictures don't have the same ratio as a standard 4" x 6" picture. To avoid unwanted chopping, develop your photos online or in a store that allows you to change the crop box, so you can get the image that you want—not the one that automatically crops itself.

"Crafty Mamas is a creative outlet that, refreshingly, doesn't involve mixing formula or reading about the million and one ways to properly raise my child."

—CRAFTY MAMA MELISSA

FINISH

11 Unzip your purse and flip it over (back side up). Cut two pieces of grosgrain ribbon long enough to accommodate your widest belt (for the belt loops).

12 Place the two ribbon pieces vertically about 2" to 3" apart on the top back of the purse. Sew them in place using a running stitch, going through only the back layer of the purse.

13 Wear your Hip Purse by first sliding your belt through the first belt loop on your pants. Then slide your belt through the first and second loops on the purse, followed by the second, third, and fourth (and so on) loops on your pants. Your purse should hang from the side of your hip. Now fill it up and hit the playground!

Share photos of your baby love with pride—now the album looks almost as adorable as he does!

MY BRAGAMUFFIN BRAG BOOK

ADMIT IT: YOU'VE BEEN SNAPPING PHOTOS LIKE A MADWOMAN ever since your baby was born. It would be a shame to let your photographic prowess go unnoticed. (C'mon, anyone would be impressed with that close-up of her sweet toothless smile!) So next time you develop your pics, swing by a craft store on your way home to buy all the materials you need to make a portable showcase for your precious love—it's one of the best bang-for-your-buck projects in this book (similar ones sell for $20 to $40 at fancy boutiques.) And for the record, it's *totally* acceptable to carry around a brag book, even when you're with your little ragamuffin! How else will your new mommy friends know how hot your husband is?

rate it:

Cost: .... $

Time: .... 🕐🕐

Skill: .... ✂ ✂ ✂

How ga-ga they'll go: ... ♥ ♥ ♥ ♥

need it:

✔ Digital photos
✔ Computer, photo editing software, and color ink-jet printer
✔ Ruler or tape measure
✔ Mini hardcover photo album (approximately 5" x 6½" x 1¼")
✔ Several sheets plain paper
✔ All-purpose scissors
✔ Iron-on transfer paper (for dark-colored fabrics)
✔ Iron
✔ Hot-glue gun
✔ Fabric hot-glue sticks
✔ ¼ yard cotton or home décor fabric
✔ Fabric scissors
✔ 16 inches of ⅜"- to ¾"-wide ribbon
✔ 2 pieces 8½" x 11" 60- to 80-pound cardstock
✔ Embellishments (optional: rhinestones, trim, satin flowers, mini mirrors)

make it:

PREP

1 Sort through your digital photos to find a horizontal or vertical image for the front of your album. Juice up that image in your photo editing program and then save it in your "Bragging Rights" folder. When you're ready to print, import the image into a text document to size it to fit your book (see page 24 for a refresher). It can be any size, as long as it's smaller than the cover of the brag book.

2 Test-print your photo at a low resolution on plain paper before you print it on iron-on transfer paper to make sure it's the exact size you want it to be. Cut out the image and check the size. Then adjust the dimensions on-screen and repeat as needed.

3 Print your perfectly sized photo on iron-on transfer paper at the highest resolution your printer allows. *Note:* To save iron-on paper, see if there's one willing mama in the group who can print everyone's pictures together. If nobody's brave enough to step up, you're it, and it's time to consult page 24 for a refresher. Also, if you're planning on making any iron-on onesies, tees, or booties later on, print those images now, too, to save paper!

4 Plug in your iron. Plug in your hot-glue gun and insert one glue stick.

5 Lay the rectangle of fabric on a flat surface, wrong side up, and use fabric scissors to trim it to size. It should be 3" taller and 2" wider than the entire album cover—front, back, and spine combined—when the album is open and laying flat.

ASSEMBLE

6 Place the closed book right side up on top of the fabric.

Grab the left edge of the fabric and fold it around your brag book to meet the right edge—centering the book inside. *Note:* If the original design on the book shows through the fabric, cut two pieces of white cardstock the same size as the cover and hot glue them onto the front and back cover of your album.

7 Open the book so that all of the photo pages fall to the right. Run a thin line of hot glue about 1" in along the left inside edge of the cover, fold the fabric over onto it, and carefully press it down. Let it dry for a minute or two.

8 Push the photo pages so they fall to the left and pull the fabric tight, but not too tight (so you can still close the book)

variations:

You Name It!
Forsake the photo on the front of your album (how could you possibly decide which was the cutest one to use anyway?) and iron on your baby's name instead. Find a font you like, print your baby's name or nickname onto some iron-on transfer paper for dark colors, and iron it on. Or, if you want to thank your wonderful mom (who's beginning to be your regular Saturday-night babysitter), print up an "I Love Grandma" transfer and iron it on the front!

Super-Size Me
You did the mini brag book, now go maxi! Buy an inexpensive *large* photo album and cover up that brown pleather, gold-etched "Our Anniversary" cover with some precious (and cheap) fabric! Iron on a photo, add some embellishments, and you have yourself a book that's coffee-table worthy!

around the right edge of the cover and repeat step 7 on the right inside cover.

9 Hold the book in place so it is open and lying flat and make two vertical cuts that line up with the spine of the book from the bottom edge of the fabric to the bottom of the book. Repeat on the top edge of the fabric.

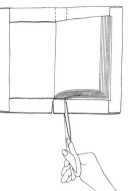

10 Fold the extra 2" of fabric at the bottom left corner into a triangle, as shown.

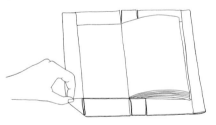

Crazy for Decoupage?

Instead of wrapping your album in fabric, wrap it in paper—comics, catalog pages, cute scrapbook sheets. Instead of hot glue, use a three-parts white glue, one-part water solution to attach the paper. Wrap your book and let it dry. Cut two pieces of decoupage paper ½" smaller than the front cover, then glue them inside the front and back covers. Let them dry. Coat the entire book cover with a thick decoupage medium to seal it. Let it dry for 10 to 15 minutes, then add some embellishments.

★ **BABY SHOWER POWER** ★

New moms always end up with about a million pictures of their baby—and that's only after his first week out of the womb! Have each guest work on a Brag Book at the shower and gift them all to the mom-to-be before the party is over so she'll have plenty of photo albums to store all of those snapshots of her little love sleeping, eating, crying, and laughing!

11 Run a thin line of glue 1" in along the bottom left edge of the inside cover, pull the extra fabric over that edge, and quickly press it into the glue. Squeeze a small amount of hot glue under the diagonal edge of fabric created in step 10 and press it down. *Note:* If you wait too long between applying the glue and pressing the fabric down, it will dry lumpy.

12 Repeat steps 10 and 11 on the top left edge of the book. Then repeat steps 10 and 11 on the bottom and top edges of the *right* side of the book.

13 Trim the extra piece of fabric at the bottom of the spine to about ¾". Run a line of glue along the edge of that piece and fold it ¼" onto itself. Run a line of glue along the bottom interior edge of the spine, fold the fabric flap over it, and press it into the glue.

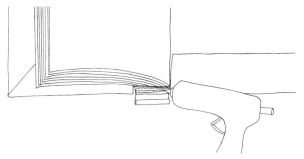

14 Repeat step 13 with the fabric flap at the top of the spine.

FINISH

15 Cut two 8" pieces of ribbon and hot glue the end of one ribbon to the inside of the front cover, about halfway down and about 1" in from the side edge. Repeat with one end of the second ribbon along the inside edge of the back cover.

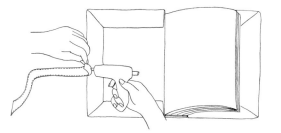

16 Cut two rectangles of cardstock with dimensions ½" smaller on all four sides than the front of your book.

17 Center one piece of cardstock on the inside of the front cover of your book, close the book to make sure it's the right size, and make any necessary adjustments. Use hot glue to attach cardstock to the inside front cover (hiding the unfinished fabric edges). Center and glue the second piece of cardstock to the inside back cover.

18 Follow the instructions on the transfer paper packaging to iron the image horizontally or vertically onto the front cover of your book. *Optional:* Use hot glue to add rhinestones, ribbon, trim, or accents to the front, back, and/or spine of your album.

19 Slip some of your adorable pictures into the sleeves of your brag book, close the book, and tie the two ribbon ends in a bow. Then head off to your high school reunion so you can casually show off your crafty skills, as well as your gorgeous child (and hot husband), to all of your old friends!

SHAPE UP!

WHAT IF I TOLD YOU THAT A CRAFT PROJECT IN THIS BOOK can pretty much get you into any shape you want? You'd be all for it, right? Well, this is your lucky day. These fabulous puzzles can totally get you into great shape— a triangle, a square, a circle, a rectangle, heck, even a hexagon! What? Not the kind of shape you were hoping for? Well, there's a lot of cutting, pasting, and gluing in this project, and that's gotta burn some calories.

rate it:

Cost: .... $ $
Time: .... 🕐 🕐 🕐
Skill: .... ✂ ✂
How ga-ga they'll go: ... ♥ ♥ ♥ ♥

The cost all depends on how much you spend on the puzzle. If you get yours at the dollar store, it's less. If you splurge on a nice Melissa and Doug puzzle, it's more.

make it:

PREP

1 Lay down a sheet of wax paper. Remove the puzzle shapes from the puzzle and paint the base over the paper. Keep it a solid color, or add stripes or polka dots. If your puzzle pieces are not already colored, take the opportunity to paint them, too. *Note:* Spray paint makes the color come out more evenly, and it dries faster.

👉 **CAUTION TIP** *If you do choose to use spray paint, make sure you're outside or in a properly ventilated space, far away from kids!*

2 Sort through your photos and lay out the ones you'd like to include. (The more you have to choose from, the better, so you can find photos that fit the puzzle shapes.) Pick a theme—"my friends," "my cousins," "all of the old people that give me lipstick-y kisses at parties"—or go with a whole mix of people in your kid's social circle.

need it:

✔ Geometric shape wooden puzzle
✔ Wax paper
✔ Acrylic paint or spray paint
✔ Paintbrush
✔ Photos
✔ Pen
✔ All-purpose scissors
✔ Tacky glue
✔ Decoupage medium or clear acrylic finish spray (optional)
✔ Foam brush (optional)
✔ Hot-glue gun (optional)
✔ Hot-melt glue sticks (optional)
✔ Embellishments (optional: stickers, jumbo rhinestones, letters, trinkets)

Cool and creative, this project shows off all your babe's loved ones and keeps her entertained!

tess' friends

3 Lay the puzzle pieces over your photos to see who will fit best under what shape. (If someone in one of your photos has big hair, she won't fit in a triangle.) Trace the shape of each puzzle piece onto its corresponding photo, taking care that each photo subject is appropriately positioned within each outline.

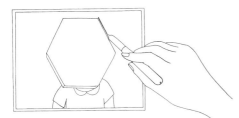

ASSEMBLE

4 Cut out the photo shapes just inside your trace lines, so they'll fit into the puzzle.

5 Wait until the puzzle base is dry, and then place the cut photos in their proper spaces on the puzzle base to make sure they fit. Trim photos additionally, as necessary.

variation:

Decoupage, Baby

If you *love* to decoupage and your little darling is into trucks or dinos, make some white glue–water decoupage solution and glue the images onto the base of your puzzle. Use a sticker or cut out letters to write "My Family Rocks!" on the base somewhere. (For a decoupage refresher, check out page 30.)

what's so funny?

To a baby, peek-a-boo is an amazing magic trick, and you're a big, lovable Houdini! Before your baby is about eight months old, he doesn't get that things still exist if he can't see them. That's why he's so thrilled when you reveal your face behind your hands. POOF! It's Mommy! After about eight months, he develops "object permanence" (meaning he understands that you're still there), but at this point, he just loves you so much that he screams with delight at the sight of your smiling face.

6 Paint the shape space in the puzzle with some tacky glue and press each photo firmly into place.

FINISH

7 Wait 5 to 10 minutes for the glue to dry.

8 *Optional:* If you choose to add embellishments, use hot glue to attach a jumbo rhinestone, trinkets, or letters to each puzzle piece (spell the title of the puzzle based on the theme from step 2). Or, simply add some fun stickers, placing one on each puzzle piece or on the frame.

9 Give Schmoopie his new puzzle and delight in the beautiful shape you're in!

Photos on the go: a great way to display pics of your little charmer and mesmerize him with the dangly, jangly beads.

PHOTO A-GO-GO

WE'RE ALL MULTITASKERS—IT'S PART OF THE MAMA CONTRACT. You juggle your kid in one hand, breakfast in the other, tuck the newspaper under one arm, and maneuver the stroller with your elbows as your cell phone's ringing furiously in your back pocket. Good luck finding room in this scenario for that brand-new Brag Book (page 209)! But I've got you covered: Slip this fabulously stylish bracelet equipped with plenty of baby glam-shots onto your wrist, and go ahead, walk the family dog while you're at it. (One woman in my Crafty Mama group got so many compliments on hers that she started a photo charm bracelet biz. Today, she makes tons of money selling them in upscale boutiques.)

rate it:

Cost:..........................$ $ $ $
Time:..........................🕐 🕐 🕐 🕐
Skill:..........................✂ ✂ ✂
✂
How ga-ga they'll go:...♥ ♥ ♥ ♥ ♥

Compared to other projects, these are a tad pricey. But paying $10 to $15 to make them yourself sure beats paying $45 to buy one in a fancy store.

make it:

PREP

1 Sort all of your materials onto little plates or into little bowls. Put beads in one, photo charms in another, jump rings in another, glass beads to be made into charms in another, and so on. Decide what you want your bracelet to look like (chunky, dangly, charm- or alphabet-filled). If you choose, follow the instructions on page 34 to make your beads into charms.

2 Wrap a length of ball chain tightly around your wrist and cut it to the exact size of your wrist. (Don't worry that it's going to be too tight; the clasp and jump rings add length later!)

need it:

✔ Plates or bowls
✔ Assorted glass beads (both with large holes and regular-size holes)
✔ Photo charms (see page 219)
✔ Charms (silver, silver-plated, enamel, glass, or rhinestone)
✔ Silver- or gold-tone base beads (holes wider than ball chain)
✔ 5mm, 7mm, and 10mm jump rings
✔ 1.2mm to 2.3mm ball chain, 6" to 8"
✔ All-purpose scissors
✔ 1 ball chain clasp
✔ Bracelet clasp of choice
✔ Chain-nose pliers
✔ Washcloth (or flocked bead board)
✔ Head pins or eye pins

ASSEMBLE

3 Attach a ball chain clasp to one end of the ball chain.

4 Take your pliers in one hand, and clamp them onto one side of a thick 7mm jump ring. Use the fingers of your other hand to pinch the other side of the jump ring near its opening. Twist the wrist of your plier hand slightly to open the jump ring. *Note:* Twist the jump ring open, rather than pulling the ends apart, so the opening will be more secure when closed again.

5 Run the open jump ring through the middle hole of the ball chain clasp, slip it through the little loop on either end of your bracelet clasp, and twist the jump ring closed using the pliers and your fingers. (Adding the bracelet clasp will keep your beads in place so they don't go sliding off your chain.)

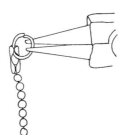

6 Lay the ball chain across the washcloth or bead board so you can get an idea of how many beads you need. Choose and lay out your beads and charms below the chain. Arrange them, rearrange them, and try a few different options until you come up with an arrangement you really like.

7 Use pliers to attach a jump ring, just as in steps 4 and 5, to any of the charms that don't already have jump rings attached (see page 34). Make sure to "over-close" the jump rings so they won't slip off the bracelet.

8 String the charms and large-holed base beads onto your ball chain until there's about ½" of unused chain left at the end. (This allows the beads to move and your bracelet to bend. If you have end-to-end beads, it will be too stiff to wrap around your wrist.)

FINISH

9 Attach a ball chain clasp on the end of your bracelet that doesn't already have one and repeat steps 4 and 5, using another 7mm jump ring and the remaining end of your bracelet clasp. (For added bling, you can attach a charm that dangles from the clasp before closing the jump ring.)

10 Clasp the bracelet onto your wrist to make sure it fits. (If you need to make it smaller, carefully remove a bead or two from either end, cut a few balls from the end of the chain, and reattach the clasps. If you need it bigger, add an extra jump ring to the one attached to the clasp.)

variation:

No Need to Bead

If your eyes and fingers just aren't up to the stringing, buy a wrist-sized piece of "large-link chain" from the bead or craft store. Cut it to size, attach a clasp to both ends, hang your charms on different links, and call it a day! Another option is to use beading wire crimp beads, a handy solution if you're having trouble finding the ball chain and large-holed beads. Or, as a last resort, dig up your old charm bracelet from fifth grade (you know, the one with the piano and Liberty Bell charms on it) and add a sterling photo charm or two to the links.

11 Follow the "Photo Charms" steps below to secure your photos to your base photo charms.

12 Clasp your bracelet around your wrist, put on a short-sleeved or sleeveless outfit so your bedecked arm is exposed to the world, go out to dinner, and talk very expressively with your hands. With all of the clinking and shimmering, someone is bound to notice both your amazing creation and your adorable kid.

NO CHOKE! *Little people like little beads, but their little throats don't. Keep a close eye on your baby's teensy fingers to make sure he doesn't grab onto any findings. For that reason, this project is best with pre-crawlers or just moms!*

photo charms

There are a few different types of photo charm bases (the charms before you've placed a photo inside) available. My favorite, and the most common, is all metal with an indentation in which to fit a tiny photo. Follow the steps below to attach your selected images and put the photo in photo charms.

Need It:
✔ Scrap paper
✔ Photo charms
✔ Ballpoint pen or pencil
✔ All-purpose scissors
✔ Small photos
✔ Clear nail polish

Make It:

1. Lay your thin sheet of scrap paper over the front of the charm. Gently press down on the paper to trace the shape of the indented space.

2. Cut out the traced shape and try placing it into the photo charm to see if it fits. (If it's too big, trim it again; if it's too small, try tracing the charm again.)

3. Select a photo you'd like to put in one of the charm frames. Lay the little paper shape on top of your photo and trace around it.

4. Cut around your photo, just inside the trace lines.

5. Place your little photo in the indented space of the charm. It's okay if you find you have to wedge it in a little bit. (If it fits, faboo! If not, trim it a teensy bit at a time; remember, you can always cut off more, but when it's too small, well, you're back to square one!)

6. Once your photo fits nicely in the charm, take a hearty dollop of clear nail polish and drop it onto the photo. Don't paint it on; simply let it fall onto the image. Cover the whole image to seal the photo in.

7. Wait at least 15 minutes for the nail polish to dry. Then, if you want to super-seal it, repeat step 6 to add a second layer of clear polish, and wait another 15 minutes for it to dry to make the charm perfectly slobber-resistant.

8. Repeat the entire process to make all the charms you want, and use them to make the Photo a-Go-Go (page 217), Album à la Neck (page 221), or Boys and Girls on the Hood (page 223) projects.

Draw attention to your décolleté and your darling daughter—now that's multitasking.

ALBUM À LA NECK

CHARM *BRACELETS* ARE FANTASTIC, UNLESS YOU CHURN butter—okay, type at a keyboard—all day long. If you just can't bear to hear the clinking and clanking every time you move your wrist, relocate your baby's adorable face to your neck! Use beads and charms to create a gorgeous, color-coordinated theme for your necklace: Go with all topaz to match the picture of your little girl in her adorable leopard-velvet party dress, or maybe choose the navy blue beads to match your little guy in his favorite Yankees jersey.

make it:

PREP

1 Sort all of your materials on little plates or in little bowls. Put glass beads in one, photo charms in another, and so on. (Keep them on the table and out of your child's reach.) Decide what charms and beads you want on your necklace.

2 Cut a piece of silk, satin, or leather cord about ½" to 1" shorter than the length you want for your necklace (the crimp coils and clasp will add extra length).

ASSEMBLE

3 Wet one end of the cord (dabbing it on your tongue is fine), twist it between your fingers, and push it into a crimp coil. Twist and turn it to get a tight fit. If it's too loose, fold over the end of the cord ½" and try again. Repeat on the other end of the cord.

rate it:

Cost: .... $
Time: .... 🕐 🕐
Skill: .... ✂ ✂
How ga-ga they'll go: .... ♥ ♥ ♥

Making beads into charms is really a meditative process, but it does take time, especially if you haven't done it before.

need it:

- ✔ Plates or bowls
- ✔ Assorted glass and crystal beads
- ✔ Photo charms (see page 219)
- ✔ Charms (silver, silver-plated, enamel, glass, or rhinestone)
- ✔ All-purpose scissors
- ✔ 1mm to 1.5mm silk, satin, or leather cord, necklace-length
- ✔ 2 crimp coils (sized to match the width of your cord)
- ✔ Chain-nose pliers
- ✔ Round-nose pliers
- ✔ Head pins
- ✔ 10 to 15 assorted jump rings
- ✔ Toggle clasp

4 Use your chain-nose pliers to pinch the last ring of the crimp coil so it catches the cord and prevents it from slipping out. Lightly tug to make sure the coil is secure on the cord.

5 Use your round-nose pliers to create any charms you want out of beads and head pins (see page 34). Gather them along with the photo charms you created by following the steps on page 219.

FINISH

6 Attach a jump ring to each charm (beaded or photo), and slide your charms onto the cord in order. Try different combinations until you find the one that you like the best.

7 Use both sets of pliers to pry open and attach the toggle clasp pieces to both ends of the crimp coils.

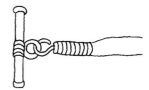

8 Wear a V-neck top to show off your mama-made necklace (as well as your hot breastfeeding cleavage), hire a babysitter, and go out on a romantic date!

☞ **NO-FRAY TIP** *If you're using silk or satin cord, finish the ends with a dab of nail polish to prevent fraying.*

a bead of a different color

Many believe that colored stones hold healing powers. If you're looking for a little luck, love, or an energy boost (because you haven't slept in months), slip a few colored beads onto your necklace and see what happens.

Red: Action, confidence, courage, and vitality. The little push you need to wear a bikini this summer!

Pink: Love and beauty. If showering in the morning is a luxury, a few pink ones for beauty might be nice!

Orange: Vitality and endurance. Husband out of town for work? You at home with the kids? Orange it is!

Gold: Wealth and prosperity. Who couldn't use a little—or a lot—of that?

Brown: Earth and order. With sixty toys on your floor at any given time, order might be just what you need.

Yellow: Wisdom, joy, and happiness. Joy and happiness you've got (you're a mom, after all), but the wisdom might not kick in until later.

Green: Life and fertility. Looking to have number two/three/four? Sport some green on your next date night.

Blue: Youth, spirituality, truth, and peace. What mom couldn't use any (or all) of those things?

Purple: Royalty and magic. You deserve to be treated like a queen, so don some purple, your majesty!

Indigo: Intuition and meditation. A tad more intuition never hurt!

White: Purity and cleanliness. Can a few white beads turn your sloppy sweetheart into a super-clean cutie?

Gray: Maturity and security. Not that you want your little guy growing up too fast, but security—I'll take some!

BOYS AND GIRLS ON THE HOOD

TIME. YOU JUST DON'T HAVE ENOUGH OF IT TO WASTE ONE more minute trying to figure out which one of the forty nearly identical strollers in the pile-up at Gymboree is yours! Admit it, the only thing that stops you from grabbing the first wheeling mass that unfolds and breaking for the door is the bag of potato chips you stashed in the bottom basket. The good news is that you can avoid all of this frustration (as well as your naughty purloining thoughts) with a little bit of bling. Accessorize your stroller with a shiny charm pin that screams to all of the hungry and frustrated moms rifling through the mass of strollers, "Hands off! I belong to that cool mom over there!" Locate your sparkle, pick it up, unfold it, take out the chips, shove a few in your mouth, and happily stroll away. A little bling goes a long way!

make it:

PREP

1 Sort all of your materials on little plates or bowls. Put colored beads in one, silver charms in another, and so on. Keep them out of your child's reach.

2 Spread out a washcloth or bead board on your working space and decide on the layout of your pin. You can make everything hang at a uniform length or vary the length of each dangle with some link chain.

rate it:

Cost: .... $
Time: .... ⏰ ⏰ ⏰
Skill: .... ✂ ✂ ✂
✂

How ga-ga they'll go: ... ♥ ♥ ♥ ♥

Be prepared: Stroller-free people (like your mom or mother-in-law) might commission you to make one for their jean jackets.

need it:

✔ Plates or bowls
✔ Assorted beads
✔ Photo charms (see page 219)
✔ Charms (silver, silver-plated, enamel, glass, or rhinestone)
✔ Washcloth (or flocked bead board)
✔ Big metal pin
✔ Silver- or gold-tone link chain
✔ Head pins
✔ Round-nose pliers
✔ Chain-nose pliers
✔ 5 to 10 assorted jump rings
✔ Eye pins
✔ Alphabet beads with vertical holes (optional)

Punk up your Maclaren with a fun and fabulous charm pin.

3 Use your round-nose pliers to make any charms you want out of beads and head pins (see page 34). Gather them along with the photo charms you created by following the steps on page 219.

ASSEMBLE

4 Attach each charm that you want to dangle from the pin to the end of a small piece of appropriately sized link chain with chain-nose pliers and a jump ring.

5 Attach each charm to your pin with a jump ring (see box, right). Make sure to "over-close" your jump rings so they don't fall off.

FINISH

6 Pin your creation onto the canopy of your stroller, the top of your diaper bag, or the lapel of your blazer, and head on over to your baby's music class.

pin theory

How and where you attach your beads and charms all depends on the kind of pin you're using. Each kind has its own quirks, so beware!

Blanket Pin, Kilt/Skirt Pin, Diaper Pin

Attach your jump rings and dangles to the side of the pin that *does not* open, so all of your bling doesn't fall off each time you open up the pin.

Charm Pin with Loops

Some metal kilt pins have little circles attached to one side. Hang your dangles from jump rings looped through the circles. Or, attach some jump rings and dangles between the loops.

Charm Pin

Some craft stores sell packs of large metal pins that look like safety pins without the circle at one end. Open up the pin, place beads over the sharp point, and pull them around to the other side (so they won't slip off when the pin's open).

variations:

The Dazzle's in the Details

There are all sorts of different ways to make your pin shine.

- For a long and glitzy dangle at the end, put several beads on a long headpin.
- For a long and glitzy dangle that features a charm, put several beads on a long eye pin and attach a charm to the end of it.
- Hang more than one charm from a jump ring.

- Hang dangles of varying lengths from the same jump ring.
- Create links out of your beads and eye pins. Attach several bead links together and hang a charm off the end.
- Use letter beads with vertical holes to spell out your child's name, nickname, or initials.
- Attach a charm onto one or two of the links of a dangling chain, as well as on its bottom link.

CRAFTYPEDIA

A to Z, every item and tool a Crafty Mama needs, how much it costs, and where to get it.

What happens when you've made a cute No-Sew Mohawk hat and don't know what to do with your remaining five yards of fleece fabric? What else can you make with the little foam brush you bought to decoupage the Little Hang-Ups closet set? And what exactly *is* a toggle clasp? The following is a glossary of sorts, where I've included every tool and material needed to complete any project in this book—plus where to buy them, how much they should cost (without you getting ripped off), and what projects they're associated with. So that when you turn to "fleece" under

F, you'll see that with those extra folds of fabric you can make a no-sew pillow, quilt, blanket, poncho, or two more kinds of hats for your munchkin! Some things to keep in mind: The prices I mention do not include tax or shipping costs added to online orders. (Most items are so inexpensive, they're not worth the shipping!) So, if you do buy online—I know, sometimes it's hard to get the little guy bundled up and out of the house to the nearest craft superstore—make your purchase the most cost-effective by buying in bulk. And always, always look for coupons!

ACRYLIC PAINT

WHAT: Acrylics are the best paints to use on wood, fabric, and metal. They're safe, fast drying, and water-resistant (when dry). Dilute them with water to make them sheer, or layer on several coats for an opaque look. Brands I love: Delta Ceramcoat, Jo-Ann Craft Essentials, Folk Art, Anita's.
WHERE: Craft, fabric, mass merchant stores; online.
HOW MUCH: 50 cents to $3 for a 2-ounce bottle.
PROJECTS: Think Inside the Box, Decou-Pail, Shape Up!

ACRYLIC SEALANT

See Clear Acrylic Finish Spray.

ALEENE'S TACKY GLUE

WHAT: This white, sticky stuff is essentially hard-core Elmer's Glue. It's thicker and stickier, but not much more expensive. Every crafter should have a bottle on hand.
WHERE: Craft, mass merchant stores; online.
HOW MUCH: About $4 for an 8-ounce bottle.
PROJECTS: Think Inside the Box, CD Snuggly, Lite the Nite, Shape Up!

ALLIGATOR CLIPS

WHAT: A lot like the clips your hairdresser uses when sectioning off your hair for a cut, these are smaller and less pointy. The two flat metal pieces of the barrette open and close on a hinge, which look, when pinched open, like an alligator's mouth.
WHERE: Mass merchant, dollar, beauty supply stores; pharmacies.
HOW MUCH: $1 to $4 for a multi-pack.
PROJECT: Ribbon Wrappuccino.

ALL-PURPOSE SCISSORS

WHAT: All-purpose scissors are great for cutting, well, just about anything except fabric.
WHERE: Craft, fabric, mass merchant stores; online.
HOW MUCH: $2 to $5, but no more!
PROJECTS: Little Hang-Ups, Think Inside the Box, Decou-Pail, Pocket Book, You-tencils, Vinyl Diner Bib, I Dream of Jeany Bib, Miracle Plate, Foto-Mat, Photo Bragnets, No-Time Frame, Hip Purse, My Bragamuffin Brag Book, Shape Up!, Photo a-Go-Go, Album à la Neck.

ALPHABET BEADS

WHAT: There are more types of alphabet beads than there are letters in the alphabet! They come in a variety of shapes, sizes, materials, and colors, and are available by the letter or by the pack. Brands I love: Darice's AlphaBeads, Westrim Alphabet Beads, Oriental Trading Company.
WHERE: Craft, bead stores; online (www.orientaltrading.com).
HOW MUCH: $4 for about 150 pieces.

PROJECTS: Think Inside the Box, Little Hang-Ups, Lite the Nite, You-tencils, Insta-Bib, Boys and Girls on the Hood, Ribbon Wrappuccino, Oh So Bow-tiful, Bootie-licious, No-Time Frame, Hip Purse, Photo a-Go-Go. *See also* Beads, Letters.

BABY

WHAT: Cute, precious, living being that likes to wake up during the night. (You'll need him or her for inspiration and for measuring.)
WHERE: This item is not available online or in stores, but can be made available in utero.
HOW MUCH: Priceless.
PROJECTS: Every single one!

BABY MEMENTOS

WHAT: Sweet little items like a positive pregnancy stick, your hospital bracelet, a lock of hair, the "It's a Boy" card that was in his bassinet at the hospital, his first booties, a silver spoon or rattle, his first comb, the striped hospital hat, and so on.
WHERE: Wherever they've been stashed.
HOW MUCH: Priceless.
PROJECT: Think Inside the Box.

BALL CHAIN

WHAT: If you ever had a dangling lightbulb in your closet or wore a dog tag in the eighth grade, you know

what this is. I use it on my jewelry projects because it's sturdy, cheap, and easy to work with. It comes in a variety of different colors and sizes, but try to get some that's 1.5mm to 2.3mm. If the thin sizes aren't available, buy one that has eight balls per inch and use it with large-hole beads.
WHERE: Hardware, craft, bead stores.
HOW MUCH: 50 cents to $1.50 per foot.
PROJECT: Photo a-Go-Go.

BALL CHAIN CLASP
WHAT: This clasp attaches to both ends of a ball chain to finish it. When shopping for one, make sure to buy the right size clasp to match the chain (otherwise it won't close properly). Also, look for those with a hole going through them, so a jump ring can be easily attached.
WHERE: Hardware, craft, bead stores.
HOW MUCH: 25 to 50 cents per clasp.
PROJECT: Photo a-Go-Go.
See also Jewelry Findings.

BANDANA
WHAT: A 21" square of fabric that you used to sport as a headband (*Xanadu*-style in the '80s or do-rag–style in the '90s).
WHERE: Craft, fabric, mass merchant, camping, dollar stores; pharmacies, street vendors; online.
HOW MUCH: $1 to $2, but no more! Buy them in a pack for a great deal.
PROJECT: Diaperlope.

BARRETTES
See Alligator Clips, Snap Clips, Double-Bar or Single-Bar Barrettes.

BASE BEADS
WHAT: Base beads are the staple bead of bracelets. Usually, they're round or square (but are available in other shapes), and made of plain gold- or silver-tone. Make sure the hole size of the base bead is *bigger* than the size of your ball chain.
WHERE: Craft stores, bead stores, online (search "silver-tone metal bead," "silvertone metal bead," or "base metal bead").
HOW MUCH: $2 to $5 for a package of 50.
PROJECT: Photo a-Go-Go.
See also Beads.

BEADED TRIM
WHAT: This dangly delight is a piece of ribbon with beaded fringe hanging down from it. Sold by the pack or yard.
WHERE: Craft, fabric, mass merchant stores.
HOW MUCH: $1.99 to $3.99 per yard.
PROJECTS: CD Snuggly, Lite the Nite, Little Hang-ups, The Better Bolder Wipey Holder, Hasta la Poncho, Bootie-licious, No-time Frame.
See also Ribbon, Trim.

BEADS
WHAT: Glass, plastic, wooden, metal, or ceramic shapes, big or little, that

have a hole in them to stick some string or wire through. (Or . . . drips of sweat that appear on your forehead when you're holding a screaming baby and trying to fold your stroller.)
WHERE: Craft, fabric, bead, mass merchant, dollar stores; pharmacies; online.
HOW MUCH: Depends on quantity and material.
PROJECTS: You-tencils, Ribbon Wrappucino, I love the 80 Barrettes, Bootie-licious, Photo a-Go-Go, Album à la Neck, Boys and Girls on the Hood.
See also Alphabet Beads, Base Beads, Charms, Foam Beads, Glass Beads, Large-Hole Beads, Photo Charms, Pony Beads, Spacer Beads.

BIB
WHAT: Piece of cloth that attempts to protect baby's shirt from getting smeared with smushed peas/blueberries/spaghetti/chocolate pudding/gooey teething biscuits. Some have better coverage than others, so trace your favorite one when making the projects below.
WHERE: Baby, dollar, mass merchant, department stores, pharmacies; online.
HOW MUCH: 50 cents to $8.
PROJECTS: Vinyl Diner Bib, I Dream of Jeany Bib.

BIRTH ANNOUNCEMENT
WHAT: Card that announces your baby's birth. But you already know

that, because you spent hours laboring over which one to choose, and then days addressing them to everyone that you (and your mom and your mother-in-law) know!

WHERE: Stationery, mass merchant stores; baby superstores; online.

HOW MUCH: It really depends on the paper type, printer costs, number of announcements . . .

PROJECT: Think Inside the Box.

BLANKET PIN

WHAT: A big metal pin that looks just like the pins you used to wear on your plaid skirts in seventh grade. When using a blanket pin as a charm pin, make sure to put the charms on the side of the pin that *doesn't* open.

WHERE: Fabric, craft, mass merchant stores; online (search "blanket pin").

HOW MUCH: 50 cents to $1.

PROJECT: Boys and Girls on the Hood.

See also Charm Pin, Diaper Pin, Skirt Pin.

BOOKS (LABEL BOOKS, CLIP ART BOOKS, DECOUPAGE BOOKS)

WHAT: Books (sometimes packaged with a CD-ROM) that offer royalty-free images specifically for craft or decoupage purposes. They may feature advertisements, cool designs from the 1950s, food and clothing labels, retro vehicles, and more.

WHERE: Craft, art supply stores;

online (search "permission-free designs," "royalty-free images," or "copyright-free images").

HOW MUCH: Less than $10.

PROJECTS: Little Hang-Ups, Miracle Plate, Decou-Pail, No-Time Frame, Foto-Mat.

BOOKS (OLD)

WHAT: Wondering what to do with that fifth copy of *Goodnight Moon*? Cut it up and decoupage it onto a bucket, of course! Buy current or retro titles but avoid the board books; they're too thick!

WHERE: Your closet; garage sales; flea markets; thrift, dollar, mass merchant stores; bookstores; mom's house, etc.

HOW MUCH: Free to $1. (You're going to chop it up, so don't pay more!)

PROJECTS: Decou-Pail, Miracle Plate, Foto-Mat, No-Time Frame. *See also* Decoupage Pictures.

BRAIDED ELASTIC

WHAT: Don't be confused by the word "braided." This regular old elastic is the same elastic that's in the waistband of all your sweats. Buy it by the yard or in a pack. It comes in black or white in a variety of widths—from ⅛" on up.

WHERE: Dollar, craft, fabric, mass merchant stores; pharmacies; supermarkets.

HOW MUCH: $1 to $3 for 2 yards.

PROJECT: Pimp My Ride, The Ten-Minute Tutu.

BUTTONS

WHAT: Plastic, glass, or metal things that keep your shirt closed so nobody sees your flabby (but soon to be flat and fabulous) stomach! They come in all shapes, materials, and sizes, and are sold by the bag or on a card.

WHERE: Craft, fabric, mass merchant, dollar stores; online (search "sew-on buttons").

HOW MUCH: 5 cents to $5.

PROJECTS: Little Hang-Ups, Think Inside the Box, Decou-pail, CD Snuggly, Lite the Nite, Insta-Bib, Wipey Clutch, The Better Bolder Wipey Holder, Tutti Bella Fontanella, Ribbon Wrappuccino, Oh So Bowtiful, Bootie-licious, Fringe 'Flops, No-Time Frame, Hip Purse, My Bragamuffin Brag Book, Shape Up!

CALENDARS

WHAT: Even though the world has gone digital, good old paper calendars still exist! The little, chunky Page-A-Day™ calendars are fantastic for decoupage because the paper is thin, and they often have at least 365 great images or quotes to choose from. Wall calendars, too, have great images, but the pages can be a little too thick. Better to save those for wrapping up a decoupaged gift!

WHERE: Bookstores; craft, mass merchant, dollar stores; online.

HOW MUCH: Free if you're using the

previous year's calendar.

PROJECTS: Little Hang-Ups, Decou-Pail, Miracle Plate, Foto-Mat, No-Time Frame.

See also Decoupage Pictures.

CATALOGS

WHAT: Just because you can't buy everything for your child doesn't mean you can't decoupage pictures of all those things onto a toy storage box. Catalogs are filled with all the stuff kids love: jungle gyms, big colorful balls, dolls, costumes, towels, and dazzling jewels. Why spend when you can decoupage?

WHERE: Your mailbox, your neighbor's mailbox, stores.

HOW MUCH: Free!

PROJECTS: Little Hang-Ups, Decou-Pail, Miracle Plate, Foto-Mat, No-Time Frame.

See also Decoupage Pictures.

CD CASE/CD WALLET

WHAT: Square or round case that looks sort of like a photo album, but holds CDs or DVDs instead of pictures.

WHERE: Music, electronic, mass merchant, dollar stores; Ikea; online (search "CD wallet").

HOW MUCH: Don't pay more than $3!

PROJECT: CD Snuggly.

CHAIN-NOSE PLIERS

WHAT: If you have needle-nose pliers in your tool box, check to see if the

inside of the metal "nose" is serrated (with little line grooves). If it is, then you are the proud owner of chain-nose pliers. The little serrated ridges are great for gripping onto metal to make it bend, twist, and crimp. Use them carefully, however, because the little serrated grooves can leave unwanted marks on your metal.

WHERE: Hardware, mass merchant, craft, bead, dollar stores; online (search "jewelry pliers").

HOW MUCH: Less than $8.

PROJECTS: You-tencils, Photo a-Go-Go, Album à la Neck, Boys and Girls on the Hood, and assorted projects around the house.

CHARM PIN

WHAT: A metal, double-bar pin that's more than 1½" long, closes at one end, and has little hoops attached to one bar specifically for hanging charms (sometimes called a "charm pin with loops"). Available in a variety of different lengths in both gold- and silver-tone (or real gold and sterling silver!).

WHERE: Craft, bead, fabric, dollar stores; online (www.orientaltrading .com).

HOW MUCH: $1 to $3 per pin.

PROJECT: Boys and Girls on the Hood.

See also Blanket Pin, Diaper Pin, Skirt Pin.

CHARMS

WHAT: Charming little things with a loop on top to dangle off bracelets, necklaces, earrings, and pins. They come in silver-tone, gold-tone, or glass, with enamel, rhinestone, or beaded accents. Some come with a jump ring attached, so they can hang right onto each creation, but others must be manually attached. When shopping, don't just look in the jewelry findings aisle; check out the scrapbook and card-making aisles, too, since they both have great charms!

WHERE: Department and jewelry stores (for pricey gold and sterling silver charms); craft, bead, mass merchant stores, or online (www .orientaltrading.com) for inexpensive ones.

HOW MUCH: Less than $1 per charm.

PROJECTS: You-tencils, Photo a-Go-Go, Album à la Neck, Boys and Girls on the Hood.

See also Beads, Photo Charms.

CLASPS

See Jewelry Findings, Lobster Claw Clasp, Spring Clasp, Toggle Clasp.

CLEAR ACRYLIC FINISH SPRAY (MATTE OR GLOSS)

WHAT: This clear spray provides a permanent, nontoxic, protective coating that's moisture-resistant and smudge-proof. I prefer the "Low-Odor Finish" by Krylon because it's not as smelly as other ones—and with all those dirty diapers around, who needs more stink?

WHERE: Craft, hardware, art supply, mass merchant stores.

HOW MUCH: About $4 per can.

PROJECTS: Miracle Plate, No-Time Frame, Shape Up!

CLEAR CONTACT PAPER/ LAMINATING PAPER

WHAT: Transparent paper that's sticky on one side. Some people use it to line their shelves; I use it to make placemats and books, and to laminate the "emergency cards" that I made for my diaper bag, kitchen, and wallet. Buy it on a roll or by the sheet.

WHERE: Hardware, mass merchant, craft, office supply, dollar stores; pharmacies; supermarkets.

HOW MUCH: A large roll is about $10 (and that makes about fourteen placemats with extra left over).

PROJECTS: Pocket Book, Foto-Mat.

CLEAR NAIL POLISH

WHAT: I'm pretty sure you know what clear nail polish is—even if you haven't done your nails in more than nine months! For the sake of these crafts, your safety, and the environment, use a polish that's phthalate-free (that's the bad thing in most nail polishes). Good brands are: L'Oreal Paris Jet-Set Quick Dry Nail Enamel, Maybelline Shades of You Nail Color, Naturistics 90 Second Dry!, Revlon Nail Enamel, Revlon

Super Top Speed, and Urban Decay.

WHERE: Pharmacies; supermarkets; mass merchant, beauty supply stores.

HOW MUCH: $4 per bottle.

PROJECTS: Foxy Boxes, Photo a-Go-Go, Album à la Neck, Boys and Girls on the Hood, Hip Purse.

CLEAR PLASTIC PLATES OR BOWLS

WHAT: Plastic plates or bowls that are transparent. The really hard ones are great, but watch out for a little plastic "navel" in the center of them. (It can cut right into your decoupage.) I like the Solo plates, which come in a few different sizes with different designs around the rim.

WHERE: Party supply, mass merchant, dollar stores; supermarkets.

HOW MUCH: $5 for a 25-pack.

PROJECT: Miracle Plate.

CLIP ART

See Books (Label Books, Clip Art Books, Decoupage Books).

CLOTHESPIN

WHAT: Little wooden (or plastic) fastener that holds wet laundry to a clothesline! Or, in our case, used to twist your T-shirt to make a swirly tie-dye.

WHERE: Mass merchant, craft, hardware, dollar stores; supermarkets; pharmacies.

HOW MUCH: $2.50 for a 25-pack.

PROJECT: To Dye For.

COAT/JACKET (CHILD-SIZE)

WHAT: Your baby's outerwear, used for sizing his fabulous new poncho.

WHERE: Baby's closet.

HOW MUCH: I hope you didn't pay full price! Most kid's coats go on sale before it's really even time to wear them.

PROJECT: Hasta la Poncho.

COLOR INK-JET PRINTER

WHAT: That big thing that's been collecting dust on your desk for the last few months. If it's a photo printer or an "all-in-one" printer, that's cool. If it's black-and-white, that'll work too. If it's a laser printer, make sure your iron-on transfer paper is for laser printers or it won't work!

WHERE: Electronic, mass merchant stores; online (try www.froogle .com for great deals).

HOW MUCH: You can get a brand-new color ink-jet printer for $25. It's not the best printer in the universe, but it will make cute iron-ons of the Fonz and your little hunk! If you spend more, ask about a rebate.

PROJECTS: Schleppy, Pocket Book, Foxy Boxes, CD Snuggly, Miracle Plate, Foto-Mat, Wipey Clutch, Diaperlope, Daily Dose of Iron, Photo Bragnets, Hip Purse, My Bragamuffin Brag Book, Shape Up!, Photo a-Go-Go, Album à la Neck, Boys and Girls on the Hood.

COMICS AND COMIC BOOKS

WHAT: Use new or old *Archie, Superman, Cathy*, or *Yu-Gi-Oh!* comics to decoupage onto buckets, frames, stools, hangers, dressers, picture frames, and more.
WHERE: Garage sales, thrift shops, the Sunday paper, or the back of your old closet at Mom's house.
HOW MUCH: Free to hundreds of bucks! (Find the free ones; chances are, you don't want to cut up the $75 one.)
PROJECTS: Little Hang-Ups, Decou-Pail, Miracle Plate, No-Time Frame.

COMPUTER

WHAT: Electronic thing that you spend way too much time in front of— blogging about your kids, browsing online sales, or reading celebrity gossip! Macs and PCs work equally well for all of the projects in this book.
WHERE: Your kitchen, den, bedroom —wherever it is.
HOW MUCH: Hopefully, you've already got it.
PROJECTS: Schleppy, Pocket Book, Foxy Boxes, CD Snuggly, Miracle Plate, Foto-Mat, Wipey Clutch, Diaperlope, Daily Dose of Iron, Photo Bragnets, Hip Purse, My Bragamuffin Brag Book, Shape Up!, Photo a-Go-Go, Album à la Neck, Boys and Girls on the Hood.

COTTON QUILTING FABRIC

WHAT: Even-weave, cotton fabric, like the stuff you'd use to make a skirt or shirt (or a quilt, for that matter). You can find nearly any print under the sun, from sock monkeys to cupcakes, plaids to batiks. This stuff is so easy and fun to work with, it may even inspire you to take up sewing!
WHERE: Fabric, craft, mass merchant stores; online.
HOW MUCH: $5 and up per yard.
PROJECTS: Pocket Book, Foxy Boxes, Lite the Nite, Vinyl Diner Bib, The Better Bolder Wipey Holder, Diaperlope, Fringe 'Flops, My Bragamuffin Brag Book.

CRAFT SCISSORS

See Decorative-Edge Scissors.

CRAFT WIRE

WHAT: Moldable, soft wire that comes in many gauges and colors, on a spool or on a roll, even water- and tarnish-resistant! And if you run out of eye pins, you can create them using this malleable wire.
WHERE: Craft, bead, mass merchant stores; online.
HOW MUCH: Less than $5 a roll.
PROJECT: You-tencils.

CRIMP COILS

WHAT: Got silk, satin, or leather cord? You can easily turn any one of them into a necklace with crimp coils! Just shove (I say "shove," because it *should* be hard to get it in) one end of the cord into the crimp coil as far as it can go. Then squeeze the very last coil into the cord with chain-nose pliers. Just make sure to buy crimp coils that are the right size for the cord being used.
WHERE: Craft, bead, mass merchant stores; online.
HOW MUCH: $3 for about ten.
PROJECT: Album à la Neck.
See also Jewelry Findings.

CUTICLE SCISSORS

WHAT: Those cute little scissors with the curved blades that most people use to cut their cuticles. But the curved edges of these scissor blades also cut paper on an angle, which makes the edges of images more decoupage-friendly!
WHERE: Pharmacies; nail salons; mass merchant, dollar stores; online.
HOW MUCH: Less than $5.
PROJECTS: Little Hang-Ups, Decou-Pail, Miracle Plate, No-Time Frame, Shape Up!

CUTTING MAT

See Rotary Cutter and Cutting Mat.

DECORATIVE-EDGE SCISSORS

WHAT: Chunky scissors with shaped blades to create decorative (scalloped, wavy, zigzag) edges on paper. The blades come in many patterns (arabesque, torn paper, zipper, volcano, cupid's bow—to name a few) and are sold individually or in sets.

It takes some practice to make the pattern continuous using multiple cuts. Aside from pinking shears (zigzag cuts), they're better on paper than fabric.

WHERE: Craft, stationery, mass merchant stores; online.

HOW MUCH: Less than $3 (I once bought 8 pairs at 99 cents each!).

PROJECTS: Little Hang-Ups, Think Inside the Box, Decou-Pail, Miracle Plate, No-Time Frame, My Bragamuffin Brag Book.

DECORATIVE HEAD PIN OR LARGE-TIP HEAD PIN

WHAT: Normally the "head" on a head pin is just plain flat (like a nail used in carpentry), but the head on this head pin is embellished, or decorative. Some even have rhinestones.

WHERE: Craft, bead, mass merchant stores; online (search "jewelry findings" and then search for "ball head pins," "bali-style head pins," "crystal head pins," "rhinestone head pins," or "large head pins").

HOW MUCH: About $3 for six.

PROJECTS: You-Tencils, Photo a-Go-Go, Album à la Neck, Boys and Girls on the Hood.

See also Head Pin, Jewelry Findings.

DECORATIVE TRIM

See Ribbon, Trim.

DECOUPAGABLE ITEM

WHAT: A picture frame, mirror,

dresser, step stool, bucket, box, plate: It's anything (big or small) that could be transformed into a masterpiece with some white glue and cute paper. Pretty much any material can be decoupaged—unfinished wood, painted wood, glass, plastic, or metal.

WHERE: Your home; dollar, craft, mass merchant, thrift, department, art supply stores; flea markets; supermarkets.

HOW MUCH: Depends on what's being decoupaged.

PROJECTS: Little Hang-Ups, Decou-Pail, Miracle Plate, No-Time Frame, Shape Up!

See also Decoupage Pictures.

DECOUPAGE MEDIUM/ DECOUPAGE GLUE

WHAT: Decoupage medium looks like regular white glue, but it's actually got some special ingredients in it to make it thicker and stronger (and more expensive). It comes in several different finishes: "matte" dries flat, muted and mod; "gloss" dries super-glossy with a lotta shine; "semi-gloss" dries with more of a sheen than matte but less than gloss; and "sparkle" has a touch of glitter in it to 'zazz up your stuff. There are a slew of different brands, but the ones I keep going back for are Mod Podge, Royal Coat Decoupage Finish, and Aleene's Instant Decoupage.

WHERE: Craft, mass merchant stores; online.

HOW MUCH: $5 per jar.

PROJECTS: Little Hang-Ups, Decou-Pail, Miracle Plate, No-Time Frame, Shape Up!

DECOUPAGE PICTURES

WHAT: Any thin, illustrated or patterned papers that can be cut or ripped and permanently affixed to a decoupagable item! Look for pictures around the house in books, brochures, catalogs, calendars, comic books, clip art books, magazines, candy wrappers, wrapping paper, photos, posters, wallpaper, or stickers. Or, go online, search for cool copyright-free images (snails, Elvis, Leaning Tower of Pisa), save them to your images folder, size them, and print them for decoupage!

WHERE: Your home; craft, stationery, art supply, mass merchant stores; online.

HOW MUCH: Free, about 50 cents per sheet for pretty papers, about $10 each for clip art and decoupage books.

PROJECTS: Little Hang-Ups, Decou-Pail, Miracle Plate, No-Time Frame, Shape Up!

See also Books (old), Calendars, Catalogs, Comics and Comic Books, Decoupagable Item, Die-cuts, Magazines, Online Fabric Swatchers, Packaging, Posters, Scrapbook Papers, Stickers, Wallpaper, Wrapping Paper.

DENIM

See Old Pair of Jeans.

DIAPER PIN

WHAT: Environmentally conscious mamas might be familiar with diaper pins, and probably have them around the house, but for those of us who use disposables, a diaper pin is just a large metal safety pin. Sometimes they have plastic tops with cute baby decals on them, but for crafting purposes, stick to the plain metal ones.

WHERE: Mass merchant, dollar, fabric, craft stores; pharmacies.

HOW MUCH: $2 for 4.

PROJECT: Boys and Girls on the Hood.

See also Blanket Pin, Charm Pin, Skirt Pin.

DIAPER WIPE BOX

WHAT: Big, horrific-looking plastic rectangular thing that mamas reach into about eleven times per day!

WHERE: Probably right next to the changing table.

HOW MUCH: Less than $5.

PROJECT: The Better Bolder Wipey Holder.

DIE-CUTS

WHAT: These look just like stickers, but they're not sticky on the back—they're just paper. Get some retro designs of cherubic angels or steam engines, or more modern hard hats and hula dancers. If you color copy a few sheets, there will be enough to make several matching projects.

Sold individually or by the pack.

WHERE: Craft, stationery, art supply stores; online (search "die-cut").

HOW MUCH: $1 to $5.

PROJECTS: Little Hang-Ups, Decou-Pail, Miracle Plate, No-Time Frame, Shape Up!

See also Decoupage Pictures.

DISPOSABLE PLATES OR BOWLS

WHAT: Paper or plastic dishes that can be thrown away, but instead, save them and use them to sort your craft ingredients from week to week. Display beads, squeeze excess dye, show off rhinestones, or pile glass globs in the bowls. Lay out trim, arrange charm pins, line up clasps, or spread out alphabet letters on the plates.

WHERE: Your pantry; supermarkets; pharmacies; dollar, mass merchant, party stores; online.

HOW MUCH: Buy the cheapest ones out there.

PROJECTS: Most!

DOUBLE-BAR OR SINGLE-BAR BARRETTES

WHAT: Each barrette is a metal or plastic clip whose top is a flat, unbendy bar (or two bars, hence the "double") that curls under on one end and bends into a joint on the other, so it looks like the metal is folded in half. Single- and double-bar barrettes

are bigger, and more powerful, hair-fastening-wise than other clips, and were super-popular in the '80s with middle schoolers.

WHERE: Mass merchant, dollar, beauty supply stores; pharmacies.

HOW MUCH: $1 to $4 for a 3-pack.

PROJECT: I Love the '80s Barrettes.

DOUBLE-SIDED TAPE

WHAT: Transparent tape that's sticky on both sides. Buy the clear stuff for items that should stick flat. Buy the foam stuff for those that should be raised a little.

WHERE: Office supply, craft, mass merchant stores; pharmacies; supermarkets.

HOW MUCH: $2.50 to $4 per roll.

PROJECT: Think Inside the Box.

ELASTIC

See Braided Elastic.

ELASTIC HEADBAND

WHAT: It looks like an oversize ponytail holder, but it's really a headband. These come in many colors and patterns, and not only do they hold back your kid's growing-out bangs, they make a great waistband for a tutu.

WHERE: Dollar, mass merchant stores, Claire's; pharmacies.

HOW MUCH: $1 to $3 for a pack of 3.

PROJECT: The Ten-Minute Tutu.

EMBELLISHMENTS

WHAT: Beaded trim, fringe trim, gimp trim, pompom trim, marabou trim, twisted satin cord, tassels, sequins, ribbon (jacquard, nylon, grosgrain, satin, organza), rickrack, patches, wooden block letters, scrapbook letters, googly eyes, silk or satin flowers, buttons, pompoms, rhinestones, felt shapes, metal words or phrases, beads, plastic toys or trinkets, and anything else you can glue on your project to make it look even more fabulous.

WHERE: Craft, fabric, mass merchant, dollar, toy, party, bead stores; online (www.orientaltrading.com).

HOW MUCH: 5 cents to $10!

PROJECTS: Almost every project in this book!

See also individual listings.

EYELET PLIERS

WHAT: Big, chunky pliers that are usually used to create eyelets (like the holes in shoes that the laces go through). In this book, use them to punch holes into fleece for hats, blankets, ponchos, and more. I love my Dritz pliers; they're easy to use and the perfect size!

WHERE: Craft, fabric stores; online (search "eyelet plier").

HOW MUCH: From $8 (on sale) to $17. If you have a 40 percent off coupon from Jo-Ann, this is a great thing to use it on!

PROJECTS: Schleppy, Vinyl Diner Bib, Hats Off to Mama, SpongeBob SquareHat, The No-Sew Mohawk, The Poncherello.

EYE PIN

WHAT: This fabulous little piece looks like a sewing needle, but it has a loop instead of a hole at one end. It comes in a variety of lengths, as well as in gold- and silver-tones, and comes in handy for transforming a bead (or beads) into a link for a bracelet, earring, or necklace.

WHERE: Craft, bead, mass merchant stores; online (search "jewelry finding" and then search "eye pin").

HOW MUCH: $3 for a pack of 12.

PROJECTS: Photo a-Go-Go, Album à la Neck, Boys and Girls on the Hood.

FABRIC

See Cotton Quilting Fabric, Felt, Fleece, Home Décor Fabric, Tulle.

FABRIC GLUE STICKS

WHAT: These glue sticks are for hot gluing embellishments to fabric. They can be very sticky, but they're worth the whole gooey hassle because the bond is super-strong and machine-washable. (You can make curtains, attach patches and rhinestones, or even hem your pants using fabric glue sticks!) There is also a slightly longer drying time involved (about 60 seconds, compared with 5 seconds with a regular hot-melt stick), so if it's not positioned correctly, there is some extra time to fix it until it's just right. At this point, they're only sized for large glue guns, and I proudly stand by the Aleene's brand!

WHERE: Craft, fabric stores; online.

HOW MUCH: $2.99 per pack of 12.

PROJECTS: Schleppy, Pocket Book, Foxy Boxes, CD Snuggly, I Dream of Jeany Bib, Insta-Bib, Wipey Clutch, The Better Bolder Wipey Holder, Diaperlope, Pimp My Ride, Tutti Bella Fontanella, Ribbon Wrappuccino, Oh So Bow-tiful, The Poncherello, Hasta la Poncho, Bootie-licious, Fringe 'Flops, Hip Purse, My Bragamuffin Brag Book.

FABRIC MARKERS/PENS

WHAT: Special pens that are permanent on fabric. (Every pen my daughter writes with seems to be permanent on fabric!) Buy special fabric pens or just use plain old Sharpies—but watch out, because they bleed a little! I like the Marvy Fabric Brush Markers because they go on easily and don't run.

WHERE: Craft, fabric, office supply, mass merchant stores; online.

HOW MUCH: $13 for a 6-pack of different colors.

PROJECT: Bootie-licious.

FABRIC PAINT

WHAT: Special paint that is permanent on fabric. It comes in bottles, as spray, in rows of pots, or in liquid pens. The finish can be matte, glossy, puffy, or sparkly. There is also "fabric paint medium" to make acrylic paint good for fabrics. I like Tulip and Delta paints and Americana fabric paint medium.

WHERE: Craft, fabric, mass merchant, art supply stores; online.

HOW MUCH: $2 to $5 for a 4-ounce bottle.

PROJECTS: I Dream of Jeany Bib, Bootie-licious.

FABRIC SCISSORS

WHAT: A nice, sturdy pair of "bent" scissors that cuts easily through fabric. Invest in a good pair of Fiskars scissors, and they'll last for life. I have three pairs of purple-handled Fiskars scissors just because I love them so much!

WHERE: Craft, fabric, mass merchant stores; online.

HOW MUCH: $12 to $15. This is a good item to use that Jo-Ann 40 percent off coupon on.

PROJECTS: No-Sew Swanky Blanky, Schleppy, Pocket Book, Spit-Up Lover Pillow Cover, Foxy Boxes, CD Snuggly, Lite the Nite, Knot in a Hurry Quilt, Vinyl Diner Bib, I Dream of Jeany Bib, Insta-Bib, Wipey Clutch, The Better Bolder Wipey Holder, Diaperlope, Pimp My Ride, Hats Off to Mama, SpongeBob SquareHat, The No-Sew

Mohawk, Tutti Bella Fontanella, Ribbon Wrappuccino, I Love the '80s Barrettes, Oh So Bow-tiful, The Poncherello, Hasta La Poncho, The Ten-Minute Tutu, Bootie-licious, Fringe 'Flops, Transforma-Tee, Hip Purse, My Bragamuffin Brag Book.

FANCY SCISSORS

See Decorative-Edge Scissors.

FAUX SUEDE LACING

WHAT: Suede string that looks like it belongs on a moccasin or drum. It's sold by the yard, roll, or wrapped around a card.

WHERE: Craft, bead, fabric stores; online (search "faux suede lacing").

HOW MUCH: Less than $3.50 for 8 yards.

PROJECT: I Dream of Jeany Bib, Fringe 'Flops.

FEATHER BOA

See Marabou Trim, Trim.

FELT

WHAT: The wool-like fabric that is a first-grade craft staple. It comes in every color of the rainbow now (not just dark green), as well as glittered. It can be bought by the sheet, by the yard, or pre-cut into letters and shapes.

WHERE: Craft, fabric, mass merchant stores; online (www.orientaltrading .com).

HOW MUCH: 30 cents per sheet.

PROJECTS: Schleppy, Pocket Book, CD Snuggly, Tutti Bella Fontanella, Ribbon Wrappuccino.

FELT LETTERS AND SHAPES

WHAT: Pre-cut felt letters and shapes with or without adhesive backing. Nearly any shape under the sun exists in felt, from Noah's Ark to a banana to soccer balls.

WHERE: Craft, fabric stores; online (www.orientaltrading.com).

HOW MUCH: $3 per bag of assorted shapes or letters.

PROJECTS: Schleppy, Pocket Book, CD Snuggly, The Better Bolder Wipey Holder, Tutti Bella Fontanella, Ribbon Wrappuccino, Bootie-licious, My Bragamuffin Brag Book.

See also Letters.

FLAT PAINTBRUSH

WHAT: Invest in a few $3 to $5 brushes (as opposed to the 49- to 99-cent ones). Cheaper brushes leave their bristles behind, and who wants a bunch of black hairs all over a project?

WHERE: Craft, art supply stores; online.

HOW MUCH: $3 to $5.

PROJECTS: Little Hang-Ups, Decou-Pail, Miracle Plate, No-Time Frame, Shape Up!

FLEECE

WHAT: Warm, cozy fabric that can be used to make hats, scarves, ponchos,

and blankets. It's perfect for a Crafty Mama because it doesn't fray when cut, it washes well, and it comes in all sorts of amazing colors and patterns.
WHERE: Fabric stores; online.
HOW MUCH: $2 to $15 per yard.
PROJECTS: No-Sew Swanky Blanky, Schleppy, Pocket Book, Knot in a Hurry Quilt, Spit-Up Lover Pillow Cover, Hats Off to Mama, SpongeBob SquareHat, The No-Sew Mohawk, The Poncherello, Hasta la Poncho, Fringe 'Flops.

FOAM BRUSH
WHAT: An approximately 2" × 3" black foam rectangle with a nice edge and a simple wooden handle. When decoupaging, it leaves fewer glue streaks than a bristled paintbrush.
WHERE: Craft, hardware, art supply stores; online.
HOW MUCH: Less than $1 each.
PROJECTS: Little Hang-Ups, Decou-Pail, Miracle Plate, No-Time Frame, Shape Up!

FOAM DOTS
WHAT: Small foam circles with adhesive on both sides to add dimension to your card-making or scrapbooking. Foam dots are sold on sheets or on tape-like rolls of paper, and come in many sizes. (If you buy the sheets, don't throw away the excess foam; cut it up and use it to decorate projects as well!)

WHERE: Craft, stationery stores; online scrapbooking sites.
HOW MUCH: $3 for about 100 dots (on either sheets or rolls).
PROJECT: Think Inside the Box.

FOAM SHAPES, LETTERS, OR BEADS
WHAT: Pretty self-explanatory, really. They are sold in several different-sized containers, from small bags to large tubs. They need to be hot-glued in order for them to be permanently affixed to something. The sticky backing isn't strong enough to endure little pulling fingers!
WHERE: Craft, stationery, mass merchant stores; online (www.orientaltrading.com).
HOW MUCH: A large tub of about 250 shapes costs around $8.
PROJECT: Little Hang-Ups. No-Time Frame.
See also Letters.

GEMS
See Rhinestones, Gems, or Jewels.

GIMP TRIM
WHAT: A braided trim that is sold by the yard in the home décor department of most fabric stores.
WHERE: Craft, fabric stores; online (search "gimp trim").
HOW MUCH: Less than $2 per yard.
PROJECTS: Lite the Nite, Vinyl

Diner Bib, Wipey Clutch, The Better Bolder Wipey Holder, Diaperlope, Hasta la Poncho, Hip Purse.
See also Ribbon, Trim.

GLASS BEADS
WHAT: You can string them on cord or thick thread to make a bracelet, or use them to make charms (see page 34). Glass beads are available in every imaginable shape, color, and size.
WHERE: Craft, bead, mass merchant, fabric stores; online (search "glass bead").
HOW MUCH: Less than $3 for 15 beads.
PROJECTS: You-tencils, Photo a-Go-Go, Album à la Neck, Boys and Girls on the Hood.
See also Beads.

GLASS GLOBS
WHAT: Glass marbles that are flat on one side. They're made for the bottom of vases and fish tanks, but they make a terrific accent or embellishment on craft projects. Glass globs come in many sizes— small (½"), medium (¾"), large (1" to 1¼"), and jumbo (1½" to 2⅓")— and in nearly every color imaginable, from "ice clear" to "electric brick swirl." They also come in three different finishes: clear, frosted (matte and frosty), and iridescent. They are also available in many shapes, like squares, hearts, stars, or moons. Glass globs are known by several

names: accent marbles, glass gems, glass nuggets, flat marbles, glass gem marbles, craft marbles, crystal accent flats, or vase gems. (You might need to try a few names before someone knows what you're talking about!)
WHERE: Craft, mass merchant, dollar stores; pet shops; online (www .megaglass.com); plant nurseries.
HOW MUCH: $12 for bag of 100.
PROJECTS: Little Hang-Ups, Think Inside the Box, Photo Bragnets, No-Time Frames.

GLITTER GLUE STICKS
WHAT: Specialty glue sticks with flecks of glitter in them (for your hot-glue gun). They're great for a messy gluer because the sparkles make a sloppy glue job look (almost) intentional.
WHERE: Craft, fabric, mass merchant, dollar, office supply stores; online.
HOW MUCH: $2.50 for a 12-pack.
PROJECTS: Little Hang-Ups, CD Snuggly, Wipey Clutch, Tutti Bella Fontanella, Ribbon Wrappuccino, The Ten-Minute Tutu, My Bragamuffin Brag Book.
See also Glue Sticks.

GLUE STICKS
WHAT: Long, cylindrical cartridge sticks of hardened glue that fit into the back of a hot-glue gun. Once the gun is hot, the glue cartridge melts to become a strong adhesive. The big sticks fit in a large glue gun, and the small sticks in a

mini glue gun. See individual entries on specific types of hot glue for more information.
WHERE: Craft, fabric, mass merchant, hardware, dollar, office supply stores; online (search "glue stick").
HOW MUCH: Less than $5 for 50.
PROJECTS: Little Hang-Ups, Schleppy, Think Inside the Box, Decou-pail, Pocket Book, Foxy Boxes, CD Snuggly, Lite the Nite, I Dream of Jeany Bib, Insta-Bib, Wipey Clutch, The Better Bolder Wipey Holder, Diaperlope, Pimp My Ride, SpongeBob SquareHat, Tutti Bella Fontanella, Ribbon Wrappuccino, Oh So Bow-tiful, The Poncherello, Hasta la Poncho, The Ten-Minute Tutu, Bootie-licious, Photo Bragnets, No-Time Frame, Hip Purse, My Bragamuffin Brag Book, Shape Up!
See also Fabric Glue Sticks, Glitter Glue Sticks, Hot-Melt Glue Sticks, Jewelry Glue Sticks.

GOOGLY EYES
WHAT: Little round plastic eyeballs that wiggle when shaken. There are a few different sizes and some even have eyelids and lashes!
WHERE: Craft, fabric, mass merchant, dollar stores; online (search "wiggle eyes" or go to www.orientaltrading .com).
HOW MUCH: Less than $3 for 100.
PROJECTS: Little Hang-Ups, Think Inside the Box, Decou-Pail,

Foxy Boxes, CD Snuggly, Lite the Nite, Insta-Bib, Wipey Clutch, Ribbon Wrappuccino, Oh So Bow-tiful, Hasta la Poncho, Bootie-licious, No-Time Frame.

GROSGRAIN RIBBON
WHAT: Matte-finish ribbon that has little horizontal grooves in it. It comes in a variety of thicknesses and is sold by the yard, the roll, or in a "ribbon assortment" package in the scrapbooking aisle. It may have cute patterns like polka dots or stripes. Most grosgrain ribbon is made out of polyester and is machine-washable.
WHERE: Craft, fabric, mass merchant, stationery stores; online (search "grosgrain ribbon").
HOW MUCH: $2.50 to $5 for a 20-yard roll.
PROJECTS: Little Hang-Ups, Pocket Book, Foxy Boxes, Lite the Nite, Vinyl Diner Bib, Insta-Bib, Pimp My Ride, Ribbon Wrappuccino, Oh So Bow-tiful, Bootie-licious, Fringe 'Flops, Hip Purse, My Bragamuffin Brag Book.

HANGING WALLET/PASSPORT PURSE
WHAT: A thin, simple rectangular purse (preferably made of canvas or denim for the iron-on projects in this book) that closes with a zipper or snap, and hangs off of a long strap.

These purses are generally used while traveling, and are just the right size for credit cards, some cash, and a passport. An oversize canvas coin purse, makeup bag, or pencil case will also do the trick.

WHERE: Craft, dollar, luggage stores; online (try www.orientaltrading.com or search "canvas purse" or "passport bag").

HOW MUCH: Less than $5.

PROJECT: Hip Purse.

HEAD PIN

WHAT: A 1" to 3" piece of straight but malleable metal with a small flat "head" on one end. Head pins are available in gold- and silver-tone, and they are essential for turning beads into charms (see page 34).

WHERE: Craft, bead, mass merchant stores; online (search "jewelry findings" and then "head pins").

HOW MUCH: $2 for 15 pins.

PROJECTS: Photo a-Go-Go, Album à la Neck, Boys and Girls on the Hood. *See also* Jewelry Findings.

HOME DÉCOR ACCENTS

WHAT: Peruse the home décor section of a local craft or fabric store and revel in all of the amazing accents that were meant for curtains and valences. I love gimp trim, fringe trim, braided cord, pompoms, and the terrific tassels.

WHERE: Fabric, home décor, mass merchant stores; online (www.joann

.com or www.fabric.com).

HOW MUCH: $1 to $5 per yard.

PROJECTS: Decou-Pail, CD Snuggly, Lite the Nite, Vinyl Diner Bib, Wipey Clutch, The Better Bolder Wipey Holder, Diaperlope, Ribbon Wrappuccino, Hasta la Poncho, Hip Purse, My Bragamuffin Brag Book.

HOME DÉCOR FABRIC

WHAT: Even-weave, cotton, canvas-like fabric used to decorate around the house—think lightweight upholstery, curtain, and valence fabric. Like quilting cotton, home dec fabric comes in an array of prints and patterns and is relatively easy to work with.

WHERE: Fabric, craft, home décor, and mass merchant stores; Ikea; online.

HOW MUCH: $5 and up per yard, depending on the print and the season.

PROJECTS: Pocket Book, Foxy Boxes, Lite the Nite, Vinyl Diner Bib, Wipey Clutch, The Better Bolder Wipey Holder, Diaperlope, My Bragamuffin Brag Book.

HOOK-AND-LOOP TAPE

WHAT: Hook-and-loop tape is best known by the brand name "Velcro." Although it can actually be hot-glued onto craft projects, it will stay more permanently if it's sewn on. Don't try to save time by using the self-adhesive kind. It doesn't stick

well enough for these projects, and it makes needles too gooey to sew it on!

WHERE: Craft, fabric, mass merchant, dollar stores.

HOW MUCH: $3 for about 18".

PROJECTS: Vinyl Diner Bib, I Dream of Jeany Bib, Diaperlope.

HOT-GLUE GUN

WHAT: A life-changing piece of machinery! Simply plug it in, fit a glue stick into the back, and wait a few minutes for the gun to heat up. Then, save hours by simply squeezing the trigger—no sewing necessary! There are large glue guns, mini ones, cordless ones, guns with interchangeable nozzle attachments, hot-melt or cool-melt versions, and many more. I love the Aleene's and Stanley brands.

WHERE: Hardware, craft, fabric, office supply, dollar, electronic stores; online.

HOW MUCH: From $1 for a mini gun to $25 for a large gun with several nozzle attachments.

PROJECTS: Little Hang-Ups, Schleppy, Think Inside the Box, Decou-Pail, Pocket Book, Foxy Boxes, CD Snuggly, Lite the Nite, Vinyl Diner Bib, I Dream of Jeany Bib, Insta-Bib, Wipey Clutch, The Better Bolder Wipey Holder, Diaperlope, Pimp My Ride, SpongeBob SquareHat, Tutti Bella Fontanella, Ribbon Wrappuccino, Oh So Bow-tiful, The Poncherello,

Hasta la Poncho, The Ten-Minute Tutu, Bootie-licious, Photo Bragnets, No-Time Frame, Hip Purse, My Bragamuffin Brag Book, Shape Up! *See also* Large Hot-Glue Gun, Mini Hot-Glue Gun

HOT-MELT GLUE STICKS

WHAT: Glue sticks that are specifically made for a hot-melt glue gun. Available for both large and mini glue guns.

WHERE: Craft, hardware, dollar, fabric, mass merchant, office supply stores; online.

HOW MUCH: $1 for a 6-pack.

PROJECTS: Little Hang-Ups, Schleppy, Think Inside the Box, Decou-Pail, Pocket Book, Foxy Boxes, CD Snuggly, Lite the Nite, Vinyl Diner Bib, I Dream of Jeany Bib, Insta-Bib, Wipey Clutch, The Better Bolder Wipey Holder, Diaperlope, Pimp My Ride, SpongeBob SquareHat, Tutti Bella Fontanella, Ribbon Wrappuccino, Oh So Bow-tiful, The Poncherello, Hasta la Poncho, The Ten-Minute Tutu, Bootie-licious, Photo Bragnets, No-Time Frame, Hip Purse, My Bragamuffin Brag Book, Shape Up!

INK-JET TRANSFER PAPER FOR DARK-COLOR FABRICS

WHAT: This iron-on transfer paper is made for use on bright- or dark-colored fabrics, and thicker fabrics as well. When ironed on, it looks like a '70s-style iron-on, like an actual photograph adhering to fabric. These iron-ons don't need to be reversed during the printing process, and the images are more clear and vibrant than those on light-colored transfer paper. However, this paper is also two to three times more expensive than paper for light-colored tees. Plus, this kind of paper is also a bit smelly when ironed, so open a window when working with it. I have found that Avery brand paper works really well, and is pretty reasonably priced.

WHERE: Craft, office supply stores; online (www.staples.com).

HOW MUCH: $15 for five 8½" × 11" sheets.

PROJECTS: Foxy Boxes, CD Snuggly, Wipey Clutch, The Better Bolder Wipey Holder, Diaperlope, Daily Dose of Iron, Bootie-licious, Hip Purse, My Bragamuffin Brag Book.

INK-JET TRANSFER PAPER FOR LIGHT-COLOR FABRICS

WHAT: This iron-on transfer paper works best for text, photos, or designs on white or light-colored cotton or cotton/polyester blend fabrics. When ironed on, the image looks more like a silk-screen print, rather than a traditional, rubbery iron-on. If a garment has ribbing, the ink won't adhere to the little grooves, so the print looks cracked when the ribbing is stretched. This type of paper (Avery brand paper's the best!) makes designs look a little distressed, in a stylish "I-paid-good-money-for-a-pair-of-ripped-jeans" kind of way. The thing to know about this paper is that designs must be printed *in reverse*. I've messed up many a tee by forgetting this little detail.

WHERE: Craft, office supply stores; online (www.staples.com).

HOW MUCH: $15 for ten 8½" × 11" sheets.

PROJECTS: Schleppy, Foxy Boxes, CD Snuggly, Wipey Clutch, The Better Bolder Wipey Holder, Diaperlope, Daily Dose of Iron, Bootie-licious.

IRON

WHAT: Metal appliance used to flatten out wrinkly clothing or, for crafting purposes, to apply funky images onto baby clothing!

WHERE: Behind all of the diapers in your linen closet; hardware, mass merchant, department, electronics store.

HOW MUCH: Less than $25.

PROJECTS: Schleppy, Foxy Boxes, CD Snuggly, Vinyl Diner Bib, I Dream of Jeany Bib, Wipey Clutch, The Better Bolder Wipey Holder, Diaperlope, Daily Dose of Iron, Bootie-licious, Hip Purse, My Bragamuffin Brag Book.

IRON-ON FLEXIBLE VINYL

WHAT: A thin sheet of vinyl that is ironed on to waterproof cotton and polyester fabrics. It's great for creating bibs, placemats, paci holders, and more. It's sold by the yard.

WHERE: Fabric stores; online.

HOW MUCH: $6 to $8 per yard.

PROJECT: Vinyl Diner Bib.

IRON-ON ITEMS

WHAT: Any garments or items onto which an iron-on transfer can be attached: shirts, onesies, pants, canvas shoes, burp cloths, blankets, socks, diaper covers, blankets, bibs, etc.

WHERE: Dollar, baby, department, mass merchant stores; baby's closet.

HOW MUCH: $1 to $15 (but look in your baby's closet first!)

PROJECTS: Daily Dose of Iron, Bootie-licious.
See also Iron.

IRON-ON LETTERS

WHAT: Pre-made iron-on transfer letters sold by the sheet or by the letter—available in just about every font and color imaginable!

WHERE: Craft, fabric, mass merchant stores; online (search "iron-on letters" or try www.createforless.com).

HOW MUCH: $4 to $8 for 36- to 50-letter sheets.

PROJECTS: Schleppy, Foxy Boxes, CD Snuggly, Wipey Clutch, The Better Bolder Wipey Holder, Diaperlope,

Daily Dose of Iron, Bootie-licious. *See also* Iron, Letters.

JACQUARD RIBBON

WHAT: Ribbon with a design— anything from tennis racquets to flamingos—woven on one side. This ribbon is beautiful, but the side without the design looks like a mess of strings. (Which is why I don't recommend it for projects where both sides of the ribbon show, like the Insta-Bib variation, Sassy Paci.) As with all ribbon, check the scrapbooking aisle for assortments. Jacquard is pricey, so it's often sold by the yard and not on a spool.

WHERE: Craft, fabric stores; online.

HOW MUCH: $1.50 per yard.

PROJECTS: Decou-Pail, Pocket Book, Lite the Nite, Insta-Bib, Ribbon Wrappuccino, Oh So Bow-tiful, Bootie-licious, Hip Purse.
See also Ribbon.

JEANS (PANTS, JACKET, SKIRT, SHORTS)
See Old Pair of Jeans.

JEWELRY FINDINGS

WHAT: This is a general term used to describe all of the little pieces used to make jewelry, minus the beads. Some examples of findings used in this book are clasps, eye pins, head pins, jump rings, and

various types of chains.

WHERE: Craft, bead, mass merchant stores; online (search "jewelry findings").

HOW MUCH: From 5 cents to $20, depending on the item and the metal it's made out of.

PROJECTS: You-tencils, Photo a-Go-Go, Album à la Neck, Boys and Girls on the Hood.
See also Ball Chain Clasp, Crimp Coils, Decorative Head Pin or Large-Tip Head Pin, Eye Pin, Head Pin, Jump Ring, Link- or Cable Chain, Lobster Claw Clasp, Split Ring, Spring Clasp, Toggle Clasp.

JEWELRY GLUE STICKS

WHAT: These special glue sticks are great for gluing glass or metal objects onto most surfaces, or for mending broken tiaras! The glue dries clear and is stronger and stickier than regular hot-melt glue, so it's great for applying jewels. These sticks are available for large glue guns only.

WHERE: Craft stores; online.

HOW MUCH: $3 per pack of 12.

PROJECTS: Anything you want to add some rhinestones to that won't go into the washing machine!

JEWELS
See Rhinestones, Gems, or Jewels.

JUMP RING

WHAT: This small metal loop is used as a connector in any jewelry item with a clasp, charm, or chain. Jump rings are available in several metals and nearly any size to fit the project's dimensions. (See page 34 to learn how to use them.)

WHERE: Craft, bead, mass merchant stores; online (search "jewelry findings" and then search "jump rings").

HOW MUCH: $3 for more than 50.

PROJECTS: You-tencils, Photo a-Go-Go, Album à la Neck, Boys and Girls on the Hood.

See also Jewelry Findings.

KILT PIN

See Blanket Pin, Charm Pin, Skirt Pin.

LARGE-HOLE BEADS

WHAT: These beads are smallish, but they have a big hole that can accommodate a ball chain or thick cord.

WHERE: Craft, bead stores; online (www.landofodds.com).

HOW MUCH: $4.50 to $10 per pack of about 20, depending on material.

PROJECT: Photo a-Go-Go, Album à la Neck.

See also Beads.

LARGE HOT-GLUE GUN

WHAT: A big hot-glue gun that takes big glue sticks. Some of the newer models come with separate nozzles that help get glue into tricky, hard-to-reach places. Some are cordless, but though they're easier to use, they're also easier to leave lying around, so I don't recommend them if there are babies present during craft time. I've had several large hot glue guns over the years, but I'm a big fan of Aleene's glue guns and Stanley glue guns. The Aleene's gun is made specifically for a crafter; it's light and comes with four fantastic nozzles. The Stanley gun is a serious "tool"; it's hotter and stickier than any glue gun I've ever used.

WHERE: Craft, hardware, mass merchant stores; online.

HOW MUCH: $8 to $25.

PROJECTS: Little Hang-Ups, Schleppy, Think Inside the Box, Decou-Pail, Pocket Book, Foxy Boxes, CD Snuggly, Lite the Nite, Vinyl Diner Bib, I Dream of Jeany Bib, Insta-Bib, Wipey Clutch, The Better Bolder Wipey Holder, Diaperlope, Pimp My Ride, SpongeBob SquareHat, Tutti Bella Fontanella, Ribbon Wrappuccino, Oh So Bow-tiful, The Poncherello, Hasta la Poncho, The Ten-Minute Tutu, Bootie-licious, Photo Bragnets, No-Time Frame, Hip Purse, My Bragamuffin Brag Book, Shape Up!

See also Hot-Glue Gun.

LATEX GLOVES

WHAT: Latex gloves used by doctors are perfect for crafting because they are light and relatively durable. If you happen to be visiting your best friend in the hospital because she just had a baby, ask the good doctor for a pair or two! Then, use them to make her new baby a tie-dye onesie.

WHERE: Hospitals; dollar, medical supply, bulk food stores.

HOW MUCH: Less than $6 for a box.

PROJECT: To Dye For.

LETTERS

WHAT: You know *what* letters are, but you might not know all of the pre-made styles available for craft purposes. Explore the scrapbooking section of the craft store to find Scrabble-like letters, metal letters, plastic letters, dangling charm letters, sticker letters, epoxy letters, glass, plastic, ceramic, and metal letter beads. And that's just to name a few. Any of these pieces are great for personalizing projects.

WHERE: Craft, bead, mass merchant, stationery stores; online (www.orientaltrading.com).

HOW MUCH: From $2.50 to $8 for thirty-two or more letters.

PROJECTS: Little Hang-Ups, Think Inside the Box, Decou-Pail, Foxy Boxes, CD Snuggly, Lite the Nite, Insta-Bib, Wipey Clutch, The Better Bolder Wipey Holder, Ribbon Wrappuccino, Oh So Bow-tiful, Bootie-licious, No-Time Frame, Hip Purse, My Bragamuffin Brag Book, Shape Up!

See also Alphabet Beads; Felt Letters

and Shapes; Foam Shapes, Letters, or Beads; Iron-on Letters; Letter Stickers.

LETTER STICKERS

WHAT: The whole alphabet in sticker sheets. Letter sizes can be from ¼" to 5" per letter. They're great for making Bubble Letters (page 32) and personalizing decoupage projects.
WHERE: Craft, stationery, art supply stores; online (www.orientaltrading .com).
HOW MUCH: 50 cents to $5.
PROJECTS: Little Hang-Ups, Think Inside the Box, Decou-Pail, Foto-Mat, Photo Bragnets, No-Time Frame, Shape Up!
See also Letters.

LINK/CABLE CHAIN

WHAT: Silver- or gold-tone chain most often sold in packs. Simply cut the chain to a desired length and use it for nearly any jewelry project. I like Daricechain and Blue Moon Beads chain—they're both easy to cut with scissors, and have links that are big enough to attach a jump ring to. Chain is also sold by the foot at bead stores.
WHERE: Craft, bead stores; online (www.joann.com or www .createforless.com).
HOW MUCH: $3.50 for approximately 50" of chain.
PROJECTS: Photo a-Go-Go, Boys and Girls on the Hood.

See also Jewelry Findings.

LIQUID MEASURING CUP

WHAT: Marked cup for measuring liquid.
WHERE: Your kitchen cabinet.
HOW MUCH: If you don't already have one, just use an old baby bottle to measure ounces (1 cup = 8 ounces).
PROJECT: To Dye For.

LOBSTER CLAW CLASP

WHAT: You may recognize this clasp from pieces of jewelry you already own. It's a secure link that opens kind of like a lobster claw when the little leverlike nub is clicked. It's the sturdiest clasp I've found. *Note:* These need a heavy-duty split ring on which to clasp.
WHERE: Craft, bead, mass merchant stores; online (search "jewelry findings" and then "lobster clasp," or try www.joann.com, www.oriental trading.com, and www.createforless .com).
HOW MUCH: About $3 for a 10-pack.
PROJECTS: Photo a-Go-Go, Album à la Neck.
See also Jewelry Findings.

MAGAZINES

WHAT: Paper things that are not only fabulous because they are an escape from reality, but also because

they have tons of delightful images that are perfect for decoupage. So go ahead and make a Tom 'n' Katie Miracle Plate, Dora and Diego hangers, or pineapple upside-down cake Decou-Pails!
WHERE: Your home, your neighbor's recycling.
HOW MUCH: Free—you already paid for them and that doesn't count!
PROJECTS: Little Hang-Ups, Decou-Pail, Miracle Plate, Foto-Mat, No-Time Frame.
See also Decoupage Pictures.

MAGNET BUTTONS

WHAT: Little, black ¾" circular magnets. They're strong, so you can keep almost anything attached to the front of your fridge. A thin magnet strip just isn't strong enough.
WHERE: Craft stores; online (search "high energy magnet buttons").
HOW MUCH: Less than $2 for ten.
PROJECTS: Photo Bragnets.

MARABOU TRIM

WHAT: Fluffy, feathery trim that looks like a feather boa. It adds a tongue-in-cheek boudoir feeling to projects like Lite the Nite and Little Hang-Ups, and looks unbelievably cute on pretty much any article of baby clothing.
WHERE: Craft, fabric, mass merchant stores; online.
HOW MUCH: About $3 a yard.

PROJECTS: Little Hang-Ups, Think Inside the Box, Lite the Nite, Ten-Minute Tutu, Fringe 'Flops.

METAL BUCKET

WHAT: Strong, durable metal container that comes in a variety of sizes. A metal galvanized bucket is waterproof, so it can be used in the bathtub. *Note:* Those with fewer ridges are easier to decoupage!

WHERE: Craft, hardware stores; plant nurseries; online (search "galvanized metal bucket").

HOW MUCH: 2-quart bucket is less than $3.50.

PROJECT: Decou-Pail.

MINI HOT-GLUE GUN

WHAT: Small hot-glue gun that uses mini glue sticks. The spout is smaller than a large glue gun, so the glue flows out slowly, giving the gluer more control and fewer opportunities to burn herself. Mini glue guns aren't great for embellishing with heavier items because they don't get as hot as bigger ones. *Note:* Make sure to buy mini hot-melt glue sticks or dual-melt glue sticks for a mini gun, not cool-melt sticks!

WHERE: Craft, dollar, mass merchant stores; online.

HOW MUCH: $1 to $5.

PROJECTS: Little Hang-Ups, Think Inside the Box, Pocket Book, Lite the Nite, Wipey Clutch, The Better

Bolder Wipey Holder, Diaperlope, Tutti Bella Fontanella, Ribbon Wrappuccino, Oh So Bow-tiful, Photo Bragnets, No-Time Frame, My Bragamuffin Brag Book. *See also* Hot-Glue Gun.

MINI PHOTO ALBUM (BRAG BOOK)

WHAT: Small photo album that holds more than forty 4" × 6" photos. It doesn't matter what's on the front of it because it's going to be covered with fabric and a photo of baby!

WHERE: Craft, dollar stores; pharmacies.

HOW MUCH: No more than $2.50.

PROJECT: My Bragamuffin Brag Book.

MITTEN CLIPS

WHAT: Small metal clips that (attempt to) hold a kid's mittens onto his jacket. One set of mitten clips makes two Insta-Bibs or four Sassy Pacis (variation).

WHERE: Craft, fabric, mass merchant, dollar stores; baby superstores.

HOW MUCH: Less than $3.

PROJECTS: Insta-Bib, Sassy Paci.

NEEDLE AND THREAD

WHAT: A 1½" hand-sewing needle and a few spools of thread in neutral colors will do the trick for all of the projects in this book (if you choose

the sewing option). See page 36 for some simple stitches.

WHERE: Pharmacies; dollar, mass merchant, fabric, craft stores; the little travel kit you took from a fancy hotel.

HOW MUCH: Free to less than $2.

PROJECTS: Pocket Book, Vinyl Diner Bib, I Dream of Jeany Bib, Diaperlope, Hip Purse.

NEEDLE-NOSE PLIERS

See Chain-Nose Pliers, Round-Nose Pliers.

NO-FRAY SOLUTION

WHAT: White, gluelike substance that stops the ends of ribbon and fabric from fraying. There are several brands to choose from—Stop Fraying, Fray Block, and Fray Check. If a no-fray solution isn't available, use clear nail polish to stop ribbons from fraying, or fold the ribbon or fabric over ¼" and hot glue the fold shut for a no-sew "hem."

WHERE: Craft, fabric stores.

HOW MUCH: $4 for a 4-ounce bottle.

PROJECTS: Foxy Boxes, Wipey Clutch, The Better Bolder Wipey Holder, I Love the '80s Barrettes, The Ten-Minute Tutu, Fringe 'Flops, Hip Purse, My Bragamuffin Brag Book.

OLD PAIR OF JEANS

WHAT: Something denim that you never wear and are willing to cut into something new. It can be a jean jacket, jean skirt, or jean shorts, or old maternity jeans.

WHERE: Your closet, your husband's closet, thrift stores.

HOW MUCH: Free to $3.

PROJECT: Pocket Book, I Dream of Jeany Bib.

ONLINE FABRIC SWATCHES

WHAT: Fabric store websites have great swatch photos of their products, which are perfect for downloading to use in decoupage projects. Enlarge an image to its biggest size, and then save it in the appropriate Crafty Mamas chapter folder. Tweak the colors if necessary, and then print on regular computer paper.

WHERE: Search online for "cowboy fabric," "monkey fabric" or "pink poodle fabric," and find really cute versions of all those, and then some.

HOW MUCH: Free.

PROJECTS: Little Hang-Ups, Decou-Pail, Miracle Plate, No-Time Frame, Shape Up!.

See also Decoupage Pictures.

ORGANZA RIBBON

WHAT: Sheer ribbon that comes in many thicknesses. It's available by the yard, but I recommend buying it by the spool for more bang for your buck!

WHERE: Craft, fabric stores; online (search "organza ribbon").

HOW MUCH: $7 for 25 yards.

PROJECT: The Ten-Minute Tutu, Fringe 'Flops.

See also Ribbon.

PACKAGING

WHAT: Want a good excuse to eat a candy bar? Candy wrappers, seed packets, and other packaging look great when decoupaged onto buckets, frames, or dresser drawers! Just make sure to wipe off all of the crumbs before gluing!

WHERE: Your pantry, supermarkets, pharmacies, corner stores, next-door neighbor selling candy for a fund-raiser, etc.

HOW MUCH: 10 cents (for the bite-size candies) to $5 (for a multi-pack of regular-size candy bars).

PROJECTS: Little Hang-Ups, Decou-Pail, Miracle Plate, Foto-Mat, No-Time Frame, Shape Up!

See also Decoupage Pictures.

PATCH ATTACH

WHAT: Gluelike adhesive that's specially formulated to stick patches onto garments and other fabric items.

WHERE: Craft, fabric stores; online.

HOW MUCH: $4.50 for a small bottle.

PROJECT: I Dream of Jeany Bib.

PATCHES

WHAT: Find your old Brownie patches, buy some snazzy new patches, or make your own patches

by simply cutting an image out of fabric and gluing it onto something else. When on the patch hunt, don't just look in the sewing section of the craft store; check out the scrapbooking aisle, too!

WHERE: Craft, fabric stores; online (www.patchsales.com, mamameritbadges.com).

HOW MUCH: Free to $5.

PROJECTS: CD Snuggly, I Dream of Jeany Bib, Diaperlope, Hats Off to Mama, SpongeBob SquareHat, The No-Sew Mohawk, Bootie-licious.

PHOTO CHARMS

WHAT: Little metal charms with an indent for photos. They come in several shapes and sizes, and in silver and gold tones. For more variety, go from the bead aisle to the scrapbooking aisle; there will be several "charmlike" things that can be made into photo charms. (To find out how to get pics into the little buggers, see page 219.)

WHERE: Craft, bead stores; online (try www.orientaltrading.com or, for real silver, search "photo frame charms").

HOW MUCH: 60 cents to $10 per charm.

PROJECTS: Photo a-Go-Go, Album à la Neck, Boys and Girls on the Hood.

See also Beads, Charms.

PHOTO-EDITING SOFTWARE

WHAT: A computer program used to edit photographs from

a digital camera. Photos can be resized, cropped, and fixed to exact specifications, so a photo-editing program is essential for printing iron-on transfers.

WHERE: Electronic, mass merchant stores; online (www.picasa.com); included with your digital camera.

HOW MUCH: Free online or with your camera.

PROJECTS: Schleppy, Pocket Book, Foxy Boxes, CD Snuggly, Miracle Plate, Foto-Mat, Wipey Clutch, Diaperlope, Daily Dose of Iron, Photo Bragnets, Hip Purse, My Bragamuffin Brag Book, Shape Up!, Photo a-Go-Go, Album à la Neck, Boys and Girls on the Hood.

PHOTO-MOUNTING SQUARES

WHAT: Little, square double-sided stickers for scrapbooking or mounting photos in an album. I love the Kolo, Fiskers, and Keep A Memory brand squares. (If you can't find them, use double-sided tape.)

WHERE: Office supply, photo, craft, mass merchant, stationery stores; online.

HOW MUCH: $3.50 for a box of 500.

PROJECT: Think Inside the Box.

PHOTO PAPER

WHAT: Special paper used to print photos, so they look like they were developed at a lab. It's thicker than regular computer paper, and comes in two finishes—matte (flat) and glossy (shiny)—and in sizes from 4" × 6" to 8½" × 11".

WHERE: Office supply, mass merchant, photo, craft stores; copy shops; online.

HOW MUCH: $12 for 100 8½" × 11" sheets.

PROJECTS: Foto-Mat, Miracle Plate, Photo a-Go-Go, Photo Bragnets, Album à la Neck, Boys and Girls on the Hood, Pocket Book, My Bragamuffin Brag Book, Shape Up!

PHOTOS OR PICS

WHAT: Digital or printed photos of your little love. To decoupage a photo, print it on thin paper (regular computer paper works), or carefully peel off the top layer of the photo paper so all that is left is the thin sheet that the photo is printed on.

WHERE: Your computer; your photo album; your camera.

HOW MUCH: How can you put a price on such cuteness?

PROJECTS: Pocket Book, Miracle Plate, Foto-Mat, Daily Dose of Iron, Photo Bragnets, Hip Purse, My Bragamuffin Brag Book, Shape Up!, Photo a-Go-Go, Album à la Neck, Boys and Girls on the Hood.

PITCHER

WHAT: Any pitcher that holds more than 2 cups will suffice. Just be sure not to use it again for beverages because it is going to be used for mixing tie-dye!

WHERE: Your cabinet or closet; mass merchant, dollar stores.

HOW MUCH: Free to $3.

PROJECT: To Dye For.

PLASTIC BUCKET

WHAT: A clean bucket used for household chores works, as long as it holds more than 10 liquid quarts.

WHERE: Hardware, dollar stores; supermarkets.

HOW MUCH: From $2.

PROJECT: To Dye For.

PLASTIC SQUIRT BOTTLE

WHAT: Clear plastic bottle with a long nose and thin tip for squirting out small amounts of liquid. Bottles that come with boxed hair dyes are great for tie-dye. So is a red-and-yellow ketchup and mustard set from the dollar store. A "sport-top" water bottle works, but may release more dye than you need.

WHERE: Craft, hardware, beauty supply, dollar stores, online (search "plastic squeeze bottles" or try S&S Worldwide at www.ssww.com).

HOW MUCH: $4.50 for 6 bottles.

PROJECT: To Dye For.

PLASTIC TABLECLOTH, BIG

WHAT: Big, plastic sheet to protect the table. (If you want your table tie-dyed or painted, skip the cloth!)

WHERE: Dollar, mass merchant stores; pharmacies; supermarkets.

HOW MUCH: Don't pay more than $2!

PROJECT: To Dye For (but it doesn't hurt to use it for others, too!).

PLASTIC WRAP

WHAT: Open up your pantry and use what you have. When you've finished tie-dyeing your garments, you'll need to wrap them in plastic wrap and let them sit overnight, so the dye can really soak in.

WHERE: Kitchen supply drawer.

HOW MUCH: Free.

PROJECT: To Dye For.

POMPOMS

WHAT: Not the big ones cheerleaders use, these pompoms are small cotton, felt, or yarn balls that can be cute and kitschy embellishments for your projects. Find sparkly ones or even pompom trim to really up the ante!

WHERE: Craft, dollar, mass merchant stores; online (www.orientaltrading .com).

HOW MUCH: $5 for 250 pompoms.

PROJECTS: CD Snuggly, Lite the Nite, Diaperlope, Hats Off to Mama, Tutti Bella Fontanella, Hasta la Poncho, The Ten-Minute Tutu, Fringe 'Flops, Hip Purse.

PONY BEADS

WHAT: The beaded braids of the Williams sisters put these large-holed beads on the map. Theirs were plastic, but I recommend using glass. Glass pony beads come in many colors and their large holes allow you to string them onto a thin ball chain.

WHERE: Craft, bead stores; online.

HOW MUCH: $3 for 12 beads.

PROJECTS: Photo a-Go-Go, Album à la Neck, Boys and Girls on the Hood. *See also* Beads.

POSTERS

WHAT: Those large, glossy images that hung all over your walls in college are great for decoupage. Posters featuring lots of little images work best (since most of us aren't interested in decoupaging our refrigerators!).

WHERE: Your old room; dollar, novelty, art stores; online.

HOW MUCH: Free to $20.

PROJECTS: Little Hang-Ups, Decou-Pail, Miracle Plate, No-Time Frame. *See also* Decoupage Pictures.

PROCION DYES

WHAT: Natural, fiber-reactive dyes that produce amazingly vibrant results on cotton fabrics. Dyes like Rit or Tintex are synthetic, so they're designed to be used on synthetic fabrics like polyester and the colors aren't as deep and vibrant.

WHERE: Craft, art supply, fabric stores; online (search "procion mix fiber-reactive cold water dye" or try www.dickblick.com).

HOW MUCH: $3.50 for ⅔ ounce.

PROJECT: To Dye For.

RHINESTONES, GEMS, OR JEWELS

WHAT: Glitzy little embellishments that add a whole lot of pizzazz to craft projects. Rhinestones come in every shape imaginable: hearts, flowers, letters, squares, dragonflies, snowflakes—even feet! They're made of glass, crystal, or plastic. And as a wise man once said: "It don't mean a thing if it ain't got that bling!"

WHERE: Craft, fabric stores; online (search "rhinestones," "plastic jewels," or www.orientaltrading .com).

HOW MUCH: $4 for 150 pieces.

PROJECTS: Little Hang-Ups, Think Inside the Box, Decou-Pail, Foxy Boxes, CD Snuggly, Lite the Nite, Insta-Bib, Wipey Clutch, The Better Bolder Wipey Holder, Diaperlope, Daily Dose of Iron, Tutti Bella Fontanella, Ribbon Wrappuccino, Oh So Bow-tiful, I Love the '80s Barrettes, The Poncherello, Hasta la Poncho, The Ten-Minute Tutu, Bootie-licious, Fringe 'Flops, Photo Bragnets, No-Time Frame, Hip Purse, My Bragamuffin Brag Book, Shape Up!

RIBBON

WHAT: There are many types, thicknesses, and styles of ribbon, such as grosgrain, satin, jacquard, nylon, and organza (see individual entries for descriptions). Each adds that something extra to your projects. Plus, a little ribbon can hide mistakes!

WHERE: Fabric, dollar, craft stores (beyond the ribbon or trim aisles, look in the scrapbooking aisle for great ribbon sets).

HOW MUCH: 33 cents to $6 per spool. Buying by the roll is much cheaper than by the yard. Think ahead and buy more than you need now, because chances are, you'll need it later!

PROJECTS: Little Hang-Ups, Think Inside the Box, Decou-Pail, Pocket Book, Foxy Boxes, CD Snuggly, Lite the Nite, Vinyl Diner Bib, Insta-Bib, Pimp My Ride, Ribbon Wrappuccino, I Love the '80s Barrettes, Oh So Bow-tiful, Hasta la Poncho, The Ten-Minute Tutu, Bootie-licious, Fringe 'Flops, Photo Bragnets, No-Time Frame, Hip Purse, My Bragamuffin Brag Book.

See also Gimp Trim, Grosgain Ribbon, Jacquard Ribbon, Organza Ribbon, Satin Ribbon or Nylon Ribbon, Rickrack, Trim.

RICKRACK

WHAT: Woven trim that resembles a continuing row of "S" shapes. It comes in many sizes and colors, and it's sold on a card or by the yard.

WHERE: Fabric, craft, mass merchant, dollar stores; online.

HOW MUCH: 25 cents to $2 per yard.

PROJECTS: Pocket Book, CD Snuggly, Lite the Nite, Vinyl Diner Bib, Diaperlope, Ribbon Wrappuccino, Hasta la Poncho, Bootie-licious, Fringe 'Flops, Hip Purse, My Bragamuffin Brag Book.

ROTARY CUTTER AND CUTTING MAT

WHAT: A circular blade (attached to plastic handle) that rotates around as it cuts straight, sharp lines through fabrics. This tool is a must for those who crave a precise cut (but do it on the cutting mat or you'll slice up your floor!). And if you want your fringe to be as perfect as possible, buy the special "fringe-cut" slotted ruler.

WHERE: Craft, fabric, hardware stores; online.

HOW MUCH: $14 to $30.

PROJECTS: No-Sew Swanky Blanky, Schleppy, Pocket Book, Spit-Up Lover Pillow Cover, Knot in a Hurry Quilt, Hats Off to Mama, SpongeBob SquareHat, The No-Sew Mohawk, Hasta la Poncho, The Poncherello, Fringe 'Flops.

ROUND-NOSE PLIERS

WHAT: These pliers are good for opening and closing jump rings and making loops at the top of your head pins and eye pins. If the round, smooth tip doesn't give you a good enough grip on your jewelry findings, try a pair of flat-nose pliers (with two flat edges for easy gripping), or chain-nose pliers with a serrated jaw. Pliers are worth the investment, because once you have a pair, you'll be able to fix all of your broken jewelry! Before buying one, check your tool box. You may already have the perfect pair.

WHERE: Tool box; craft, bead, hardware stores; online.

HOW MUCH: Less than $6.

PROJECTS: You-tencils, Photo a-Go-Go, Album à la Neck, Boys and Girls on the Hood.

RUBBER BANDS

WHAT: Buy varied sizes and thicknesses for different tie-dye looks.

WHERE: Dollar, office supply, craft stores.

HOW MUCH: $1 to $3.50 for 100.

PROJECT: To Dye For.

RULER

WHAT: A standard 12" measure will do the trick for most of the projects in this book.

WHERE: Your desk drawer; dollar, office supply, mass merchant stores.

HOW MUCH: 50 cents to $2.

PROJECTS: Schleppy, Pocket Book, No-Sew Swanky Blanky, Spit-Up Lover Pillow Cover, Knot in a Hurry Quilt, Insta-Bib, Hats Off to Mama, SpongeBob SquareHat, The No-Sew Mohawk, I Love the '80s Barrettes, The Poncherello, Hasta la Poncho, The Ten-Minute Tutu, Fringe 'Flops, Transforma-Tee.

SAFETY PINS

WHAT: These are used in this book to help feed elastic through fabric casing at waistbands and other stretchy hemlines, as well as to keep fabric in place while working. Don't use a teensy one, because it will most likely get lost in the fabric.

WHERE: Your sewing box; dollar, craft, fabric stores.

HOW MUCH: $1 to $3 for a pack of 25.

PROJECTS: Pimp My Ride, Hats Off to Mama, SpongeBob SquareHat, The No-Sew Mohawk.

SATIN FLOWERS

WHAT: Small roses, daisies, peonies, and more made of satiny material. These make gorgeous and classy accents on projects for your little lady.

WHERE: Craft, fabric, dollar, mass merchant stores.

HOW MUCH: $1 to $1.50 for a pack of 8.

PROJECTS: Little Hang-Ups, Think Inside the Box, CD Snuggly, Lite the Nite, Wipey Clutch, The Better Bolder Wipey Holder, Diaperlope, Tutti Bella Fontanella, Ribbon Wrappuccino, The Poncherello, Hasta la Poncho, Fringe 'Flops, No-Time Frame, Hip Purse, My Bragamuffin Brag Book.

SATIN OR LEATHER CORD

WHAT: Smooth, thin cord used for making bracelets, necklaces, or as an embellishment. It comes in a ton of hot colors and a few thicknesses and is sold by the yard or the spool. Crimp coils need to be fitted onto

each end of the cord to attach a clasp to a necklace or bracelet.

WHERE: Craft, bead, fabric stores; online.

HOW MUCH: $1.50 for 5 yards.

PROJECTS: I Dream of Jeany Bib, Album à la Neck.

SATIN OR NYLON RIBBON

WHAT: Smooth and shiny ribbon that lends a classy air to any project. But buyer beware, satin and nylon (a cheaper material with a similar look) ribbon tends to fray easily, so if you choose to use them, be sure to bring out the No-Fray Solution.

WHERE: Craft, fabric, dollar, mass merchant stores; online.

HOW MUCH: Depends on the width of the ribbon. About 50 cents per yard for thinner satin ribbon; $3 per yard for thicker ribbon. Nylon is generally less expensive at 25 cents to $1.50 per yard, again, depending on width.

PROJECTS: Little Hang-Ups, Decou-Pail, Pocket Book, Foxy Boxes, Lite the Nite, CD Snuggly, Vinyl Diner Bib, Insta-Bib, Pimp My Ride, Ribbon Wrappuccino, I Love the '80s Barrettes, Oh So Bow-tiful, Hasta la Ponch, The Ten-Minute Tutu, Bootie-licious, Fring 'Flops, Photo Bragnets, No-Time Frame, Hip Purse, My Bragamuffin Brag Book.

See also Ribbon.

SCISSORS

See All-purpose Scissors, Fabric Scissors.

SCOTCH TAPE

See Transparent Tape.

SCRAPBOOK EMBELLISHMENTS

WHAT: All of those neat metal letters, words, and shapes, woven tags, tiny frames, fancy fabric and paper stickers, ribbon assortments, plastic tiles, slide mounts, buttons, tags, alphabets, and more. These magnificent minis look great as accents on tons of projects. Between Making Memories, Creative Memories, Creating Keepsakes, and Jo-Ann Scrap Essentials, there's nothing you won't be able to find.

WHERE: Craft, stationery, dollar stores; online (www.orientaltrading.com, www.createforless.com, other scrapbooking sites).

HOW MUCH: 50 cents to $6 per pack.

PROJECTS: Little Hang-Ups, Think Inside the Box, Foxy Boxes, CD Snuggly, Lite the Nite, Wipey Clutch, The Better Bolder Wipey Holder, Tutti Bella Fontanella, Ribbon Wrappuccino, Bootie-licious, No-Time Frame, Hip Purse, My Bragamuffin Brag Book.

See also Letters.

SCRAPBOOK PAPERS

WHAT: Themed, patterned papers, primarily used for scrapbooking, that come in packs of 8½" × 11" sheets or 12"-square sheets. It's available in just about any style or theme imaginable—pretty and preppy, funky and classy, flames, Cheerios, argyles, and more!

WHERE: Craft, stationery stores; online (bulk).

HOW MUCH: 15 cents to $1 per sheet. Don't pay more!

PROJECTS: Little Hang-Ups, Think Inside the Box, Decou-Pail, Miracle Plate, Foto-Mat, No-Time Frame, Shape Up!

See also Decoupage Pictures.

SCRAP FABRIC

WHAT: Buy new stuff or just use all the scraps from your bibs, blankets, hats, old clothing, brag books, night lights, and so on.

WHERE: Your house.

HOW MUCH: Free.

PROJECTS: Schleppy, Pocket Book, Knot in a Hurry Quilt, Vinyl Diner Bib, SpongeBob SquareHat, No-Sew Mohawk, Fringe 'Flops.

SCRAP PAPER

WHAT: Anything will do—an old newspaper, a piece of an envelope, an expired coupon, or a paper bag.

WHERE: Your desk or recycling pile.

HOW MUCH: Free.

PROJECTS: Decou-Pail, Foxy Boxes, Album à la Neck, Photo a-Go-Go.

SELF-ADHESIVE NIGHT LIGHT

WHAT: Night light that comes with a self-adhesive shade so it can be

decorated. They come in a variety of shapes and sizes.

WHERE: Craft, lighting stores; online (search "Hollywood Lights™ Self-Adhesive Night Light").

HOW MUCH: About $7 per fixture.

PROJECT: Lite the Nite.

SEQUINS

WHAT: Small, metallic discs that have a tiny hole in them. They are sold by the pack or threaded on strings by the yard. They add lots of pizzazz to any project.

WHERE: Craft, fabric, dollar stores.

HOW MUCH: 50 cents to $1 per pack; $1 per yard for sequin trim.

PROJECTS: Little Hang-Ups, CD Snuggly, Wipey Clutch, The Better Bolder Wipey Holder, Diaperlope, Ribbon Wrappuccino, Hasta la Poncho, Fringe 'Flops, Hip Purse, My Bragamuffin Brag Book.

SHADOW BOX

WHAT: It looks like a picture frame, but it has depth, so three-dimensional items can be put beneath the glass. My favorite is the EK Success 6" square shadow box because it's small and classy looking. But they're available in all shapes and sizes.

WHERE: Frame, craft, dollar stores; Ikea; online (www.createforless.com, search for "EK Maple Lane Studio Shadowbox 6" × 6" Keepsake").

HOW MUCH: $1 to $30. (EK Success brand frames are about $12 each.)

PROJECT: Think Inside the Box.

SHOEBOX

WHAT: A box that shoes or boots came packaged in. (If you didn't save one, then a shoebox craft project is a great opportunity to go and buy a new pair!) For a small box, use one that held baby shoes. For storing a lot of stuff, use your husband's boot box!

WHERE: Your closet, garage, or attic.

HOW MUCH: Free—unless you go out and spring for that new pair of shoes!

PROJECT: Foxy Boxes.

SHOES (BABY)

WHAT: Buy canvas pairs with soft or rubber soles, Chinese slippers, or anything plain that's just itching to be jazzed up!

WHERE: Craft, dollar, mass merchant stores; department stores (sale rack); baby superstores; Payless.

HOW MUCH: $1 to $10.

PROJECT: Bootie-licious.

SKIRT PIN

WHAT: A skirt pin is what you've probably been calling a "kilt pin" for all these years. It's a large metal pin that holds together kilt fabric. Real kilt pins, however, are very fancy—decorated with swords and lions!

WHERE: Craft, fabric stores.

HOW MUCH: 50 cents to $1.50 per pin.

PROJECT: Boys and Girls on the Hood.
See also Blanket Pin, Charm Pin, Diaper Pin.

SNAP CLIPS

WHAT: Metal barrettes that snap open when bent gently one way and then snap shut when bent the other. They come on a card, or in a bag. Buy the ones *without* a plastic coating for the projects in this book.
WHERE: Pharmacies; supermarkets; mass merchant, craft, dollar, bead stores.
HOW MUCH: Shop around and you can get a pack of 10 for about $1. (Don't spend more than $3.50 for a 10-pack!)
PROJECT: Ribbon Wrappuccino, Oh So Bow-tiful.

SODA ASH

WHAT: Powder to mix with water for pre-soaking tie-dyeable garments and other items. It gets the molecules in clothing all ready to adhere to the fiber-reactive dye.
WHERE: Craft, art supply stores; online at dickblick.com.
HOW MUCH: $5 for a 5 pound bag.
PROJECT: To Dye For.

SPACER BEADS

WHAT: These nice, simple staple beads come in gold- and silver-tone, as well as in a variety of sizes and designs. They will complement more ornate beads in jewelry designs. They are usually the major component of bracelets and necklaces, despite playing second fiddle! Look for ones with large holes, so there is more flexibility with the width of the chain or cord they're being strung on.
WHERE: Craft, bead stores; online (search "jewelry findings" and then "spacer beads").
HOW MUCH: $3 for thirty-five beads.
PROJECTS: Photo a-Go-Go, Album à la Neck, Boys and Girls on the Hood.
See also Beads.

SPLIT RING

WHAT: Similar in size and shape to a jump ring, a split ring features a second coil for added strength (especially for attaching clasps). However, if your fingers aren't so nimble, split rings require investing in a new tool—split ring pliers. Split rings can be difficult to maneuver, and despite their sturdiness, they *can* stretch out or break if pulled too far.
WHERE: Craft, bead stores; online (search "jewelry findings" and then "split ring").
HOW MUCH: $3 for 12 rings.
PROJECTS: You-tencils, Photo a-Go-Go, Album à la Neck, Boys and Girls on the Hood.
See also Jewelry Findings.

SPRAY ADHESIVE

WHAT: Gluelike spray that affixes lighter objects to various surfaces. I love 3M, Krylon, and Scotch brands. Just be sure to buy one that is for "crafts" or "fabric" (rather than those labeled for "photos" or "paper crafts," which won't adhere as well). These sprays are stinky, so use them outdoors or in well-ventilated areas—with no babies around!
WHERE: Craft, hardware, art supply stores.
HOW MUCH: $5 per can.
PROJECT: Foxy Boxes.

SPRING CLASP

WHAT: Everything from your baby bracelet to the name necklace you got for your sweet sixteen was probably closed with this old-school clasp that's a little circle with a tiny lever that slides over to close. They're not as cute to look at as the toggle or lobster clasp, but they function just as well. Be wary of inexpensive "gold tone" or "silver tone" clasps that come in packs of twenty or more, as they break pretty easily.
WHERE: Craft, bead, mass merchant stores; online (www.orientaltrading .com, or search "jewelry findings" and then "spring clasp").
HOW MUCH: $3 for a pack of 12.
PROJECTS: Photo a-Go-Go, Album à la Neck.
See also Jewelry Findings.

STAINLESS STEEL BABY FLATWARE

WHAT: Any metal flatware, with or

without a rubber coating, will suffice (plastic or ceramic handles are next to impossible to bead). For a ritzier utensil, go for sterling silver!

WHERE: Pharmacies; mass merchant, dollar, department, jewelry stores (for a sterling utensil); baby superstores; supermarkets.

HOW MUCH: 50 cents to $1.50 per piece of stainless steel; $15 to $50 for sterling silver.

PROJECT: You-tencils.

STICKERS

WHAT: Paper shapes or designs that have self-adhesive sticky stuff on the back. (But you know that.) Any image on a sticker is great for decoupage, but stickers can't be decoupaged while the adhesive is still active, or they'll slide right off when being painted over with decoupage medium. Instead, stick stickers to a thin piece of paper first, cut them out, and glue them on. Or, make a bunch of color copies of your stickers so you can use the designs again.

WHERE: Craft, stationery stores; pharmacies; online.

HOW MUCH: 50 cents to $5 per sheet.

PROJECTS: Little Hang-Ups, Think Inside the Box, Decou-Pail, Miracle Plate, Foto-Mat, No-Time Frame, Shape Up!

See also Decoupage Pictures.

TAPE MEASURE

WHAT: Metal, flexible plastic, or cloth strip with measurement markings. Use a tailor's tape measure (flexible plastic or fabric) or a carpentry one (it pulls out from the coil inside its metal case and retracts).

WHERE: Craft, fabric, hardware, mass merchant, domestic merchandise, dollar stores.

HOW MUCH: 50 cents to $10.

PROJECTS: Pocket Book, Insta-Bib, Hats Off to Mama, SpongeBob SquareHat, I Love the '80s Barrettes, The Ten-Minute Tutu, Fringe 'Flops.

THIN CARDBOARD BOX

WHAT: Any cereal box, cracker box, or pasta box will do. If there isn't an empty one in the recycling, pour your Cheerios into a zip-top bag and cut up a box in your pantry. Use it to create reusable patterns, as well as to stop globs of hot glue from dripping onto your countertop.

WHERE: Your pantry, garbage, or storage closet.

HOW MUCH: Free. (You paid for the cereal, not the box!)

PROJECTS: No-Sew Swanky Blanky, Decou-Pail, Spit-Up Lover Pillow Cover, Knot in a Hurry Quilt, any project with a glue gun.

TINY TOYS

See Trinkets.

TOGGLE CLASP

WHAT: A two-piece metal clasp comprised of a simple ring and a small bar that goes through the ring to clasp two ends of a necklace or bracelet together. If a simple circle seems too ordinary, toggles come in all sorts of shapes, including hearts, keys, stars, and even mermaids!

WHERE: Craft, bead, mass merchant stores; online (www.orientaltrading .com, www.createforless.com, or search "jewelry findings" and then "toggle clasp").

HOW MUCH: About $3 for a 6-pack.

PROJECTS: Photo a-Go-Go, Album à la Neck.

See also Jewelry Findings.

TRANSPARENT TAPE

WHAT: Wrap it around the end of your ribbon (like the end of a shoelace) to make it easy to thread through things like Vinyl Diner Bib and Bootie-licious laces.

WHERE: Your desk drawer; office supply stores.

HOW MUCH: Free (if you already have it) to $1.50 per roll.

PROJECTS: Decou-Pail, Vinyl Diner Bib, Bootie-licious.

TRAVEL WIPE CASE

WHAT: Flat, rectangular wipe case that becomes like a credit card for moms with babies—don't leave home without it! Buy your regular

Huggies or Pampers versions, or check out the dollar store for unfilled cheapies.

WHERE: Pharmacies; dollar stores.
HOW MUCH: $1 to $2.50.
PROJECT: Wipey Clutch.

TRIM

WHAT: Anything decorative that's sold by the yard or on a spool that gives a project a jazzy edge. There is beaded trim, fringed trim, gimp trim, pompom trim, eyelet trim, pearl trim, rhinestone trim, crochet trim, rickrack, flower trim, and more. Check out the scrapbooking aisle for variety packs.
WHERE: Craft, fabric, dollar, mass merchant stores; online (search fabric and scrapbooking sites).
HOW MUCH: 25 cents to $4 per yard.
PROJECTS: Decou-Pail, Pocket Book, CD Snuggly, Lite the Nite, Vinyl Diner Bib, Wipey Clutch, The Better Bolder Wipey Holder, Diaperlope, Ribbon Wrappuccino, Hasta la Poncho, Fringe 'Flops, Hip Purse, My Bragamuffin Brag Book, any other project in this book where you want to add some 'zazz.
See also Beaded Trim, Gimp Trim, Marabou Trim, Ribbon, Rickrack, Sequins.

TRINKETS

WHAT: Miniature trains, cars, dolls, soldiers, lizards, farm animals, rings, and more that are sold in multipacks intended for party favors, creative play, or decoration.
WHERE: Dollar, mass merchant stores; pharmacies; online (www.orientaltrading.com).
HOW MUCH: 50 cents to $3 for about 12 pieces.
PROJECTS: Little Hang-Ups, Think Inside the Box, Decou-pail, The Better Bolder Wipey Holder, No-Time Frame.

T-SHIRTS

WHAT: All those boxy tees brought back from Grandma's trips that have been stashed at the bottom of your kid's drawer because throwing them away just seemed wrong!
WHERE: Dresser drawer; dollar, thrift, mass merchant stores; souvenir stands.
HOW MUCH: Free to $2.
PROJECTS: Daily Dose of Iron, To Dye For, Transforma-Tee.

TULLE

WHAT: Netted fabric sold by the yard and by the spool. (Your wedding veil may have been made of tulle. Once you find it by the yard in a fabric store, you're going to wonder what on earth made your veil so darn expensive—I did!). It comes in a bunch of different colors, as well as netting gauges (size of the "holes").
WHERE: Fabric stores.
HOW MUCH: 50 cents to $2 per yard.
PROJECT: The Ten-Minute Tutu.

UNFINISHED WOODEN PICTURE FRAME

WHAT: Just as the name describes, it's an unpainted picture frame where the wood is raw and unvarnished with no designs or shapes etched into it. (It's hard to paint, glue, or decoupage onto ornate frames.) Picture frames come in all different shapes and sizes. I like the ones with a generous wooden border, so there's more space to decorate.
WHERE: Dollar, craft, mass merchant stores, Ikea.
HOW MUCH: 75 cents to $3 each.
PROJECT: No-Time Frame.

VINYL PLACEMAT

WHAT: A ¼"-thick placemat made out of semi-squishy vinyl or foam.
WHERE: Dollar, mass merchant, domestic merchandise stores; Ikea.
HOW MUCH: 50 cents to $5.
PROJECT: Foto-Mat.

WALLPAPER

WHAT: I'm sure you're familiar with wallpaper from home improvement projects. Use the extra sheets or rolls still lying around from your hallway revamp, and cut or tear it up for use on decoupage projects.

WHERE: Basement or attic; mass merchant, textile stores (look for big sales on discontinued patterns).
HOW MUCH: Free to $7 per roll.
PROJECTS: Little Hang-Ups, Think Inside the Box, Decou-Pail, Miracle Plate, No-Time Frame, Shape Up! *See also* Decoupage Pictures.

WATER-BASED VARNISH
See Clear Acrylic Finish Spray.

WAX PAPER
WHAT: Wax-coated paper that keeps baked goodies from sticking to pans. If the glue on a decoupage project is a little bit wet, but it's time to turn a project over, do so on a piece of wax paper so it doesn't stick to the table or anything else around it.
WHERE: Your kitchen drawer (next to the aluminum foil); supermarkets, dollar, mass merchant stores; pharmacies.
HOW MUCH: Free to $4 for a roll.
PROJECTS: Little Hang-Ups, Decou-Pail, Miracle Plate, No-Time Frame, Shape Up!

WHITE GLUE
WHAT: This is the same white stuff third-graders use to stick googly eyes onto paper bag puppets. A "white glue solution" (three parts white glue to one part water) works great for attaching decoupage images; however, it's not great to use as a decoupage topcoat because it's too

thin and it dries very, very matte.
WHERE: Craft, office supply, dollar, mass merchant stores; supermarkets; pharmacies.
HOW MUCH: $1 to $2.50 per 7.5-ounce bottle.
PROJECTS: Little Hang-Ups, Think Inside the Box, Decou-Pail, Miracle Plate, No-Time Frame, Shape Up!

WIPE BOX
See Diaper Wipe Box.

WOODEN HANGERS
WHAT: Things your kids' clothing hangs on—that is, if there's ever time to hang it up! They come in a few different shapes: flat and slightly arched, upside-down wide V-shaped (like a suit hanger without the bar at the bottom), and skirt hangers with the metal clips on them. For the project in this book, choose wooden ones.
WHERE: Dollar, mass merchant stores; baby superstores; online (search "children's wooden hanger" and look for the best price).
HOW MUCH: $1.50 per hanger (but I recommend buying in bulk).
PROJECT: Little Hang-Ups.

WOODEN PUZZLE
WHAT: It's far easier to cut a picture of Grandpa into a triangle than a fire truck shape, so I recommend using a puzzle with geometric pieces. That said, if a pic of Auntie Marsha would look awesome cut into the shape of a

peacock, go for it. Buy a new puzzle or use the one in Junior's toy box.
WHERE: Craft, dollar, thrift stores; online (www.orientaltrading.com, www.ssww.com, and www.discountschoolsupply.com).
HOW MUCH: $1 to $20.
PROJECT: Shape Up!

WRAPPING PAPER
WHAT: It's not only good for wrapping up mama-made gifts, but it's also great for making them, too! Save it for decoupaging onto buckets, picture frames, hangers, and more. Use the cheap stuff on rolls or splurge on the beautiful stuff sold by the sheet.
WHERE: Craft, dollar, stationery, office supply stores; Ikea; The Container Store; online.
HOW MUCH: $1 to $8 per roll.
PROJECTS: Little Hang-Ups, Think Inside the Box, Decou-Pail, Miracle Plate, No-Time Frame. *See also* Decoupage Pictures.

INDEX

about the author

Abby Pecoriello has worked as a writer and producer at Disney, Scholastic, and Nickelodeon. During her maternity leave after the birth of her first child in 2003, Abby turned to crafting (as she had at many life-altering times in her life) to find that a little hot glue, rhinestones, beads, and fabric were just the thing to diffuse the overwhelming feelings of new motherhood. Inspired by her new muse, the results were adorable: one-of-a-kind projects for the nursery, diaper bag, and wardrobe. Abby hosted her first Crafty Mamas get-together during her playgroup so that she and her new mommy friends could navigate the crazy and exciting world of parenthood together as they cut up fleece, tie-dyed onesies, and decorated diaper wipe boxes. Abby continues to write and produce and lead Crafty Mamas groups in New York City, where she lives with her husband and two daughters.

Visit **www.craftymamas.com** to find out more about the projects in this book or to contact the author with questions, comments, or your own crafty triumphs.

The author with her family.